Australia's Vietnam War

TEXAS A&M UNIVERSITY MILITARY HISTORY SERIES 77

Texas A&M University Military History Series
Joseph G. Dawson III, General Editor

Australia's Vietnam War

Jeff Doyle, Jeffrey Grey, and Peter Pierce

Texas A&M University Press
College Station

Manufactured in the United States of America

First edition

The paper used in this book meets the minimum requirements
of the American National Standard for Permanence
of Paper for Printed Library Materials, Z39.48–1984.
∞
Binding materials have been chosen for durability.

Frontispiece:
Australian, U.S., and ARVN personnel on parade
at Long Hai, South Vietnam, in January, 1972.
Courtesy Australian War Memorial
Photo by William James Cunneen

Library of Congress Cataloging-in-Publication Data

Australia's Vietnam War / Jeff Doyle, Jeffrey Grey, and Peter Pierce.—1st ed.
p. cm.—(Texas A&M University military history series ; 77)
Includes bibliographical references and index.
ISBN 1-58544-137-6 (cloth : alk. paper)
1. Vietnamese Conflict, 1961–1975—Australia. 2. Vietnamese Conflict,
1961–1975—Particpation, Australian. I. Doyle, Jeff, 1952– II. Grey, Jeffrey.
II. Pierce, Peter, 1950– IV. Series.
DS558.6.A8 A97 2002
959.704′3394—dc21
2001005499

For Ian McNeill
(1933–98)
soldier, scholar, friend

CONTENTS

ILLUSTRATIONS

PREFACE

We first came to the study of Australia's Vietnam War in a concerted fashion in the late 1980s, and the results of that interest appeared in several volumes of essays from a variety of authors and scholarly perspectives published between 1990 and 1992. This was a high-water mark of public interest in the Vietnam War in Australia, bracketed by the "Welcome Home" march in 1987 and the dedication of the national monument to Vietnam veterans in 1992. At decade's and century's end that interest had plateaued, but after Gallipoli and the First World War, the Vietnam War remains the conflict best known to modern Australians and the only one of which the majority have any experience, however indirect.

As authors we have many debts and owe thanks in many quarters. A Large Grant from the Australian Research Council supported some of the original work on which these essays are based. Emeritus Prof. Harry Heseltine, then professor of English at University College, Australian Defence Force Academy (ADFA), and Prof. Alan Gilbert, then professor of history at the same establishment and now vice chancellor of the University of Melbourne, were early supporters of the work. In different ways and for different reasons we also acknowledge the support and assistance of Prof. Peter Dennis of the School of History, ADFA. Thanks are due as well to Prof. Joseph G. Dawson III of the Department of History at Texas A&M University. He first brought us together with Texas A&M University Press, and the rest is history.

Our two contributing authors merit special recognition. Peter Edwards, the Official Historian of Australian Involvement in Southeast Asian Conflicts 1948–75, held that office from 1982 to 1996. As author of two seminal volumes in that series and editor of the series as a whole, he has made a sizable scholarly impact upon Australians' understanding of the subject—one with which students at all levels will have to grapple for decades to come. We are gratified by his agreement to publish in this volume a reworked form of his original essay on Australia's commitment to the war. Our saddest task is to acknowledge the work of our friend and colleague Ian McNeill. Author of several major works on the Australian Army and the war, he died suddenly and far too soon in late 1998, with his crowning achievement, a study of the Australian Task Force in Phuoc Tuy between 1967 and 1971, incomplete and unpublished at this writing. We are doubly grateful to his wife, Gwen, for permission to present his lengthy summary essay on that topic between these covers.

Mrs. Margaret McNally assisted with word processing and John Connor provided advice and assistance, while Susan Cowan provided some last-minute help with references. Our families deserve our final thanks for putting up with us and with projects like this.

INTRODUCTION

Australia's Vietnam War

The history of the Australian-American relationship is a long and uneven one, and something of its course needs to be understood if we are to appreciate the context in which Australia went to war alongside the United States in Vietnam in the 1960s. In the nineteenth century, Britain's Australian colonies had periodically viewed the United States as a threat. In November, 1839, two U.S. warships threw Sydney into panic when they slipped into anchorage quietly and unannounced one night, to be discovered by the colonists at their breakfast the following morning, thus confirming the gravest fears for the vulnerability of the colony. During the last stages of the American Civil War the Confederate raider *Shenandoah* found safe harbor in Melbourne to refit before recommencing commerce raiding in the northern Pacific. It is said that she left port with a larger crew than when she had berthed. Some of these additional men were possibly Americans (or, at least, Southerners) who had sought a livelihood on the Victorian gold fields of the 1850s and 1860s, but the suspicion is that a few of them were sympathetic Australian colonists. The Australian colonies proved welcoming to defeated Confederates also, with perhaps a hundred or more emigrating to the distant Antipodes after 1865.

At the beginning of the twentieth century, Australians undoubtedly knew more about America than the other way around. The visit of the Great White Fleet in 1907 when it circumnavigated the globe in celebration of American power brought near-delirious responses in a country then in the throes of a debate about the acquisition of a navy of its own. In the early years after the federation of the colonies in 1901, Australian governments continued to build a social welfare structure well in advance of anything in the English-speaking nations of the northern hemisphere (including the extension of the franchise to women), but Australian politicians knew enough of America's experience after the Civil War to oppose the extension of generous workers' compensation provisions to members of the new nation's armed forces. By the time U.S. forces reached France in strength in 1918, the Australian Imperial Force had been at war for over three years and had passed some of the skills it had acquired to green American divisions in the spring and summer of that year through training and advisory missions specially attached to the American Expeditionary Force.

Relations between the United States and Australia deteriorated between the wars, especially during the 1930s, as a result of the closed trade preference within the British Empire designed to keep American commercial enterprises out of Empire markets. The ominous strategic situation in the Pacific following the outbreak of war in Europe in 1939 did little to ameliorate this condition. An increasingly anxious Australian government sought to interest the United States in the defense of the South and Southwest Pacific but received little comfort or reassurance from Washington. This was especially the case in 1941 with the Anglo-American decision in March to "beat Hitler first"—of which the Australian government was not officially informed—and the movement of part of the U.S. Pacific Fleet to the Atlantic in May to help bolster Britain. The deliberations at the Arcadia conference in Washington from December, 1941, to January, 1942, in which the strategic priorities and command relationships governing the war against Japan were resolved, had enormous implications for Australia. However, the views of the Australian government again were not sought; nor were Australian interests and priorities taken into consideration. This is frequently the lot of small powers in great power conflicts.

The Second World War marks one of a succession of watersheds in the Australian-American relationship in the second half of the century, most of them entirely dependent on circumstance. The collapse of the American position in the Philippines left Washington with a dilemma: A strategic base from which to prosecute the war with Japan was required, with neither the remaining American base in the Pacific, Hawaii, nor the West Coast of the United States entirely suitable for the purpose of relieving embattled U.S. and Filipino forces at Bataan and Corregidor. Australia, on the other hand, provided a more or less developed Western infrastructure and stable political framework, while strategically it posed a threat to the security of the newly acquired Japanese Southern Resources Zone in Southeast Asia—something that the Japanese recognized through their efforts in 1942 to isolate Australia and sever its communications with the United States. General Douglas MacArthur's arrival in April, 1942, to take command of the Southwest Pacific Area (SWPA) signified American commitment to that theater, at least until the Japanese were beaten.

Australia was the most important American ally in the Pacific War. China proved a broken reed, and until the war's last months the British engaged the Japanese Empire only on its peripheries (although the Burma campaign was vital to the defense of India). Australia fielded five divisions, plus air and naval forces; provided a vast base for the buildup of U.S. troops and supplies; and met many of America's needs in the theater by providing raw materials and foodstuffs. In addition, during the critical fighting in Papua New Guinea in 1942–43, in which the defense of Australian territory was at stake, Australian forces engaged in by far the larger share of combat, and they continued to outnumber American forces in the SWPA until well into 1943. Australia was one of the few belligerents to end up as a net creditor under the lend-lease scheme at war's end, but the traffic was by no means all one way. Australians were badly frightened by the speed with which Japanese aggression had triumphed in Southeast Asia, and particularly by the fall of Singapore in February, 1942, the defense of which had been the key to interwar military planning in the Far East. The influx of U.S. forces helped to reassure them, while MacArthur's presence and his close and mutually advantageous collaboration with Australian prime minister John Curtin gave the Australian government access to American strategic thinking previously denied it, and probably available in no other way. In the absence of local vehicle and aircraft industries, Australian forces were also dependent on the Americans for various kinds of heavy equipment, not least because the traditional source of supply for such items, Britain, was too busy meeting its own needs to have anything to spare for the Dominions.

By 1945, Australian and American strategic priorities had markedly diverged. With the defeat of Japan, the United States rapidly withdrew from the Southwest Pacific—an area in which it once again had little or no political, strategic, or economic interests, and certainly no compelling ones. In the late 1940s the Australian government attempted to reinterest Washington in the region, but with conspicuous lack of success. It thus sought once again a reinvigorated British Commonwealth system of cooperative military endeavor as compensation for the absence of the United States. This prove to be a fruitful partnership in the 1950s and 1960s insofar as it helped to defeat insurgency in Malaya and guaranteed Malayan independence against an internal communist threat, and subsequent Malaysian independence against an external threat from Indonesia. But Britain made it clear as early as 1957 that it would withdraw from "east of Suez" and, although this process was delayed far longer than originally intended, it was clear to Australia's leaders by the late 1950s that Australian security would not much longer be underwritten by London. For this reason if for no other, the treaty signed between Australia, New Zealand, and the United States (ANZUS) in 1951 (flawed though it was and is) gained increased importance in Australian eyes as a security guarantee.

The ANZUS treaty was the second major development in the relationship and as unexpected as the wartime alliance of convenience had been. In short, the Australian government of Sir Robert Menzies managed to secure in 1950–51 that which its predecessor under J. B. Chifley had been unable to bring about despite strenuous efforts from 1946 to 1948. The objective circumstances in the Southwest Pacific had not changed; the United States still possessed no significant national interest in that region. The ANZUS treaty was the price the United States was willing to pay in order to moderate continuing Australian antagonism to the idea of a revived Japan in a period when Americans were discovering that their vital interests in Northeast Asia were being challenged by the triumph of mainland Asian communism in China and North Korea. The treaty subsequently became a key document in the Cold War relationship between the three signatories, but that was not how it began.

These were the contexts, both general and more narrowly defined, in which Australia's commitment to the American intervention in Vietnam took place. In the opening essay in this book, Peter Edwards shows that Australian decision making in the early 1960s was fashioned both by the Cold War in Europe and Asia and by the decolonization of the European empires, principally in Asia. While fear of communist expansion was of concern, it was not only or mainly its manifestation in Indochina that occasioned consternation in Canberra. Rather, the growth and influence of the Indonesian Communist Party (PKI) and its influence on an ailing President Sukarno in Jakarta were the goads to an Australian policy that looked for a reemphasized American capacity to intervene on our behalf against an Indonesian attack, together with the willingness to do so. The Vietnam commitment was the price Australia paid to secure that countercommitment from Washington, or so it thought.

That commitment saw an army training team sent in 1962 to work within the U.S. advisory and Special Forces systems, aiding the Army of the Republic of Vietnam (ARVN) and forces formed from the Montagnard tribes in the interior in their fight against the Vietcong and the North Vietnamese forces being infiltrated south. The trainers were followed by ground combat troops beginning in early 1965, and the Australian force in Vietnam reached a peak strength of eighty-three hundred men, including air and naval units working with the U.S. Fifth Air Force and U.S. Seventh Fleet. Ian McNeill's essay concentrates on the deployment and operations of the 1st Australian Task Force, which operated in Phuoc Tuy Province in the III Corps Tactical Zone/Military Region 3 from 1966 to 1971. He demonstrates the differences in operational methods and assumptions that the Australian force brought to Vietnam, which were based on tactics and techniques refined in a decade of counterinsurgency warfare in Malaya and Borneo beginning in the mid-1950s.

Although initially, and for some time thereafter, the government's commitment of Australian forces received widespread support at home, there was always opposition to Australian involvement. Over time this grew in both size and intensity in common with the experience in the United States and much of the rest of the Western world. There are two points of focus in considering the ways in which popular dissent expressed itself. The first involves a more generalized discussion of the idea of "the Sixties" as a socio-cultural and political phenomenon. Peter Pierce shows that in its Australian manifestation much of the alleged radicalism in Australian culture so often associated with the impact of the Vietnam War in fact predates it, often by a significant margin. In keeping with Eric Hobsbawm's notions of "the long Nineteenth century" (c. 1789–1914) and "the short Twentieth century" (c. 1914–89), we can see that the 1960s was a period that may have lasted less than the ten years common to the standard division by decades and that it does not conform to the same time span in different countries. To put it another way, depending on one's viewpoint, one might, as an American, consider that the 1960s began with Pres. John F. Kennedy's assassination in 1963 or with the civil rights disturbances and troop commitments to Vietnam in 1964–65. Many Americans would end the 1960s in 1973–74 with Watergate and Pres. Richard M. Nixon's resignation, although others might point to 1968 and the violent confrontations at the Democratic National Convention. These observers might in turn argue that the 1960s began in 1961 with Kennedy's election, the end of a long period of Republican rule, and the beginning of the whole "Camelot" fantasy. In Australia, the cultural and political signposts are quite different. Although Australia's commitment of troops began in 1962 and escalated in 1965, many commentators would agree that the 1960s really only began with the retirement of long-serving conservative prime minister R. G. Menzies in 1966 after seventeen years in office. The height of anti–Vietnam War protests on the streets of Australian cities came about in 1970–71, while the agitation on major university campuses only really subsided after 1974. It might further be argued that the political end of the 1960s is best marked by the vice-regal dismissal of the Whitlam government in 1975 and the return of the conservative parties to office in December of that year. Pierce charts these cultural processes, while Jeffrey Grey discusses the forms taken by protest and dissent during this period.

Australian forces were withdrawn slowly but progressively from Vietnam beginning in 1970, when the third battalion in the task force was not replaced on rotation, and by December, 1971, the majority of Australia's forces had left the theater in line with the American drawdown and in keeping with the policy of Vietnamization. The fall of Saigon elicited little response in Australia in 1975, and for almost a decade after the Australian withdrawal Vietnam disappeared from the public sphere. By the early 1980s, however, a section of the veteran community had begun to agitate in an organized manner around a number of issues on which it felt aggrieved or disadvantaged. This aspect of Australia's Vietnam involvement has closely paralleled American behavior and experience in the same sphere of activity. (The term *veteran* is an Americanism and had little or no popular application in Australia before Vietnam, the "Australianism" of choice and common usage being "returned serviceman" or simply "returned man.") Extraparliamentary political activism; a heavy public campaign on the issues of herbicide exposure, birth defects, and post-traumatic stress; the disparagement of traditional veterans' organizations; and governmental veteran welfare structures are common themes in the two national experiences. So too is the distinctly minority status of the disaffected within the total of Vietnam veterans and the process of gradual reintegration of that group within the broader community. In the Australian case, the enveloping national martial myth of Anzac has made this a somewhat less traumatic process than in the United States, but the timing and the staging posts of that process in Australia have taken their cue from the American experience, as Jeff Doyle's first essay makes clear.

In keeping with the broad theme of the second half of the volume, which examines the impacts and outcomes of the national experience of Vietnam, Grey and Pierce look in successive chapters at the ways in which the war has been dissected and disseminated in the national literatures of Australia, with a sideways glance at American practices as appropriate. Australia has a long tradition of distinguished nonfiction writing about the nation's war experience, one that has transcended national boundaries on occasions. This is especially the case with the writing of the official historian of the First World War, C. E. W. Bean, whose notion of "democratic history" was clearly influential elsewhere in the English-speaking world when the official histories of the next world war came to be written after 1945. Australia's Vietnam War is still imperfectly and unevenly understood, which reflects the state of the historical writing, and it is still capable of exciting occasional controversy along lines familiar to those who witnessed the politics of the war experience itself. The response to early volumes of the official history is an excellent case in point.[1] Fictional writing is in many ways a less satisfactory case. Many of the fictional narratives of the Australian war were written by people who were not there or who saw no combat, in marked contrast to the participant-novelists in the United States. The latter have greatly enhanced our understanding of the experience of men, and especially of young men, in a conflict that has helped to redefine ideas about war in the English language in the twentieth century.

Following from the discussion of the response to veterans after 1972, Doyle's second chapter picks up on the ways in which Australia and the United States have chosen to memorialize the Vietnam War by looking at each national monument, both individually within its own context and comparatively. In the Australian case, the Vietnam monument and its associated memorializing attempts to fit with a tradition of public commemoration and celebration associated with the national martial myth of Anzac. It also operates within long-standing practices of public commemoration at the national level, epitomized both by the Australian War Memorial and the memorial avenue, Anzac Parade, in the heart of the national capital, Canberra.

Australia is an outrider of an English-speaking empire whose symbolic capital once was London and is now Washington. In cultural terms, the received view of the Vietnam War, its nature and course, is overwhelmingly an American one. While there were a number of film and television versions of Australia's war produced in the 1980s, the ideas that shape Australians' understanding of the war are heavily influenced by *Rambo* and *China Beach,* neither of which has anything much to do with the Australian war. The issues that continue to wrack the public and private spheres of American life, such as the alleged role of the media in losing the war; the racial, disciplinary, and drug problems within the U.S. military that the war accentuated; and the long-festering wound of the missing-in-action (MIA) issue have no Australian equivalents. In the 1990s the focus of Australian memorializing has shifted to more specifically Australian sites—August 18, the date of the battle of Long Tan in 1966, is now observed as Vietnam Veterans' Day—but the images this conjures up often have more to do with homogenizing the Vietnam experience along the lines of earlier wars, to make it comprehensible in terms other than those that actually applied in Phuoc Tuy at the time.

The full consequences of Australia's Vietnam involvement have yet to be properly identified, much less understood. In domestic politics, the

Western failure to prevail in Indochina challenged the conservative parties' presumption of moral authority—their semblance of a natural right to govern—for twenty years, and their resurgence in the mid-1990s at the federal level is owed to quite different external and globalizing factors. No Australian prime minister can now claim the quietly assumed authority that was Menzies's natural and customary position. Nor is the American alliance viewed with the same implicit confidence that it was accorded before 1965. In matters of defense, although the official position has been enunciated as one of "self-reliance within an alliance framework," the Vietnam experience makes it still politically sensitive to talk of force projection in the region, of expeditionary forces, or of "forward defense." Veterans' issues remain unresolved, and a portion of that group at least remains unreconciled to the broader Australian community. If the issues that attach themselves to glib headline usage of terms like "Agent Orange" and "PTSD" appear to have lost something of their intensity, at least in public in the 1990s, it is because they are now being pursued in a more systematic manner through the legal and appellant processes of the veterans' benefits system, the Repatriation Commission. This, too, provides an echo of other, older wars and their aftermaths.

The Vietnam War divided both countries, although the divisions were less deep and less lasting in Australia than in the United States. Involvement in Vietnam characterized an older way in which Australians looked at the world. We no longer think about the world or the Asian region in that way, and both the world and the region are vastly different now from what they were then in any case. Australian relations with the United States survived the defeat of Western aims in Indochina, perhaps even were strengthened by it; but we no longer think about that relationship in the same way, either. In Australia, though not the United States, the Vietnam War is increasingly firmly consigned to history, but it is a history that retains the power to influence the present.

A Note about the Anzac Legend

At the level of popular culture in Australia, the "Anzac legend" and its heritage would be in little need of explanation, however (arguably) imperfectly understood. For a U.S. audience it is perhaps worthwhile to offer a summary of the salient features of the legend because it is not without a substance large enough of itself for several volumes and because it is, like so many "well trammeled" beliefs, malleable if not universally accommodating. In brief, then, the Anzac legend is hardly fixed, as recent events with the Australian involvement in the International Force for East Timor (INTERFET) have shown from 1999 to the present. This ongoing commitment of troops has as much adapted as it has used the Anzac legend as its implicit template of behavior and results. Not dissimilar modifications to Anzac have also been conjured up during the celebrations and analyses of the Centenary of Australian Federation throughout 2001. But while Anzac is hardly fixed, there is a core or axis around which the historically differing people and events of the twentieth century Australian armed services constellate. It is this core that is outlined here.

C. E. W. Bean wrote his multivolume history of Australia's participation in the First World War with an eye to setting in place the idea of a new kind of armed service commensurate with the ideas and ideals of the newly federated state of Australia. Much was and is still made of Australia's origins in 1901 as a constitutional democracy founded in a series of legal acts rather than in acts of rebellion and warfare. Yet the new nation seemingly felt the need to be "blooded" and was anxious to aid the Empire in its time of need. It may be curious then that such anxieties also gave rise to the first signs of uneasy relationships with the mother state. Among many abiding concerns with its own possible identities when nineteenth-century Australia measured itself against the ideals of empire, it often found the core culture lacking or inferior. As a frontier culture, predicated on seeing itself as pioneering the conquest of an antagonistically harsh land—summed up in the notion of "the Outback" or "the Bush"—Australians saw themselves as better men than those bred by the urban and industrialized ghettoes of the mother country. The Australian "bushman" as fabricated in the writings of Henry Lawson, Banjo Paterson, and others in the pages of the magazine *Bulletin* and elsewhere, is still discussed critically. The precise origins and meanings are not totally clear, but the trajectory through the late 1880s and 1890s, the Boer War, the 1914–18 war, and into the 1920s is well traveled. When called upon to defend the Anglo-European culture, the margins, the edge of the Empire, provided the best troops and showed the Empire how to fight. In the Boer War the Australians provided quantities of horsemen—allegedly excellent irregular cavalry that predate and predict the famous Light Horse of the First World War.[2] When the Australian and New Zealand governments sent forces to fight in World War I, the tradition was born in the combined acronym of ANZAC: Australian and New Zealand Army Corps. Characteristically, the Anzacs were excellent and natural fighters. Taller, stronger, more rugged than the British "Tommy Atkins," and with long, lean, chiseled features, "Aussies" also possessed a strong sense of individualism, laconic personalities, and ironic dry humor and were spare with words.[3] These men were also spare with hierarchy. It was not so much that they were not given to following orders, but that they were indifferent to the, as they saw it, class-ridden superfluities of the British system and the poor, if not ludicrous, leadership skills of the British. They were gifted with superior fighting skills allied to the democratic talent of skilled individual initiative, something lacking from the cowed underclasses forming the imperial soldiery. Where British society was structured vertically by class, the colonies were decidedly horizontal. The individual was supreme, but he also valued his cohort, his friends, emphasizing the idea of the mate and mateship. Allegiance to the nation or the state was important, but *the* most important feature was one's mates. It was almost inevitable, and in a way necessary, for the legend that there were to be major disasters on the battlefields, as well as regular clashes of rank and class behind the lines. The most significant event, the 1915 Gallipoli campaign, occurred early in the First World War and acted then and throughout the twentieth century as a defining moment against which all others are measured and seems likely to continue as such.

On 25 April 1915, Anzac troops, part of a larger imperial force, undertook amphibious assaults along the Dardanelles coast at Gallipoli in Turkey in an attempt to remove a German ally from the war and secure the Bosphorus and Middle East. The assault was a disaster since the Anzac landing took place at the wrong beaches, leaving the infantry to assault enfilading positions on the cliffs above them. To add to the legend, British forces at a later landing at Suvla in August sat down to "tea" while the Anzac attacks were being shot up by the Turks. A long period of modified trench warfare followed and the campaign was finally terminated with a brilliant Australian withdrawal. The foundations of the Anzac legend are riven thereafter by a sense of loss, waste, and betrayal. To compound this Australian version of the "we was robbed" syndrome during the ensuing months of near-futile siege, the Australians often suffered withering casualties during bayonet charges against Turkish trenches supposedly neutralized by British artillery barrages. The most famous, or rather infamous, example is the charge of 7 August at the Nek, a diversion that cost two thousand Australian lives. In Peter Weir's 1981 film *Gallipoli,* this incident is presented as typical of British incompetence—and worse—callous disregard for Australian troops. The barrage lifted early and the men were ordered to assault even though the Turks were ready for them. In this version, historical accuracy gives way to the legend of the betrayal of superior troops, courageous even under suicidal orders.

By 1916 the Anzacs were fighting on the western front, often used as shock troops but still with a reputation for indiscipline. There they became known as "diggers," a term applied to the miners on the goldfields of the 1850s and which presumably stuck to the Anzacs as apposite for soldiers fighting in trench warfare.

In the 1920s, Bean wrote this legend into his official history, and, if that was not enough, aided those who made it concrete, almost literally, in the design, building, and contents of the Australian War Memorial, which is more a combination shrine, archive, and museum. Briefly, both edifices, the official history and the War Memorial, presented a soldier's-eye-view of the First World War. Grand strategy—the hierarchical war of the imperium—was seconded to the individual digger, the Anzac soldier, as *the* central image.

The Second World War and the Korean actions followed, and in both conflicts Anzac commitments were substantial in comparison to their nations' populations and resources. More importantly, in both wars Australian soldiery hit harder than its weight. The legend of the natural fighting man and of certain levels of "larrikin" indiscipline continued, and the Anzacs thrived on it. Indeed, Lord Haw Haw's naming them the "rats" of Tobruk merely reinforced the digger identity. Put against the First Anzacs, the actions at Tobruk, El Alamein, and in Greece measured up. Kapyong and other Korean actions likewise were taken into the fold, though in less publicly spectacular fashions.[4] When Singapore fell, the Second Anzacs had their large-scale betrayal, too. The New Guinea and Pacific campaigns, especially the battles of the Coral Sea and the Kokoda Trail only reinforced the imagery of the natural soldier and of the political need to stand alongside other major powers, albeit with due care to their potential for inconsistency and betrayal.

That sense of one or another empire cutting Australia adrift profoundly affected the national identity from the middle of the Second World War to the end of the Cold War (and even to the present) and influenced the way Australia viewed the Vietnam conflict. Indeed, that war saw the Australian military designated by itself and the state as the next generation of Anzacs. As the essays in this volume show, the transformation of the Anzac legend through and in the aftermath of the Vietnam War is still active and still central to the national identity. For many, the congruencies of the Anzac legend and the diggers who served in Vietnam were slight, too slight, and the legend seemed unable to accommodate them. That failure raised many issues, not the least about the timeliness of the Anzac legend itself in the later part of the twentieth century. This volume is one product of that incongruence.

Australia's Vietnam War

PETER EDWARDS

1 Some Reflections on the Australian Government's Commitment to the Vietnam War

By mid-April, 1965, the Australian government's senior ministers had decided, but not yet announced, that an Australian battalion would be made available for service in South Vietnam.[1] Meanwhile, a group of Anglican bishops had engaged the Liberal prime minister, Sir Robert Menzies, in a public exchange of letters over Australia's policy toward Vietnam. As this debate continued, the government's principal official adviser on foreign policy, the newly appointed secretary of the Department of External Affairs, Sir James Plimsoll, urged Menzies to make his next contribution short and "unbelligerent" because "there are some aspects of the Vietnam situation which are so hazy that anything written, no matter how carefully, can be open to rebuttal."[2] It was sound advice that bears repeating even today as the Vietnam War passes from politics into history.

The April, 1965, decision to deploy troops was seen then, as now, as the biggest single step by which Australia came to be committed to the Vietnam War, but it can best be understood as the culmination of twenty years of Australian involvement in Southeast Asia. During the decades following Hiroshima, two great historical movements dominated international politics. One was the Cold War, and the other was the decolonization of the European empires. These two great processes were interwoven in perhaps their most complex and challenging form in Southeast Asia. In trying to understand the events in the region to their immediate north during this period, Australians tended to fall into one of two camps. Those of a more conservative disposition, including not only the leaders of the Liberal and Country Parties that held office in Canberra for most of this period but also a significant portion of the Labor Party, tended to interpret events in Cold War terms. Every development was seen as either a gain or a loss for the anticommunist cause. By contrast, those of a more left-liberal persuasion—including many in the Labor Party as well as a number of academics, clergymen, journalists, and other commentators—tended to place greater emphasis on the decolonization process, decrying the conservative emphasis on communism and stressing the importance of the anticolonial urge for independence. In retrospect, neither school of thought can claim a monopoly of wisdom or success.

Australian policy makers were first forced to choose between these two approaches in the Indonesian revolution of the late 1940s. The Labor government, led by Prime Minister J. B. Chifley, gave firm and effective support to the nationalist rebels, despite conservative criticism, and it proved to be a wise choice. The nationalist revolution was successful and Australia's role laid the foundations for a good relationship with the new government, until soured by the dispute over West New Guinea in the late 1950s.

An insurgency erupted in Malaya in 1948, leading to the twelve-year conflict known as the Malayan Emergency. It seems clear that Chifley, like some of his principal advisers, was immediately inclined to see this dispute as essentially similar to the one in Indonesia, despite the strong advice of the Australian diplomats in Malaya that the two positions were in fact quite different. The secretary of the Department of External Affairs, the youthful J. W. Burton, even advanced the remarkable assertion that Chinese sympathetic to the anticommunist Kuomintang government in China largely instigated the insurgency. One of the principal Australian diplomats in Malaya, Francis Stuart, has described this as "extraordinary in its naivety, inaccuracy and looniness," given that the avowedly communist insurgents were killing more Kuomintang sympathizers than Europeans.[3] Chifley's comments were more moderate, indicating that he saw the struggle as essentially an anticolonial uprising by exploited workers.

Notwithstanding his general sympathy for Clement Attlee's Labour government in Britain, he took steps to ensure that Australia did not become substantially involved in giving military support to the British colonial administration in Malaya.[4] Under pressure from the opposition and the press, he sent some small arms and radio sets, but remained firmly against any suggestion that Australian troops or other servicemen might be sent to Malaya.

The Menzies government, elected in December, 1949, took a different view. It regarded Malaya, like Korea and Indochina, as essentially another theater in the global struggle between democracy and communism. In 1950 it sent both transport aircraft and bombers from the Royal Australian Air Force to assist in the campaign against the communist-led insurgency. More significantly, in 1955, as part of the creation of the British

Commonwealth Far East Strategic Reserve, it sent a battalion to Malaya, the first Australian troops to be committed overseas in peacetime.

The reaction of those who opposed these commitments is significant. The first public debate over Malaya, in April, 1950, coincided with a controversial visit to Australia by the dean of Canterbury, Hewlett Johnson, widely known as "the Red Dean" for his frequent expressions of admiration for Joseph Stalin and the Soviet Union. Johnson, who described communism as "a Christian movement that is surging upward in every part of the world," also described British policy in Malaya as "imperialistic" and aimed at the encirclement of the Soviet Union.[5] Other respected commentators, such as Macmahon Ball of the University of Melbourne and Peter Russo in the *Argus,* expressed similar views in more moderate terms. More notably, the subsequent commitment of troops to Malaya in 1955 followed not only the Indochina crisis of 1954, centering on the fall of Dien Bien Phu, but also some highly divisive controversies in Australian domestic politics, from the defection of Soviet diplomat Vladimir Petrov to the disastrous split in the Labor Party. In this supercharged atmosphere, the phrase "no troops to Malaya" became a slogan of great political and emotional significance in Labor politics. It also marked the divide between those who formed the Anticommunist Labor Party, which later became the Democratic Labor Party, and those who remained in the Labor Party proper, which adopted a more radical foreign policy. (Until quite recently, the graffiti message "no troops to Malaya" could still be seen in railway culverts around Melbourne.)

In 1955 and 1956, Labor members argued that the dispatch of Australian troops to Malaya was opposed by the local population, and would lead to lasting and bitter resentment when an independent government took power. In fact, Malaya gained its independence in 1957 and the elected government—especially its prime minister, Tunku Abdul Rahman—explicitly welcomed the continued presence of Australian and other Commonwealth forces. In 1959, during a visit to Australia, Rahman expressed strongly anticommunist and pro-Commonwealth sentiments, which delighted his hosts. The following year, the Emergency was declared over throughout Malaya. The Australian government could thus draw positive conclusions from its policies on Malaya. In the face of domestic and external criticism it had joined one of its principal allies in a military intervention in a former European colony in Southeast Asia in order to combat a communist-led insurgency. The deployment of Australian troops had led not to hostility but to warm relations with the freely elected government of an independent, prowestern country that had good prospects of economic prosperity and political stability.

This experience was clearly fresh in the minds of the Menzies government when it first faced the possibility of intervention in Indochina in the early 1960s. Just as the Chifley government approached Malaya in the light of its experience with Indonesia, so the Menzies government approached Indochina in the light of its experience with Malaya. In May, 1962, less than two years after the end of the Emergency, the government decided to send to South Vietnam a group of army instructors that became known as the Australian Army Training Team Vietnam (AATTV). The cabinet minute recording this decision explicitly drew the parallel with Malaya, comparing the Vietcong with the Malayan "bandits" and asserting that Australian personnel in Malaya after independence had "played a useful part in countering aggression."[6]

Similarly, when critics of the government began to raise arguments against western policy in Vietnam in the 1960s, their effectiveness was reduced by the fact that similar arguments had been raised over Malaya and evidently proved wrong. We now know that, for example, the Anglican bishops who tackled Menzies in March and April, 1965, had good reason to point to the risks of a military commitment; but the tone and substance of his replies suggest that Menzies saw them as essentially the successors to the Red Dean and the other clergy, known as the "peace parsons," who had challenged his policy on Malaya in the 1950s.

This is not to say that the insurgency in Vietnam was seen as simply a repetition of that which had been defeated in Malaya. At least some on the conservative side of politics understood the major differences. During the parliamentary debate on the Gulf of Tonkin incident in August, 1964, for example, Malcolm Fraser, a young Liberal backbencher and future prime minister with a strong interest in defense and foreign affairs, accurately noted some of the political, ethnic, geographic, and military differences which meant that "[t]he task in this struggle [Vietnam] is infinitely more difficult."[7] Nevertheless, the fact that he raised this question, and the way in which he did it, underlines the wider point. If we are to understand how and why particular decisions were made, we must understand the mind-set of those making the decisions, the information and the comparisons that they brought to the task. At the risk of oversimplification, it could be said that those who got Vietnam wrong did so partly because they had previously gotten Malaya right; and those who got Vietnam right suffered a loss of credibility because they had previously gotten Malaya wrong.

This chapter has dealt at some length with Australia's commitment to Vietnam while scarcely mentioning the United States. That is quite deliberate. It is an exaggeration to argue, as many have, that Australia became involved in Vietnam solely because of its relationship with the

United States. Just as the Australian experience in Vietnam was not identical to the American experience, so too were the two nations' paths there also quite different. The American route to Vietnam lay through Europe and Northeast Asia, owing much to the perceived need to see both France and Japan established as economically strong and politically stable partners. Australia, for obvious reasons, was much less concerned about France or even Japan than it was about Malaya, Indonesia, and the other countries in Southeast Asia. Australia's concerns about developments in the region were separate from, if often parallel to, those of the United States. Even if the United States had not existed, the Australian government would have been deeply concerned over the perceived threat from communism in Southeast Asia. Nevertheless, it must be said that the Australian-American relationship was vitally important in shaping Australia's reactions to this perceived threat.

The Asian and American dimensions to Australian policy were well summarized immediately after the commitment of the AATTV in May, 1962. In the Melbourne *Herald,* Denis Warner, an Australian journalist with extensive experience in Southeast Asia, wrote an article in question-and-answer form that began: "Why is Australia getting involved in the Vietnam War? Partly because we think a Communist victory there would threaten the rest of South-East Asia and jeopardise our security and partly because of the need to convince the Americans that we are more than paper allies." Expanding on the latter point, he added, "It's a sort of life insurance cover we're taking out." This marked perhaps the first public use of that famous phrase.[8]

Several general comments about the American dimension in Australian policy need to be made before turning to one particularly important aspect. The Menzies government consistently emphasized that its foreign and defense policies, especially after a statement on 1 April 1955, were based on collaboration with "great and powerful friends." This enabled it simultaneously to point to the perceived danger of Asian communist expansionism while keeping Australian defense expenditures under strict constraints. In 1952–53, reflecting the current concern that the Korean War might be the prelude to a third world war, Australia spent £215.3 million on defense, or 5.1 percent of its gross national product. For almost a decade thereafter, defense spending was kept below £200 million, not creeping beyond that level until the early 1960s, by which time it represented only 2.7 percent of the gross national product. This is well known, but perhaps the extent to which the government pursued this line has not been fully understood. In 1959, the Defence Committee, composed of the government's senior military and civilian advisers on defense policy, presented a major paper proposing that Australian forces should be developed in such a way that they could act independently of allies. The cabinet explicitly rejected this advice and returned the paper to the Chiefs of Staff for reconsideration. The chiefs stressed that they were seeking greater military independence only as a long-term goal, not an immediate aim, but even this was not enough for the cabinet. The government's formal statement on defense policy later that year emphasized that Australia's defense forces were being designed to act with allies under collective defense arrangements in Southeast Asia.

The Menzies government deliberately rejected the idea of self-reliance, even as a long-term goal. When defense expenditures began to rise markedly from 1963–64 onward, it was still within the framework of a policy based on alliances.

In a sense, this approach worked. The consistent policy of restraining defense expenditures and instead giving high priority to developing Australia's economic infrastructure was fundamental to the country's steadily growing prosperity in the 1950s and 1960s. But when the United States began to tire of carrying what it regarded as an excessive proportion of the Western defense burden, Australia had little option but to respond to American pressure to support U.S. policies in Southeast Asia, notably in Indochina. In that sense, it may be said that Australia's commitment to Vietnam was the price that had to be paid for its post-1945 prosperity.

Nevertheless, none of this should be taken to mean that the Australian government was as supine in its diplomatic dealings with the United States as has sometimes been deduced from its public statements. The records indicate that Australian and American perspectives did not always coincide, and to coordinate the two nations' policies required more effort than was publicly apparent. One major concern in Canberra, strange as it may seem in retrospect, was that the U.S. government might not be sufficiently concerned with the security of anticommunist governments in Southeast Asia. This was particularly evident in the early 1960s, when the Menzies government for some time feared that John F. Kennedy's Democratic administration might not be as resolute in its anticommunism, especially in that part of the world, as its Republican predecessor. American historians generally portray Kennedy as a rather blinkered Cold Warrior, confrontational in his relations with the communist bloc; but that was not the view held by the Australian government at that time.

This was most evident in May, 1962, when the ANZUS Council, the ministerial body set up by the ANZUS treaty of 1951, met in Australia for the first time. Dean Rusk, Kennedy's secretary of state, visited Canberra for this meeting, and the Australian cabinet decided it was an excellent opportunity to try to elicit "the inner political thinking and defence planning" of the United States—something of a Holy Grail for Australian policy makers for decades.[9] The Australian minister for external affairs, Sir Garfield Barwick, QC, had been a brilliant and aggressive barrister before going into politics, and he interpreted this as a brief to cross-examine Rusk. In a way that visibly irritated the American and startled the New Zealanders present, he interrogated Rusk at some length on whether the United States had made a fundamental decision to defend the anticommunist government in South Vietnam "come hell or high water." Rusk answered positively, indicated that he was looking for support from allies, and, in response to Barwick's persistence, referred pointedly to the fact that the United States already had some eight thousand men in South Vietnam, whereas Australia had none. Rusk's performance under Barwick's questioning led directly to the Australian commitment of the AATTV.

But if Australia was sometimes worried that the United States was not sufficiently committed to the defense of anticommunist governments in Asia, another recurring theme was the fear that it might go too far in that cause. On several occasions in the 1950s and 1960s, most notably during the "off-shore islands" crises, Australian policy makers were worried that Washington, under pressure from "the China lobby," might unleash Chiang Kai-shek, allowing him to precipitate a full-scale attack on the communist government on the mainland. Similarly, Australian ministers held a persistent fear that the United States might, under extreme pressure in Indochina, take action that could lead to a major war with China, possibly including the use of nuclear weapons. This fear had been a significant factor in Australian policy during the 1954 Indochina crisis, when R. G. Casey, as minister for external affairs, had shared many of the concerns that Britain and other Commonwealth countries held about the policies generally associated with Secretary of State John Foster Dulles and Adm. Arthur Radford, the chairman of the Joint Chiefs of Staff.

This concern emerged again in 1961 in the context of the major crisis over Laos. In that year, the Australian cabinet twice formally decided that it would follow an American lead and, if called upon, join a Western military intervention in Laos. But these decisions, which marked a major step toward the eventual commitment to Vietnam, were not taken with equanimity. The Australians were deeply concerned that a relatively small intervention against the communist forces in Laos might precipitate an overt response not only by the communist government in Hanoi but also by China. (Memories of the Chinese intervention in the

Korean War no doubt played their part in this concern.) Such an intervention might in turn induce the military leaders of the Western force to demand the use of nuclear weapons to avoid being overrun by hordes of enemy forces. A special cabinet committee met twice to consider this issue, after which Menzies drew the attention of both the British and American governments to Australia's concerns on this score. Beyond that, there seemed little that Australia could do.

This concern does at least help to explain one of the puzzling features of Australian policy in the early 1960s: Australia's continued strong adherence to the Southeast Asia Treaty Organization (SEATO), established by the 1954 Manila treaty. The weakness of that organization had long been manifest, especially since the Laotian crisis of 1960–61, when it was clear that the eight member nations held markedly different views on the feasibility of Indochina intervention. Nevertheless, Australian ministers continued to give SEATO strong rhetorical support and to base Australian military plans for the region on those developed by the SEATO Military Planning Office in Bangkok. The cabinet records suggest that at least two factors lay behind this continued support. First and most obviously, SEATO's Asian membership meant that intervention under its aegis would avoid, or at least lessen, the appearance of a conflict between whites and nonwhites. But the second reason, which could not be stated publicly, was that the Australian government believed there would be a reduced risk that the military commander might call for the use of nuclear weapons if the Western intervention was conducted as a multinational operation under a SEATO plan rather than under unilateral U.S. leadership.

Concerns of this nature never became the dominant strand in Australian policy. They were never allowed to outweigh the factors that led Australia to give strong political and eventually military support to the United States in Southeast Asia. But these fears were real, forming an undercurrent of Australian involvement in Southeast Asia that should not be totally neglected.

There were, therefore, many more aspects and nuances to the Australian-American relationship over this period than many accounts have suggested. A further consideration was particularly important: Indonesia. Both the United States and Australia found it difficult to make policy toward Indonesia because of the complexities of the relationship between nationalism and communism there, further complicated by the personality of President Sukarno. Differences between Canberra and Washington became evident over the disputed territory of West New Guinea. Australia supported the Dutch claim to maintain this territory, which had not been included when the rest of the Netherlands

East Indies had become independent as the Republic of Indonesia. The Australian government feared that if Indonesia acquired West New Guinea, a subsequent takeover in Jakarta by the Indonesian Communist Party would bring communism right up to the borders of the Australian-administered territories on the eastern half of New Guinea. The Americans, by contrast, were more inclined to accept the argument, persuasively put by President Sukarno and Foreign Minister Subandrio, that the Indonesian acquisition of West New Guinea would be the best way to ensure that Jakarta did not come under a communist regime. In early 1961, American policy swung decisively in this direction and the Australian government was forced to accept the inevitable.

This controversial and highly publicized episode exposed the dependence of the Australian government on the support of its great and powerful friends, especially the United States. It was clearly at the front of ministers' minds when, in 1963, Indonesia announced a policy of confrontation toward the proposal to form a federation of Malaysia from the states of Malaya, Singapore, and British territories on the island of Borneo. It seemed that Sukarno was intent on applying the same mixture of military and diplomatic measures that had won him success over West New Guinea, a prospect that could only alarm the Australians. For its part, the United States made it clear that it regarded this as essentially a concern for the relevant Commonwealth countries—Britain, Australia, and New Zealand—and that American support was to be considered only as a last resort. At the same time, Washington indicated that even this degree of support was conditional on support for American policy elsewhere—and by 1963 it was becoming increasingly clear that "elsewhere" meant Vietnam.

This implicit quid pro quo was most clearly indicated in June, 1963, when a senior State Department official, Averell Harriman, visited Canberra. The Australian minister who seemed most concerned by it was one whose influence on critical issues in Australian foreign policy has often been underestimated: John McEwen, the deputy prime minister and leader of the Country Party. In an important meeting with the Australian cabinet, Harriman linked American support for the Australian position in Indonesia with Australian support for the United States in Vietnam. The discussions initiated at this meeting led to a famous "piece of paper" in which the United States delineated its degree of support under ANZUS for Australian involvement in Indonesia. Ill-chosen words about this document probably precipitated Barwick's sudden removal from office in April, 1964. The public controversies over this matter underlined the extent to which Australia relied on American defense support in general, and over Indonesia in particular. The cabinet records suggest that McEwen was perhaps less inclined than his Liberal colleagues to see events in Indochina as constituting a direct threat to Australia, but even more concerned over the trend of developments in Indonesia. In effect, he applied a farmer's logic to the two simultaneous crises in Southeast Asia: You help your friend to put out the brushfire that concerns him, because you might need his help to put out another brushfire even closer to your property. His constant advocacy of this view proved vitally important in the crucial meetings of the cabinet's Foreign Affairs and Defence Committee in April, 1965.

British historian C.V. Wedgwood once wrote: "History is lived forwards but is written in retrospect. We know the end before we consider the beginning and we can never wholly recapture what it was to know the beginning only."[10] In looking back at Australian involvement in Southeast Asia between 1945 and 1965, Australians cannot exclude the knowledge that it ended in a disastrous commitment to Vietnam, and all developments tend to be seen in that light. But Vietnam was not seen as a major problem until very late in the day, whereas Indonesia was a far greater preoccupation, to an extent that has usually been overlooked. In particular, the impact of the Indonesian military buildup in December, 1964, and January, 1965, has not been adequately recognized. In the early months of 1965, Australian ministers were deeply concerned by the simultaneous pressure from the British to assist in the confrontation with Jakarta and from the Americans to assist in Vietnam. McEwen, as acting prime minister in January, told the British that these two conflicts were "coming to form part of a common pattern and a common threat."[11] The commitment of the Australian battalion to Vietnam in April, 1965, has now become established in popular memory, but the preceding commitment of another battalion, together with a squadron of the Special Air Service, to Borneo in January and February of the same year, is usually recalled only by specialists.

The wisdom of C. V. Wedgwood's dictum, that "History is lived forwards but written in retrospect," is well illustrated by the difficulties we have in identifying the motives for the government's introduction of conscription in November, 1964. The conscripts chosen by ballot under this scheme served in Vietnam, a fact that contributed enormously to the public controversy over the war. There has therefore been a tendency to assume that the scheme was introduced for precisely this purpose, despite the fact that comment at the time centered on the developing conflict between Indonesia and Malaysia. The documentary evidence makes it clear that the underlying concern within the government was that Australia might simultaneously face commitments in three areas of conflict: the Indonesian-Malaysian Confrontation, which appeared to be on the brink of major escalation; Vietnam or some other part of mainland Southeast Asia; and the possibility of incursions across Australia's only land border, that between West New Guinea, which was controlled by Indonesia, and the Australian-administered territories in eastern New Guinea. We now know that the confrontation with Indonesia eased in 1965 and ended in 1966 without requiring a greater involvement by Australian forces, and that the feared Indonesian incursions into New Guinea never eventuated. But the decision makers in late 1964 could not foresee that. Indeed, there is clear evidence that, on the day the cabinet decided on conscription, the fear uppermost in the minds of both Menzies and McEwen was the potential conflict against Indonesia in New Guinea, the one that never happened. At that time, American policy toward Vietnam was in limbo. The specific approaches that ultimately led to the Australian commitment did not begin until early December, a full month after the conscription decision had been made.

Moreover, it would also be wrong to assume that, insofar as a commitment to mainland Southeast Asia was contemplated in late 1964, the location for such a commitment would be South Vietnam. A careful examination of the papers prepared by the senior advisers on defense and foreign policy suggests that they had virtually written off the prospects of survival of the anticommunist government in Saigon, together with the governments of neighboring Laos and Cambodia. They seemed to expect that Australia might be asked to send forces to help bolster the next "domino," Thailand. This deduction is supported by looking at the exercises conducted, usually annually, by the Chief of the General Staff (CGS)—exercises that indicated the location and type of conflict the army felt it was most likely to face. The scenarios for the 1959 and 1960 CGS exercises involved conflict in South Vietnam, in 1961 Laos, in 1962 South Vietnam again, but in September, 1964, the hypothetical trouble spot was Thailand.

That prompts some comments on the so-called domino theory, the idea that a communist victory in South Vietnam would lead almost inevitably to communist domination of Southeast Asia and more. One wonders if Australians, as the residents of the only nation to occupy an entire continent, have found it especially difficult to grasp the subtleties of the effects of political change on adjoining countries. The domino theory was neither the undeniable truism that its proponents asserted (and often exaggerated for electoral purposes), nor the groundless folly that its critics later contended. There were many reasons why so many observers of Southeast Asia—not only Australians, but also Americans, Europeans, and not least many Asians—believed in some form of domino theory. In the late 1940s and early 1950s, communists and anticommunists alike tended to believe, whether in hope or in fear, that a communist victory in Indochina would have a huge psychological effect, not only in Southeast Asia but throughout the underdeveloped world. After what we might call the anticommunist domino effect of events in Eastern Europe in 1989 and among the republics of the Soviet Union in 1991, the idea of a chain reaction no longer seems quite so absurd as it was held to be in the immediate aftermath of the Vietnam War.

But in the Southeast Asian context there were also practical reasons for taking such an approach. In a closely fought struggle between an established government and a rebel movement, the existence of political, economic, and military support from a close neighbor, together with sanctuaries across the border, could mean the difference between victory and defeat for the insurgents. The victory at Dien Bien Phu in 1954 was won by communist Vietnamese, not Chinese, but it owed much to the support received from China and the sanctuaries provided in that country over the preceding five years. It was no coincidence that the two major communist insurgencies that were defeated in the 1950s took place in an archipelago and on a peninsula. If the Philippines and Malaya had shared long land borders with, say, China or North Vietnam, the outcome of those insurgencies might well have been different.

None of this is to justify the simplistic application of the domino theory to Indochina in the 1960s, when much had changed since the late 1940s and early 1950s. By 1961, when President Kennedy and British prime minister Harold Macmillan were discussing the Laotian crisis, neither side doubted that a communist victory in Laos would have wider ramifications. The issue was whether Western military intervention could achieve a positive result. Similarly, in 1964–65, few Western observers doubted that the apparently imminent fall of South Vietnam would be closely followed by that of Laos and Cambodia, so that the Cold War front line would become the Mekong River border between Laos and Thailand—as eventually happened in 1975. The real question in 1965 was whether the benefits of Western military intervention could outweigh the costs, given the balance of internal and external forces at work in South Vietnam; and that was the question to which both Washington and Canberra gave the wrong answer. The central flaw here can best be illustrated by returning to the comparison between Vietnam and Malaya, with which this essay began. In both the Malayan Emergency and the Indonesian-Malaysian Confrontation, western intervention was designed to support Tunku Abdul Rahman's alliance government, which enjoyed genuine popular support. By contrast, the successive juntas in Saigon never commanded the degree of popular support necessary to counter the claims of the National Liberation Front and its creators, the communist regime in Hanoi. In December, 1964, and January, 1965, the United States and its allies were still hoping desperately that a sufficiently strong government could be formed in Saigon on which a western military intervention could be based. In February, 1965, Washington and Canberra came independently to the decision that military intervention did not depend on political stability in Saigon, but would somehow help to create it. If one is forced to identify a particular point at which western policy made a fatal error, it was then.

Three broad conclusions suggest themselves: the Australian policy making that led to involvement in Vietnam was conditioned not only by the relationship with the United States but also by Australia's independent concerns and experiences with Malaya, Malaysia, and Indonesia; that both the Southeast Asian and the American dimensions of Australian policy making were rather more complex than has often been assumed; and, above all, that Plimsoll was right when he urged Menzies to be cautious and not dogmatic when saying anything about Vietnam.

IAN McNEILL, *with an addendum by Jeffrey Grey*

2 The Australian Army and the Vietnam War

The Defence Committee met in Canberra on 5 March 1971 to consider the future direction of Australian defense policy. The 1st Australian Task Force was still fighting in Phuoc Tuy Province, South Vietnam, but substantial withdrawals already had taken place. Others were soon to be ordered. The committee determined that Australia would not be likely to commit ground forces to counterinsurgency operations again unless its own security was directly affected. These words underscored the end of an era in Australian strategy, during which forces were sent to Southeast Asia in defense of the Australian mainland and trust territories against communist encroachment. It was then the height of the Cold War, a time when the deep ideological hostility between communist and noncommunist powers threatened global war. This chapter outlines military and strategic developments that led to the Vietnam involvement and discusses some of the operational issues.

Defense Changes

As Robert O'Neill concludes in his official history, the Korean War accelerated changes to Australian defense and foreign policies already in train.[1] Successive governments recognized that security in the Pacific region rested on the United States, that the United Kingdom still had a significant role in the Southeast Asian and western Pacific area, and that, mindful of recent experience against Japan, Australia required strong defense forces (although little had been done to achieve this).[2] But the disadvantage of Australia's continuing strategic link with Britain was that it involved a commitment of Australian forces to the security of the Middle East in a global war without a commensurate guarantee of sufficient British forces to hold Malaya against a significant communist threat.

A conference of defense leaders from Britain, New Zealand, and Australia in Melbourne in 1953 resolved that the defense of Malaya was the key to defense in Southeast Asia. It recommended the creation of the Far East Strategic Reserve of one infantry brigade with air and naval units to be based in Malaya and to be maintained by Britain, Australia, and New Zealand. Its purpose would be to deter communist aggression and, as a subsidiary role, it would be available to counter "communist terrorists," the armed forces of the Malayan Communist Party.

The committee further identified a potential direct military threat to Australia should Malaya fall. It foresaw communist infiltration of Indonesia and the possible eventual confrontation of Australia by an enemy within bombing range of the mainland and who shared a common frontier in Papua New Guinea.[3] Manifestations of Australia's concern over Indonesian intentions loomed large in defense planning well into the following decade. The defeat of the French Union forces at Dien Bien Phu on 7 May 1954 and the subsequent Geneva agreements concluded on 21 July crystallized the government's unequivocal acceptance of Southeast Asia as Australia's area of strategic interest.

The agreements provided for the division of Vietnam at the 17th Parallel into two separately administered zones, communist in the north—the Democratic Republic of Vietnam (DRV), commonly referred to as North Vietnam—and noncommunist in the south, the Republic of Vietnam (RVN), or South Vietnam. The division was to be temporary, pending a countrywide plebiscite on reunification to be conducted by July, 1956. The agreements further provided that neither side would use force to overcome the other. As a shield against external communist aggression against member nations in Southeast Asia, and aimed particularly at any attempt by North Vietnam to extend its influence by military means, the United States negotiated the Southeast Asia Defense Treaty in Manila on 8 September 1954. Australia joined with the United States and six other member nations to create the South East Asia Treaty Organization (SEATO).[4] Vietnam, Laos, and Cambodia were nominated as protocol states.

By 1956 it became clear that the new president, Ngo Dinh Diem, had survived and was strengthening his position in the south. He refused to hold elections, claiming that they could not be free in the north. In this move he had the moral backing of the United States, which encouraged the retention of the partition of Vietnam into communist and noncommunist states in the pattern set by Korea and Germany. On its side, the DRV received only limited support for the holding of elections from the Soviet Union and China.[5] Both the DRV and RVN entered into ruthless campaigns to suppress opposition and consolidate their zones. A land reform program instituted in North Vietnam in 1955 and 1956 seemed less dedicated to reform (which was, in effect, collectivization of private farmland), than it was to the violent eradication of a social class and therefore potential communist opponents. It led to widespread killings and punitive measures and finally to a peasant revolt before being checked.[6] In the south, Diem apparently almost extinguished the whole clandestine communist apparatus in a campaign of persecution of former Vietminh and possible rivals for power.[7] But the widespread killing and incarceration of former resistance fighters alienated many groups and contributed to the later success of the communist-led insurgency.[8] Both the DRV and the RVN consolidated during the remainder of the 1950s, each receiving extensive aid from its allies, with the DRV receiving at least $578.5 million in economic assistance from the Soviet Union, China, and Eastern Europe, while the RVN received $1.393 billion from the United States.[9]

In December, 1960, in response to appeals from the growing insurgency in the south, the Central Committee of the Communist Party in Hanoi proclaimed the National Front for the Liberation of South Vietnam. Having already sanctioned the use of force against the RVN in 1959 the Central Committee in effect assumed leadership of the revolution. The so-called National Liberation Front (NLF) consisted of a coalition of groups opposed to the Diem regime, not necessarily communist themselves, but communist-led for ultimately communist ends. Its aim was to overthrow the Diem regime and sever its connection with its U.S. ally. Less publicized was the aim of reunification under communist rule. The "liberation" was from "American imperialism," South Vietnam being dubbed an American colony.[10] Jeffrey Race describes the creation of the NLF as a facade to conceal, for international consumption, the true role of North Vietnam.[11] The assumption of primacy by Hanoi and the flow of soldiers and materiel to the south, which were essential to the success of the war against the RVN, prompted American and RVN cries of "aggression from the north" and determined the events that followed.

Raising an Army

Australian membership of regional security organizations, more particularly SEATO, brought with it the requirement to nominate forces to contribute to planned contingencies. These would be put into effect if member nations or the protocol states were threatened by subversion or overt aggression by a communist state. But the army had no standing forces to offer beyond the single battalion and supporting elements allotted to the British Commonwealth Far East Strategic Reserve (BCFESR) in Malaya. Raising that battalion in 1955 had proved just as difficult as sending a battalion to Korea five years earlier. In an effort to overcome this predicament, the cabinet in 1957 directed that the three-month national service scheme be reduced and that "absolute priority" be given to building up, equipping, and maintaining a regular brigade group.[12]

The decision was a milestone in the development of the standing army. For the first time in peace, precedence would be given to the maintenance of a well equipped, highly trained, and self-contained force for rapid deployment overseas. The emphasis in defense planning had been transformed from a leisurely state of preparedness by an uncertain future date to the maintenance of a force in being which could be sustained over a long period. Large manpower numbers gave way to modern equipment, mobility, and firepower. The allocation of forces for participation in new regional security arrangements was becoming a more realistic proposition.

Shortages of manpower in a time of full employment continued to prevent the army reaching the manpower ceiling necessary if the regular brigade group was to be at full strength. To provide additional manpower, the national service scheme for training youths was fully suspended in January, 1960. That same year, the army reorganized into the Pentropic formation, again primarily to conserve manpower.[13]

By mid-1964, regional tensions were becoming critical. Beginning in May, 1963, Indonesia intensified its confrontation with Malaysia. As a result, Britain requested direct military assistance that could only be supplied at some expense to SEATO commitments. Border incidents had occurred between Papua New Guinea and the new state of West Irian. Should Australia accede to British requests for assistance in Borneo, the Confrontation could spread to Papua New Guinea. Furthermore, appeals could be expected from Britain and the United Nations over the situation in Cyprus. Finally, the situation in Laos and Vietnam was becoming of pressing concern. In the light of these events, the Chief of the General Staff, Lt. Gen. Sir John Wilton, concluded that it was necessary to be able to commit ground forces to two or more areas simultaneously. Time to raise these forces might run out, as international tensions could resolve themselves unfavorably well before 1972, when the planned ceiling of thirty-three thousand troops was to be reached.

Following the Gulf of Tonkin incident in August, 1964, the cabinet agreed with the Defence Committee's new strategic assessment that Australia faced the possibility of being committed in three widely separated areas: the Southeast Asian mainland, Malaysia, and Papua New Guinea. But Australia did not have the combat forces to become deeply involved in three areas at the same time.[14] Faced with mounting international tensions and the need rapidly to expand the army, the government almost immediately made two decisions of critical importance to

Australia's defense preparedness. In November, 1964, it revived the national service scheme. This provided for the call-up of twenty-year-old males selected by a birthday ballot for two years' service which could include service overseas.[15] With intakes commencing in early 1965, the army was soon well on the way to achieving its desired manpower ceiling of thirty-three thousand. The following January it approved the abandonment of the large Pentropic organization in favor of the smaller conventional battalions. As Wilton remarked, "it is not the size of the battalions but the number of battalions which counts." Just four months later an Australian battalion was able to fit neatly into an American brigade in Vietnam.

A Counterinsurgency Doctrine

As these events were taking place, the direction of the army's preparation for war was changing from conventional war in Southeast Asia to counterinsurgency. It was becoming apparent in 1962 that South Vietnam, a protocol state that SEATO was designed to protect, was "going under" without any overt invasion. Alarmed by this development, SEATO planners were forced to take notice of the possibility that military assistance could be required in circumstances that were not so clear-cut as had been envisaged. Communist revolutionary warfare, which presented few targets for nuclear weapons or massed allied forces, was now being recognized as a distinct and formidable threat.

The army published an interim tactical doctrine on counterrevolutionary warfare in December, 1962. It derived from the Australian experience in Malaya, the French experience in Indochina, and the teachings of Mao Tse-tung, and was worked out in conjunction with British experts at General Headquarters, Far East Land Forces, Singapore. Intensive training in counterinsurgency operations was conducted throughout the Field Force from 1963.[16] Units and formations adapted elements of the doctrine for their individual training programs, while Army Headquarters (AHQ) schools, in particular those concerned with officer promotions, were required to include problems on antiguerrilla operations.[17] Information on the enemy and the conduct of operations in Vietnam was collected at AHQ from Australian Army advisers in Vietnam, military intelligence, the U.S. Military Assistance Advisory Group Vietnam (USMAAG), and the regular visits to Vietnam of Australian observers from Malaya. This information was disseminated to army schools and commands.[18]

Training in units generally followed the pattern of small-unit operations as these had been practiced in preparation for Malaya, although the skills and techniques of conventional warfare (advance, attack, defense, and withdrawal) were not forgotten. New terms and techniques were introduced such as search and clear, search and destroy, and cordon and search. Officers were required to lecture their troops on the appeal and threat of communist ideology. Individual battalions and the Jungle Training Centre erected their own Vietnamese-style hamlets, complete with hideouts, tunnels, and booby traps to practice cordon and search and attack techniques. The whole army was given over to counterinsurgency.

Australian Army Training Team Vietnam

As an expression of its concern over communist gains in Indochina, the Australian government dispatched thirty officers, warrant officers, and sergeants to Vietnam in July, 1962, to form the Australian Army Training Team Vietnam (AATTV).[19] Expert in jungle warfare and with many members possessed of Malayan experience, the predominantly infantry group joined the growing influx of American advisers, which reached eleven thousand by the end of 1962. America had requested a contribution from Australia not so much for the military value of such a token force but for its political significance. In assisting the Republic of Vietnam to put down the insurgency that was directed and supported from Hanoi, Washington wanted to forestall communist charges of "U.S. imperialism." The Americans thus wanted as many countries as possible standing by them and the Republic of Vietnam in what became known as the "more flags" program.

The AATTV grew to one hundred officers and warrant officers by 1965. Deployed throughout South Vietnam but predominantly in the northern provinces until the closing stages of the allied presence, they served in all of the many kinds of units that made up the South Vietnamese armed forces and distinguished themselves by becoming probably the most highly decorated unit of its size in the Australian Army. With further increases in strength, the AATTV remained in Vietnam for twelve months after the departure of Australian combat forces, leaving shortly before the cease-fire agreement of January, 1973.

A Suggestion of Combat Forces

In early December, 1964, the Australian ambassador in Washington, J. K. Waller, was briefed by Assistant Secretary of State William Bundy.[20] Describing the situation in Vietnam as "fragile but not unhopeful," Bundy outlined new American plans for increasing the pressure on North Vietnam. He referred to a U.S. proposition to deploy one division and two battalions of marines in northern South Vietnam but added that the marines could be reinforced with whatever troops Australia and New Zealand might be able to provide. American planners had in mind an international force based near the Demilitarized Zone (DMZ) to deter ground invasion from the north, block attacks down the coastal plain, and shield against infiltration. Bundy concluded by welcoming comments from respective governments. He added that the possibility of deploying combat forces could be discussed at the military staff level if Australia and New Zealand thought this might be useful.[21] For the moment, however, the United States would be asking Australia for an additional two hundred advisers.[22] Waller's report of this briefing initiated formal consideration in Canberra of the introduction of ground forces. At AHQ, Wilton immediately summoned his staff.[23]

The "South Vietnam Problem"

Behind the assessment of the service chiefs was the continuously deteriorating military and political situation in Vietnam. The government of Ngo Dinh Diem had consolidated its position during the late 1950s. This success was reversed when the Communist Party took over the insurgency and the NLF was created. Even the increase in American advisers and the economic and material assistance provided in 1962 had arrested only temporarily the downward slide. Attempts to bolster the South Vietnamese position had been counteracted by the Buddhist crisis in 1963, which shook national confidence, and the increasing government instability following the 1963 coup against President Diem. A report by the National Intelligence Board in Washington in October, 1964, noted that "Coup after coup, intractable Buddhists, Montagnard revolt, and strikes were all evidence of the lack of leadership, and no charismatic leader was in sight."[24]

By December, 1964, Vietcong strength was assessed as up to 34,000 regulars operating from five main base areas, compared with 25,000 only six months earlier.[25] These troops were actively supported by 100,000 locally recruited part-time guerrillas. Infiltration from North Vietnam had reached 1,000 per month, with an estimated 10,000 in 1964 alone. Where previously infiltrators from North Vietnam had been mostly southern Vietminh who had moved north in keeping with the 1954 Geneva agreements, an increasing proportion of northerners were included in their ranks. Although North Vietnamese Army (NVA) units had not yet been identified in the south, North Vietnam was providing the senior Vietcong officers, key cadre, and military specialists as well as military and communications equipment.[26] Supplies from North Vietnam followed similar infiltration routes to personnel, skirting the demilitarized zone and entering the northern and central provinces of South Vietnam through central Laos. Victories in Laos by North Vietnamese and communist-led Laotian forces (Pathet Lao) in the first quarter of 1964 had virtually assured the safety of this passage.[27]

Perilous as the situation was, the full dimension of the catastrophe was only recognized when, for the first time, formations of North Vietnamese regular forces were reported leaving their bases between November, 1964, and February, 1965, destined for South Vietnam. A whole division was established in and around Kontum Province by the end of February, 1965.[28] According to Gen. William C. Westmoreland's intelligence chief, the infiltration of regular units into the south became one of the "hinge events" in the Vietnam war, changing it from an insurrection into an invasion.[29] For this reason, the Hanoi leadership went to great lengths to disguise its dominant role and foster instead the illusion of the independence of the southern movement.[30]

Ranged against these forces the Army of the Republic of Vietnam (ARVN) totaled 205,000, supported by 21,000 U.S. advisers. An additional 215,000 men were distributed among the Regional Forces and Popular Forces and paramilitary groups. Whereas until 1960 aid from the Soviet Union, China, and Eastern Europe to the DRV outstripped that from the United States to the RVN, American aid had risen to approximately $1 million per day. Although equipped almost completely by the United States and reasonably well trained, the ARVN was unable to counter the insurgents in the field. Australian intelligence assessments of the reasons for this failure were damning, listing variable morale, war weariness, a lack of political and ideological motivation, overreliance on heavy weapons and vehicles, and inadequate leadership. The desertion rate was approximately 0.6% per month. On the other side, the Vietcong enjoyed the security and intelligence that flowed from their domination of the countryside.

Colonel O. D. Jackson, incoming commander of the AATTV in Vietnam, spent most of January and February, 1965, touring the country. His observations reinforced the assessments contained in intelligence briefs:

> I saw in I, II, and III Corps areas almost every important government post. I certainly saw every place where Australians [advisers] were deployed. The impression I gained, a very real impression, was the war was lost from a military point of view . . . Wherever I went there were Vietnamese Army forces on hilltops, behind barbed wire. They very rarely went outside that wire. If they did go outside to relieve one post by another they were frequently ambushed in strength by the VC—and it was nothing for a whole battalion or more of South Vietnamese troops to be butchered. There was very

> little in the way of offensive action from anywhere in the Vietnamese Army; the Viet Cong were thoroughly on top from a military point of view. I would have said that it was just a matter of weeks or months before the war militarily was lost in Vietnam—it was as bad as that in my opinion, and a lot of people agreed with me.[31]

The Defence Joint Planning Committee recognized the discord in Vietnam between the government, the Buddhist factions, and the strongly anti-communist Catholic element. Together with the deteriorating military position, it considered the present situation could be beyond recovery. The deployment of one or even two allied divisions, the committee believed, might not be sufficient to reverse this. The most optimistic view was for a long, drawn-out struggle.[32]

The Stakes

The stakes were high for both the American and Australian governments. Three major factors lay behind the American policy of resisting communist expansion: the general will to support countries trying to resist communist subversion and attack; the consequences of communist control of South Vietnam and Laos on the security of other countries in Southeast Asia; and the worldwide implications of the portrayal of South Vietnam, and to a lesser extent Laos, as a test case of communist "wars of national liberation."[33] The defense of South Vietnam was considered vital for the defense of Southeast Asia against communism. Southeast Asia was located astride east-west air and sea lanes, dominated the route between the Indian and Pacific Oceans, and flanked India, the Philippines, Australia, and New Zealand. Part of America's forward defense depended therefore on keeping Southeast Asia non-communist.[34] In assisting the government of South Vietnam to resist a communist takeover, the United States made no secret of the fact that it was acting in its own interests.[35]

North Vietnamese leaders clearly saw their struggle as part of an irreversible global transition from capitalism to communism. Already partly achieved in Europe, Asia, and South America, such a transition was to be accomplished by a process of revolutionary class struggle on both an international and national basis.[36] The struggle was aimed primarily at the United States and its influence but embraced all Western countries. It was the policies that sprang from this worldview, the pivotal position of Vietnam in Asia at that time, and North Vietnam's direction and support of the insurgency in South Vietnam, that led the ten-year-old DRV regime into violent confrontation with the United States.[37]

Consistent with Le Duan's proclamation that "the ultimate goal of all the communist and workers' parties is the establishment of socialism and communism throughout the world," the DRV opposed America's "shameful" role in the Korean War and supported communist insurrection in Asia, South America, South Korea, Laos, and northern Kalimantan—in fact, anywhere communists opposed the established government.[38] Challenging Australian strategic interests, Pham Van Dong expressed strong support for Indonesia, Australia's principal antagonist, and endorsed President Sukarno's policy of confrontation in 1965.[39] North Vietnam's public and unrestricted declaration of solidarity with both the Soviet Union and China and the profound gratitude the North Vietnamese leadership expressed for the support of these two countries exemplified the international aspects of the insurgency.[40] Indeed, Ho Chi Minh taught that international unity was indispensable to the victory of the Vietnamese revolution.[41] Leaders of both the DRV and the People's Republic of China used the analogy of lips and teeth to express the closeness of the relationship between the two regimes, the Chinese emphasizing that as fraternal socialist neighbors they were comrades in arms and shared the same destiny.[42]

North Vietnam's support for communist revolutionary movements in neighboring countries as well as its resort to force in Indochina had as its stated objects both the unification of Vietnam under communist rule and the emergence of an enlarged and cohesive communist bloc in Asia antipathetic to the West. Just as Robert S. McNamara, the U.S. secretary of defense, saw the Vietnam War as a test case against communist insurgency everywhere, Pham Van Dong regarded a communist victory in Vietnam as serving the cause of communist revolution throughout the world.[43]

In contemplating military intervention in Asia, the paramount concern of Australian strategists was that political and military developments there were inimical to Australia's ultimate safety. At the same time, they were not unmindful that Australia's willingness to contribute promptly to the common defense in Southeast Asia could influence any obligation which the United States might feel to come to Australia's assistance in an emergency.[44] Such a consideration was aimed principally at obtaining military support from the United States if Australian and Indonesian relations deteriorated into open hostilities.

An Appropriate Response

As foreshadowed in the 4 December cable from the Australian ambassador in Washington, on 14 December Pres. Lyndon B. Johnson appealed to Prime Minister Robert Menzies for an additional two hundred advisers. But the service chiefs saw the addition of more advisers, ships, or nonmilitary props to the Vietnamese economy in a continuation of the present campaign as merely reinforcing failure.[45] The communists would have agreed, judging by their assertion that the battle of Binh Gia marked the defeat of the "special war" strategy.[46] The air strategy did not amount to much. As General Westmoreland wrote later, Operation Barrel Roll into Laos, which began as scheduled on 14 December, involved so few aircraft that "it was hardly surprising that the North Vietnamese failed to discern that a new program was underway."[47] The approval for retaliatory bombing of North Vietnam was not put to any immediate use. As a consequence, the Joint Chiefs of Staff eschewed the "more of the same" approach proposed by President Johnson, and responded instead to the broader invitation for comment extended by Bundy.

In Australia, the Departments of External Affairs and Defence considered that if military discussion confirmed that the importance of preventing further North Vietnamese interference justified the risks of escalating the war by the introduction of ground troops, and if the practicability of isolating South Vietnam was established, then Australia should offer a battalion. The cabinet decided that Australia should indicate its willingness to consider an infantry battalion as a contribution and that the provision of ground forces should be the subject of further military staff discussion.[48] Menzies replied to Johnson in those terms the following day.[49]

Committing a Battalion

In early 1965 the Vietcong targeted American advisers for the first time. On Christmas Eve a three-hundred-pound bomb was detonated under the bachelor officers' quarters in Saigon, killing 2 Americans and wounding more than 100 others, including an Australian.[50] After a weeklong truce at Tet, the enemy executed a well-planned attack against the American advisers' compound and airstrip at Pleiku on 7 February 1965, killing 9 Americans and wounding 128, and damaging or destroying 122 aircraft. According to the U.S. Marine Corps's official history, it was "a provocation that altered the entire course of the war." Three days later, the U.S. enlisted men's quarters at Qui Nhon was destroyed, resulting in the death of 23 American soldiers and the wounding of 22 others.[51] The United States responded with punitive air attacks on North Vietnam on both occasions and the introduction of air force ground-attack aircraft against targets in South Vietnam. The U.S. Joint Chiefs of Staff, declaring that retaliatory air strikes seemed not to be enough to deter the Vietcong, recommended a series of measures including a continuous bombing campaign against North Vietnam, naval bombardment, and the deployment of American ground troops in South Vietnam. Operation Rolling Thunder, the systematic bombing of military targets in North Vietnam, was approved by President Johnson on 13 February but was delayed until 2 March because of continuing political instability in Saigon and bad weather.[52]

The demonstrated vulnerability of bases at Bien Hoa, Pleiku, and Qui Nhon amid the continuing political instability aroused General Westmoreland's concern for the safety of the airbase at Da Nang, which was essential for the air campaign against North Vietnam.[53] Doubting the capability of the ARVN to defend such a large complex, he requested a contingent of U.S. marines. In late February, with the agreement of Prime Minister Quat, President Johnson approved the introduction of a two-battalion marine brigade into Da Nang. Its mission was to protect the airfield and support installations from enemy interference. The marines were expressly forbidden to engage the Vietcong on a day-to-day basis.[54] At 9 A.M. on 8 March, troops of one marine battalion landing team came ashore on the beach at Da Nang, transported by amphibian tractors from ships lying forty-five hundred yards off the coast. More men and materiel followed in flat-bottomed landing craft. That same day, troops from a second battalion based on Okinawa landed on the Da Nang airfield in C-130 Hercules aircraft.[55]

General Westmoreland saw the marines' arrival as a welcome first step in U.S. force escalation in Vietnam. Washington, on the other hand, regarded the commitment of marines as a "one shot affair to meet a specific situation."[56] While their arrival did not guarantee a further American buildup, their presence eased the way for subsequent decisions.

Military staff talks involving representatives from the United States, Australia, and New Zealand were held in Honolulu from 30 March to 1 April, 1965. Admiral Ulysses S. G. Sharp, the U.S. commander in chief, Pacific, conducted the conference. Air Chief Marshal Sir Frederick Scherger led the Australian delegation, and Rear Adm. Sir Peter Phipps, chief of the Defence Staff, led the New Zealand delegation. However, the talks fell far short of providing the range and depth of information the Joint Planning Committee thought necessary before a firm recommendation on whether to commit ground forces could be made to the government. A balance had to be drawn between the risks and likely outcomes of deploying or not deploying ground combat forces to Vietnam. One of Scherger's tasks had been to discuss the feasibility of isolating South Vietnam by a force deployed near the DMZ. This had been the concept for which the Americans had first suggested an Australian contribution. Indeed, the Defence Committee had predicated the commitment of a battalion on the viability of such a strategy. There is no evidence that Scherger even raised the many issues posed by the Joint Planning Committee and the government. The questions of strategy, of isolating South Vietnam, of the risks inherent in the presence of foreign troops, or even the chance of victory, appear not to have been discussed. It seemed that the United States itself had not thought through for itself a strategy or the ramifications of the employment of ground troops.[57] Sharp merely advised Scherger of his general assessment of the alternatives. The admiral then stated his chosen course, which was the creation of enclaves, and extended an invitation to the Australians to join in.

Following Scherger's visit to Honolulu, the cabinet on 7 April agreed to the provision of a battalion when requested by the United States,[58] and on 29 April 1965 the prime minister announced that the commitment would be made. He stated that in view of the gravity of the situation in Vietnam and the importance to Australia of preventing its fall to externally directed communism, the commitment of a battalion would be the most useful contribution Australia could make. Referring to the ANZUS and SEATO treaties, he added that alliances, besides providing guarantees and assurances, also made demands.[59] The Defence Committee reasoned that it was "vital to Australia's strategic interests to have a strong United States military presence in South East Asia," and it was therefore "essential to show a willingness to assist the United States to achieve her aims in South Vietnam."[60] The prime minister then included a reference to a China threat: "The takeover of South Vietnam would be a direct military threat to Australia and all the countries of South and South East Asia. It must be seen as part of a thrust by Communist China between the Indian and Pacific Oceans."[61]

The statement was overstated and inaccurate, hyperbole designed to stimulate support for military intervention from an uninterested Australian public.[62] Its insertion had been arranged the day before by the recently appointed permanent head of the Department of External Affairs, Sir James Plimsoll. The Plimsoll version, however, continued after "oceans" with "exploiting weeknesses [*sic*] in the multi-racial and economically underdeveloped countries of the region." Someone deleted this phrase, compounding the exaggeration. In fact, no strategic assessment had envisaged a direct military threat to Australia if South Vietnam fell to the communists.[63] The government did see China as having expansionist aims in Asia, but through subversion and support of communist insurgency, not by direct invasion.[64] The only direct threat to Australia and its territories, strategists believed, came from Indonesia.[65] The Defence Department distanced itself from the assertion. In a paraphrase of the prime minister's statement shortly after, it changed "direct threat" to "direct defence significance," while leaving out altogether any reference to a thrust by China.[66]

The oft-quoted statement helped throw rational debate off the tracks for years, concentrating too much attention on China rather than Vietnam and the remainder of Indochina. The reply to the prime minister by the opposition leader, Arthur Calwell, gave a foretaste of what was to come. Quoting the passage, he scoffed at the notion of a direct military threat and declared the commitment of troops to be the result of an erroneous assessment: "the true nature of the threat from China is not military invasion but political subversion."[67] Ironically, this was precisely the government's unstated position, but it was stuck with what had been said.

At 1 A.M. on 27 May, HMAS *Sydney,* escorted by the destroyer HMAS *Duchess,* departed from Sydney Harbour. On board were B Company, 1st Battalion, Royal Australian Regiment (RAR), and support personnel, together with weapons, vehicles and stores, and five Australian journalists.[68] Confirmation of the precise destination of the troop transport was kept secret. It was not until HMAS *Sydney* passed Manus Island, site of a Royal Australian Air Force (RAAF) refueling base and the last mail takeoff point, that the commander of B Company, Maj. I. D. McFarlane, was permitted to break open his orders. These gave his destination as Bien Hoa, the location of the U.S. Army's 173rd Airborne Brigade (Separate) and the site of one of the three largest airfields in Vietnam. Shortly afterward, chartered civilian aircraft and a RAAF Hercules transport began ferrying the advance party and main body of the Australian contingent.

The force was destined for a bitter war whose ferocity and tempo had risen well beyond that of local guerrillas. The next few months were critical as Vietcong and North Vietnamese forces were poised to drive a wedge across the middle of South Vietnam. The *Sydney Morning Herald,* while noting the beginnings of dissent and controversy over the involvement, affirmed that all Australians would wish the troops Godspeed. There was no doubt, the editorial continued, that "they would acquit themselves well in whatever demands are made of them. No better trained or better equipped military force has ever left Australian shores."[69]

The enemy also was preparing. In Hanoi, the secretary general of the Central Committee of the Communist Party of Vietnam, Le Duan, was responsible for the direction of the insurgency. Even as the 1st Battalion, RAR, was on the water and in the air, he wrote prophetically to his followers in the south: "If the Americans switch over to 'local war' in the South with from 250,000 to 300,000 troops, they will be confronted with our protracted war of resistance. To have to fight a long-drawn-out war is the US Achilles' heel."[70]

The introduction of ground forces to the Vietnam War was a direct extension of strategic policies that had their genesis in the mid-1940s. It was fully consistent with the perceived threat of militant communism that had crystallized in defense and foreign-policy thinking and which had received practical recognition in the development of plans and the creation of standing forces since the mid-1950s. Not only was Australia taking direct action in accordance with its own strategy of forward defense, but the government also had the satisfaction of seeing the United States commit forces to Southeast Asia, thus fulfilling an important foreign-policy objective. Moreover, the Australian government's seizure of the opportunity to offer the political and military support that America sought in Vietnam augured well for any future appeal it might make to the American government. However, in achieving these objectives the government and its advisers had forfeited the opportunity to inject their own assessment into the creation of an appropriate military strategy.

Deploying a Task Force

The 1st Battalion, RAR, had barely arrived in Vietnam in May, 1965, when Lieutenant General Wilton began to consider the problems involved in increasing the battalion to a task force (brigade group) should the situation require. A fundamental belief of both Wilton and his successor as Chief of the General Staff, Lt. Gen. Sir Thomas J. Daly, was that a task force was the most suitable minimum Australian contribution in the event of limited war.[71] Such a condition was fast approaching. It was also basic to defense planning that the smallest national contribution to a larger allied force in Southeast Asia would consist of a task force or its brigade equivalent.[72]

In 1965, however, the army was understrength, with one battalion in Malaysia, a hundred officers and warrant officers already in Vietnam as advisers, and home resources given over to the training of national servicemen who were not yet filling the ranks. The most the army could provide on short notice and sustain in the theater was a single battalion. But a battalion was not a self-contained force; to ensure its operational viability it had to be amalgamated with an American brigade, just as in Korea, Malaya, and Borneo Australian battalions operated as part of a Commonwealth brigade.[73] Wilton always had in the back of his mind that when manpower and resources were available, the battalion would be increased.[74] Yet unless the government was willing to disrupt the army's planned reorganization and expansion, a major buildup of the force in Vietnam could not take place before March, 1966.[75]

The strong army persuasion toward a task force stemmed from its being able to operate independently for indefinite periods. Commanded by a brigadier, the headquarters had the capacity for forward planning at the same time as it controlled current operations. It could consist of between two and four battalions, with other units drawn in for a particular mission, although the preferred number of battalions for maneuver purposes was three. Apart from these advantages, when compared with a battalion group, the deployment of an independent task force would allow Australian troops to employ their own operational concepts and procedures, regarded by Australian strategists as superior to U.S. doctrine in South Vietnam.[76] It could operate in a role readily identifiable as an Australian effort, a condition that would satisfy both political and military interests. Although it would necessarily function under American operational control, its relative independence would permit it more easily to respond to military and political guidelines from Australia.[77] Of these, the main requirements were national identity and independence. As Wilton expressed it: "Although for military tactical reasons we really had to be under operational control of the US command, I preferred not to be included in an American position. I wanted to have as much independence within the force limitations as I could so I could keep a closer eye on it."[78]

Wilton had been concerned not only with whether a task force would be readied for Vietnam, but where in Vietnam it would be sent.[79] He rejected several areas proposed by Westmoreland before alighting on Phuoc Tuy Province. The strategic importance of Phuoc Tuy was its dominant position in relation to both the port of Vung Tau and Route 15, the highway between the port and Saigon. As the port became increasingly congested, so Vung Tau and the connecting highway grew in strategic importance as a means of commerce and entry for military supplies.[80] The port would also be useful for Australian resupply and would provide a withdrawal route if the situation went bad. The province was virtually in communist hands but for the capital, Baria, and the narrow strip connecting Baria to the Vung Tau peninsula. This was of pressing concern to the Vietnamese not only for the security of the province itself but because in Vietcong hands it contributed to the isolation of Saigon. The province was situated in an area conducive to brigade-sized operations. Terrain and vegetation suited Australian operating methods, while demographic patterns in Phuoc Tuy appeared to favor the separation of enemy units from the population and their source of replenishment, a basic condition in the Australian concept of counterrevolutionary warfare.[81]

Phuoc Tuy was mostly flat. Two-thirds of the province was covered with rainforest, and the remainder rice paddies and grassland. Three groups of mountains rose sharply from the countryside, the Long Hais

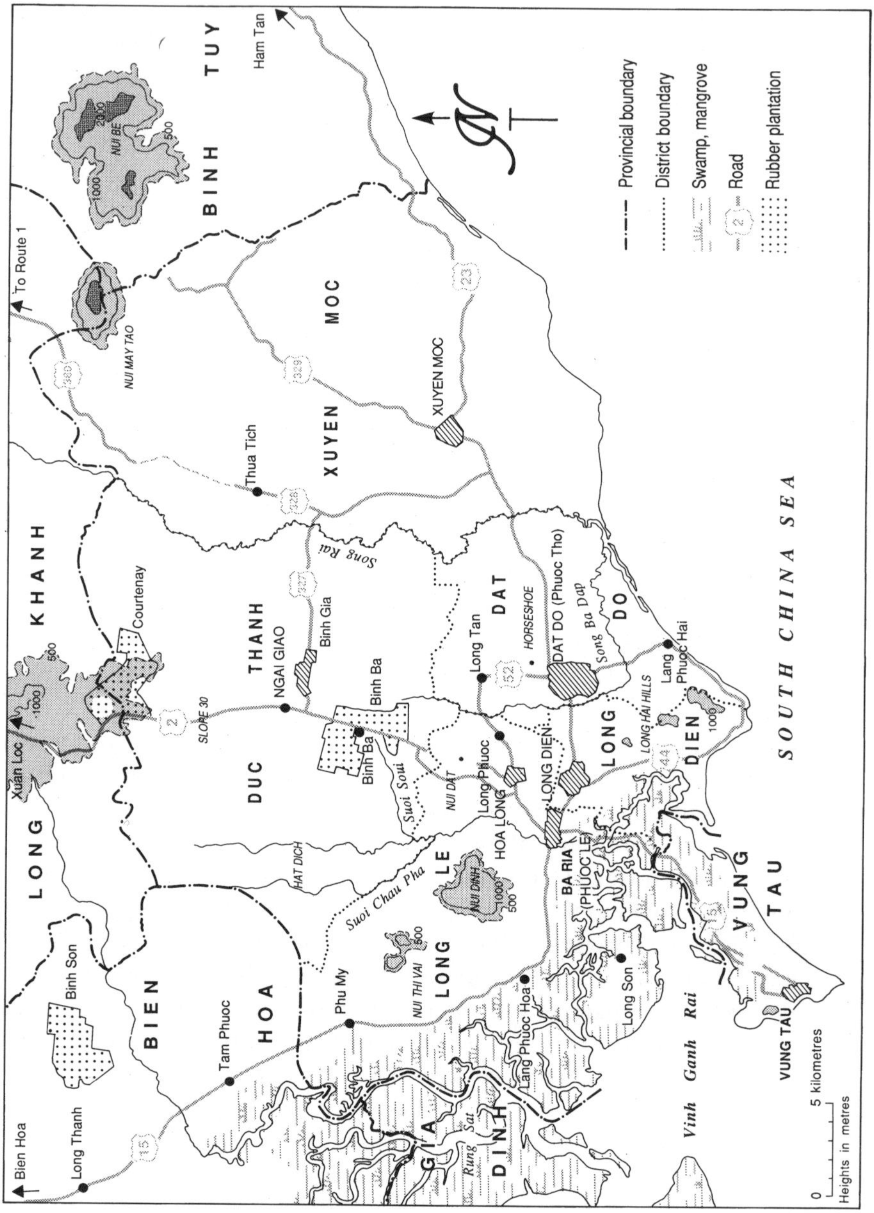

Phuoc Tuy Province, 1966. The whole province, excluding the populated areas, was included in the Tactical Area of Responsibility of 1ATF by July, 1967.

in the south being of greatest significance. In these cavernous hills lay the Minh Dam secret zone, a resistance base since the war against the French. Communist-led insurgents had been present in Phuoc Tuy since 1945 and had formed a center of resistance against the French. After the 1954 Geneva agreements, former Vietminh cadres that had fought against the French were ordered underground in anticipation of renewing their armed struggle against the Diem government. Communist-inspired insurgency increased in 1959, leading to the major victory at Binh Gia in 1964.

By the time the Australian task force arrived, the enemy forces in and close to Phuoc Tuy were assessed to be a divisional headquarters, two main-force regiments totaling 3,850 men, the D445 Regional Battalion with a strength of 550, local forces up to company size, infrastructure in the hamlets, and some logistic installations.[82] This could be enough to defeat a sizable Australian force and severely threaten the Nui Dat base.

Defence Department submitted requests to the cabinet to increase the force to a task force in 1965 and 1966, but the government vetoed any such consideration until it was satisfied that additional forces were not required for New Guinea or Malaysia. The long-deferred decision was finally reached on 2 March 1966. The force would contain two battalions, a Special Air Service (SAS) squadron, and combat and logistical support units. It would be supported by a flight of eight Iroquois helicopters. The cabinet further decided that the task force should embody the whole of the Australian force in Vietnam, that is, it would include the AATTV and RAAF Caribou flight already stationed in the country.[83] The total contribution (including units already in the country) would be approximately forty-five hundred men, with national servicemen fully integrated into the force. With a battalion and support troops already in Malaysia and other forces in Singapore, this new commitment was considered to be the upper limit of Australian contributions to Vietnam short of the declaration of a defense emergency.[84]

In resolving to deploy a task force, the cabinet stated: "The prime consideration for Australia is the continued commitment of the United States to the defence of South East Asia, and thus to play what the United States will recognize as a full part in the defence of South Vietnam."[85] This reflected Australia's concern over communist expansion in Southeast Asia and the acceptance that it alone could do little to prevent it. The cornerstone of Australian defense policy was therefore to encourage the presence of powerful allies in the region to whose forces Australia could contribute.

The new prime minister, Harold Holt, deferred disclosure of the decision to commit a task force until Parliament resumed on 8 March. This meant that tight security was maintained for an additional six days, thus curtailing military preparations. In announcing the dispatch of a task force, Holt placed the ceiling at forty-five hundred men, enumerated the units involved, and stated that it would be deployed in May and June, 1966.

The Defence Department, and especially the army, finally had the go-ahead. But despite what may have been sound political reasons, many problems that affected the task force in Vietnam had their genesis first in a planning embargo, then in the delay of the decision. The availability for deployment in May and June was predicated on an announcement in mid-February. The embargo on planning, especially at lower levels, resulted in important matters being overlooked. The prohibition on consultation with the Americans and the absence of a detailed reconnaissance of the area to be occupied, especially the logistics area, before submitting manning figures and unit lists to the cabinet meant that the ability of the U.S. system to provide the agreed logistic support was never questioned. Similarly, the full requirement in units and materiel to establish a logistics area could not be calculated. Ships and aircraft were not given sufficient warning and instead were used largely on the basis of availability. This, rather than priority for deployment in Vietnam, largely determined the order of departure of units.

Phuoc Tuy Province was at last formally chosen as the location and principal area of operations for the Task Force. The selection of a suitable base within Phuoc Tuy was a separate issue. Wilton and others of his staff had flown over Phuoc Tuy often. He was well briefed also by Brigadier O. D. Jackson, commander of Australian Army Forces Vietnam (COMAAFV), who, as the task force commander designate, had already singled out Nui Dat as the most suitable location. In the course of his duties as commander of the AATTV, Jackson had visited the province on several occasions to speak with Australian soldiers serving there. He had conferred many times with the province chief, Lt. Col. Le Duc Dat, whom Jackson knew to be trustworthy, able, and brave.[86]

The first requirement for the base was that it should stand between the enemy and the main civilian population areas. It had to provide space for an airfield and maintenance area, and allow sufficient room to fight should it come under heavy attack. It needed to be on ground that would be above water level during the wet season, and relatively open so that maximum use of firepower, rather than manpower, could be used for its defense. It had to be located close enough to Vung Tau to avoid the diversion of forces for line of communication duties or, alternatively, maintenance by air. It also needed to be centrally located so as

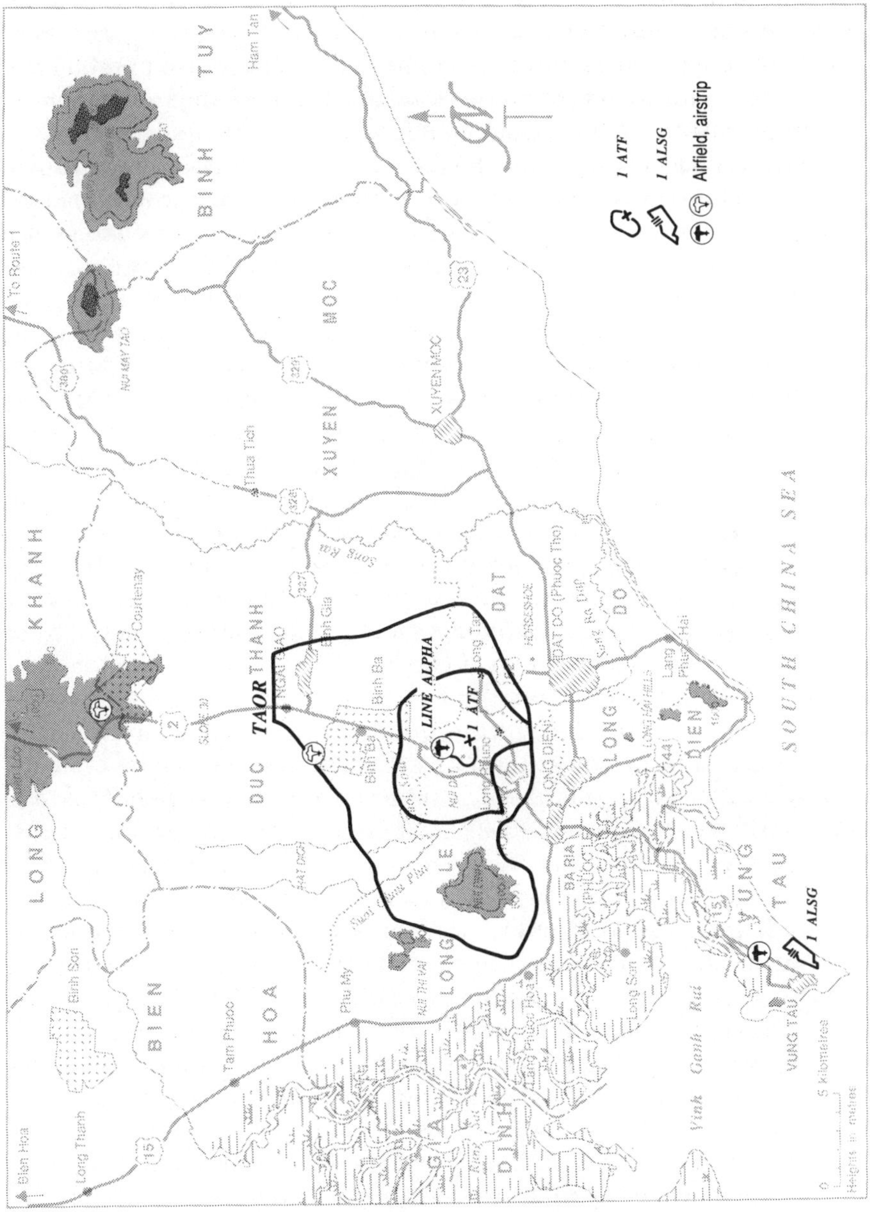

Phuoc Tuy Province Tactical Boundaries, June, 1966. Note that the initial Tactical Area of Responsibility, although small, was designed to include the Nui Dinh hills in order to protect Route 15.

to facilitate operations anywhere in the province.[87] Nui Dat best answered these requirements.

Wilton had little hesitation in confirming Jackson's choice, although it seemed to surprise both the Americans and the Vietnamese—the Americans because they believed that location adjacent to the province capital would be most convenient and would provide direct protection to it, and the Vietnamese because they thought the Australians would follow the American pattern. But setting up outside Baria was not Wilton's idea of dominating Phuoc Tuy. "We thought we had to get out and establish our presence as near as we could to the centre of the province," he said, "so that we could move in any direction with the minimal amount of travelling involved. Secondly I wanted to get my forces clear of the problems and temptations which arise when you have a too ready access to the civilian population and they are many and varied."[88]

The commander of the new Australian Force Vietnam (COMAFV) would be a two-star general whose headquarters would be near Westmoreland's in Saigon. The Australian commander would place the operational elements of his force under the operational control of the relevant U.S. military command. While control of operations would be with the Americans, COMAFV, as national commander, was responsible to the Australian government for the safety of the force and the national interest. He thus had authority to scrutinize all operations involving Australians in the planning stage and with this, the power of veto. Operational control of the 1st Australian Task Force would be vested in the commanding general of the U.S. II Field Force Vietnam (II FFV). This headquarters became operational on 15 March and functioned as a corps headquarters under Westmoreland. Wilton was especially satisfied that the task force would be under the control of a higher U.S. field headquarters at corps level rather than a U.S. division. As he noted to Scherger, this would allow it greater freedom of operation and give the task force the chance to demonstrate the Australian Army's operational concepts and tactical doctrine for counterinsurgency warfare.[89]

Arriving in Vietnam aboard the HMAS *Sydney,* chartered aircraft, RAAF Hercules transports, and army small ships, the force was operational in Phuoc Tuy on 14 June 1966.

A Question of Role

The Vietnam debate in Australia has spread to encompass the operational context of the Australian involvement. One historian has argued that the task force was deployed in Vietnam with an "imprecisely defined role," one that "had not been sufficiently delineated" and which on the ground in Phuoc Tuy was hardly coherent or militarily effective.[90] These and some other problems have been described as intractable. The only way of being sure to avoid them, it is maintained, would have been not to go to Vietnam at all.[91] I rely heavily on testimony attributed to Maj. Gen. C. M. I. Pearson, the task force commander from October, 1968, to August, 1969, to support these contentions.

On examination, the assertions appear to be overstated, deriving from a misunderstanding of Pearson. I believe that the role given to the task force was both appropriate and clearly understood by its commanders. While the role extended the force, especially before the arrival of the third battalion and tanks in late 1967 and early 1968, it was within its capacity when prearranged support and combined operations are taken into account. The generalized nature of the directive, which left the initiative with field commanders, actually contributed to the task force's effectiveness.

Frank Frost explains that General Pearson "felt that the government's failure to develop a detailed concept for a specific function for the Task Force was indeed a substantial problem."[92] Pearson is quoted to the effect that the government had three main options when deploying the force in 1966: to conduct operations in depth against NVA and Vietcong main-force units, to conduct pacification operations in and around villages to secure them from local Vietcong units, or to conduct a combination of both. The first two tasks had different support requirements, and the third, a combination of the first two, would have required a much larger force. According to Frost, Pearson maintained that the government should have specifically directed the task force to carry out operations either against the North Vietnamese and Vietcong main-force units (the first alternative) or operations concerned with pacification (the second). But the government did not. In Frost's most telling passage, Pearson is alleged to have said that it had been a major problem for the army that "we weren't given a task, an aim . . . It's the first war we've gone into without a political aim that's expressed as an aim."[93] Not only do these issues raise fundamental questions regarding the efficacy of the task force, but Pearson also comes across as disillusioned.

A colleague of Frost's endorses the substance of the argument. With proper attribution to Frost, Greg Lockhart highlights Pearson's observation that Vietnam was the first war without an aim. So that there is no mistaking the drift, the word *political* is dropped. Pearson is thus quoted as saying: "we weren't given a task, an aim . . . It's the first war we've gone into without an aim that's expressed as an aim." "In at least one general's view, therefore," Lockhart proclaims, "the Australian Army was aimless in Vietnam."[94] He repeated this in a later publication, again to allege that the task force's aim was obscure.[95]

Pearson is clear in his recollection of the statement, and firmly refutes the inferences drawn. He says: "I cannot understand how he [Frost] could misinterpret my views about aims, political or otherwise. I was referring of course to the national, political aims of committing troops to Vietnam. No force commander and certainly no Brigade Commander could be expected to receive from the Government the precise military aims, but he should be, generally speaking, directed to achieve the political aims."[96] Pearson was not commenting on the aim or role of the task force. He was concerned that the nation did not articulate an aim that was capable of attracting popular support.[97]

Pearson's expounding of the possibility of three separate roles for the task force flows from the chief of the General Staff's exercise in 1971, which reviewed Australian experiences in Vietnam. The exercise report presented the complete bill of requirements if Australian forces in Vietnam were to take on the full responsibility for confronting large enemy forces in depth, local guerrillas in a pacification role, or a combination of both. The 1st Australian Task Force in Vietnam did not take responsibility for all these functions. It did assume responsibility for securing the Tactical Area of Responsibility (TAOR) allotted to it. The TAOR was not a fixed area. It was expanded in line with the increasing capacity of the task force to secure areas farther from the base. It was always delineated carefully but did not encompass the whole of Phuoc Tuy Province until more than twelve months after the task force's presence was established. In keeping with agreements between Vietnam and its allies, the Vietnamese retained full responsibility for the populated areas. These, therefore, were not part of the TAOR. Although task force commanders recognized the fundamental objective of restoring government control of the population, it could only assist, not take over, the government measures. It always required the continuing presence of the U.S. provincial military and civil advisory structure.

Pearson acknowledged that the Australian government made a compromise by taking an area role that involved both main-force and pacification operations.[98] "During my time," he said, "there were two major concepts: in the first six months or so, the bulk of the Task Force supported by US, Vietnamese and sometimes by Thais, and Philippines engineers operating against NVA (North Vietnamese Army) and Viet Cong mainforce units; and the last six months or less the Task Force conducting pacification tasks against local Vietcong units, assisting and training local SVN (South Vietnamese) forces and so on."[99] In so doing, Pearson felt that the task force achieved its aim.

As Wilton had arranged, Westmoreland provided the additional support needed by the task force to fit it for operations against the enemy's

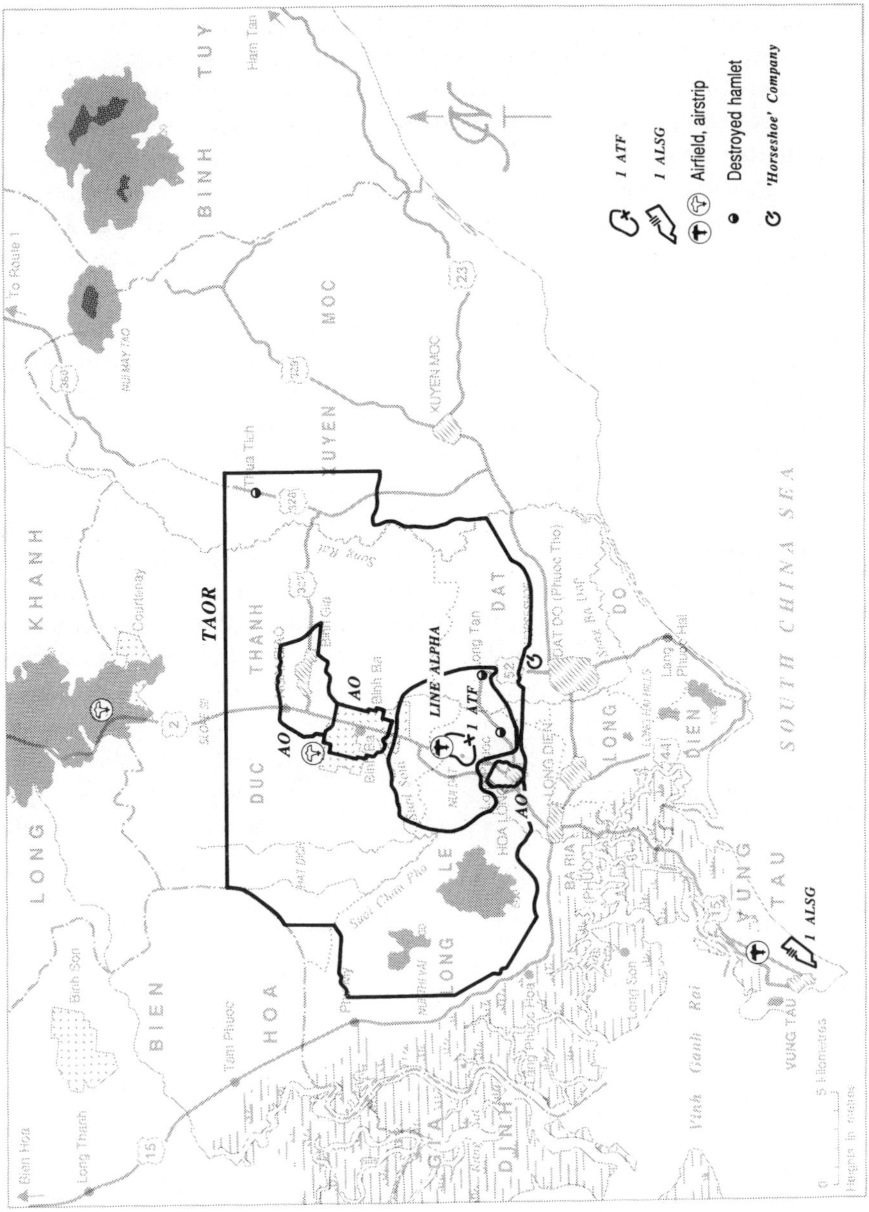

Phuoc Tuy Province Tactical Province Boundaries, December, 1966. The Tactical Area of Responsibility now covered almost half the province.

main forces. "We were lucky though," said Pearson, "in that the Americans had in my time ample forces and logistics and were willing to support our efforts for the overall benefit of the allies."[100] From the beginning, the task force's firepower was stiffened when it received a battery of six self-propelled medium guns, two self-propelled heavy guns, and two eight-inch guns. The task force had more artillery in support of it than did the Americans' own 173rd Airborne Brigade (Separate) at Bien Hoa. In addition, American or Vietnamese units could reinforce the task force for operations in depth. American aircraft on the runway at Bien Hoa were ten minutes away.

Nevertheless, Pearson is talking of the period when the task force consisted of three battalions of infantry, a squadron of medium tanks, and a squadron of armored personnel carriers mounted with machine guns. This force was far more effective than the two-battalion task force that operated without tank support during the first eighteen months. During that time commanders found the pressures of pacification, base defense, and operations in depth to be more than the task force could handle effectively at the same time. Compromises were made. The first task force commander, Brigadier Jackson, eschewed operations against the main force in favor of steadily expanding base security out to mortar range and beyond, and pacification operations amongst the population.

Pearson saw nothing lacking regarding his directives:

> Our actual directive for the Task Force, as far as I was concerned, was sound, given we were precluded from fighting outside the Province except on special occasions. The way it worked was that we would develop a concept for a particular operation, then put it to the weekly II FFV [II Field Force Vietnam, the U.S. headquarters that had operational control of the task force] conference or more likely to the Commander, privately first, gain his approval which was essential to receive all the support elements—and then set about it. . . . So there would not seem much awry with the aims of the Task Force, and I was never in doubt about what we had to do. . . . I could not therefore agree with the inferences put forward either by Frost or anyone else regarding the aims of the Task Force or that the Task Force was aimless in my period there.[101]

Other task force commanders received similar instructions. Brigadier R. L. Hughes, who had immediately preceded Pearson as task force commander, visited the II FFV commander each week, and at least once each month the II FFV commander visited Hughes. "In Vietnam," said

Hughes, "there was an annual MACV (Military Assistance Command Vietnam) directive which covered the whole country that was written in conjunction with the Vietnamese Chief of Staff. It was elaborated on by II Field Force Victor in conjunction with Headquarters III Corps. We had a general outline directive which gave priorities of operations; priorities of tasks that were to be undertaken . . . The Australian Task Force's method of doing things was different to the way the Vietnamese, the Americans, or the Koreans, would do the same things. I found no difficulty working with the directive we had."[102]

A comment by the first task force commander, Brigadier Jackson, could be misinterpreted: "No formal orders or mission were given to 1 ATF by any higher authority other than the rather bald statement of 'take over Phuoc Tuy'."[103] At first sight, the statement suggests that Jackson felt he was barely given any direction. There is no doubt, however, that Jackson knew what was expected of his force. Major General K. Mackay, COMAFV to Brigadier Jackson, has stated that he had discussed the whole concept of operations and problems with Jackson and that there was no need for a formal directive. "Who the hell's going to sit down and write a stupid directive on this?" said Mackay in explanation of his dealings with the task force. "You are only dealing with two or three people and if the slightest thing gets out of hand you sense it and put your finger on it immediately and correct it. So you don't need directives, you give yourself much more flexibility and much more understanding if you operate this way."[104] Mackay's successors apparently agreed, as no written national directive was ever produced for the task force.

Jackson understood precisely the provisions of the directive for the Australian force and the tasks contained therein.[105] He had been in Vietnam six months already as national commander. He knew the province well, he had had long discussions with and assisted Wilton on reconnaissances, he had frequent meetings with the province chief, and it was he who had selected the site in Phuoc Tuy Province for the task force's base. What he wanted was independence from II FFV to get on with his job. This independence was not difficult to achieve as there also seemed some reluctance on the part of the II FFV commander, Lt. Gen. Jonathon O. Seaman, to interfere too much with the Australians.[106] In his "take over Phuoc Tuy" statement (which Jackson and everybody else knew then and later was never the task force role), Jackson was trying to indicate that II FFV did not try to spell out his tasks in detail. Immediately after this comment Jackson added: "1 ATF general concept of operations was of course known and agreed to by Lt. Gen. Seaman CG II FFV. What the Task Force was setting out to do therefore purported to be the Australian way of conducting operations in the Vietnam theatre, as distinct from anyone else's."[107]

In a separate but related vein, Lockhart contends that the task force "was . . . caught in a web of strategic dilemmas." Supporting this he refers to a one-line extract from historian Capt. Robert O'Neill, the 5th Battalion's intelligence officer during its tour of Vietnam in 1966. Lockhart relates O'Neill's observation that scarcely a week passed in which his commanding officer, Lt. Col. J. A. Warr, "did not ask me what our aim in Phuoc Tuy was and then proceed to debate the matter for half an hour or so."[108] It might seem that Lockhart intends to convey that either Warr knew of no aim or that he was absentminded. Or perhaps Warr, having discovered that the insurgency was not "simply" aggression from the north but also included southerners, had lapsed into a state of helpless quandary.

The extract from O'Neill is from the chapter titled "A Re-evaluation of Strategy" in his history of the 5th Battalion, RAR.[109] After six months of fighting against the Vietcong it was time to rethink, he writes. The knowledge that had been gained of the enemy's weaknesses, where formerly it had been mostly of the enemy's strengths, presented a basis for "ruthlessly scrutinizing both our aim and our methods to see if we were acting to bring the war to a successful end in the shortest possible time with the least number of casualties." To take best advantage of the initiative given to battalions by the task force commander, the senior officers carried on a continual debate concerning operations. "The driving force behind this rethinking of our attitudes was Colonel Warr," O'Neill writes. "He had been stimulating discussion of our methods ever since the battalion had been raised and scarcely a week passed in which he did not ask me what our aim in Phuoc Tuy was."[110] This is hardly a man caught in a "web of strategic dilemmas." Using the benefit of the discussions, O'Neill was directed to prepare a paper for his commanding officer. This document rigorously examined the operational experience of the battalion for the first six months and established the operating principles for the next six.[111] In Hanoi and in the jungles of Phuoc Tuy, the enemy were reevaluating their strategy, too.

The Australian system of command and control in Vietnam revolved around the condition that the 1st Australian Task Force was placed under the operational control of II FFV headquarters. It could not have been fully independent, and the government would not have it under the command of the Vietnamese. As a result, Wilton, who had been promoted to chairman of the Chiefs of Staff Committee, could not direct the task force from Canberra even if it were practicable. Nor could the COMAFV issue directions on operational matters from Saigon; he was responsible solely for overseeing the national interest and matters of Australian administration.

The basis of government influence over the task force was the directive issued by Wilton to the COMAFV. The provisions of this document were agreed upon between Wilton, Westmoreland, and the chief of the Vietnamese forces. Establishing the broad reason for the commitment, it began: "At the request of the Government of the Republic of Vietnam and in consultation with the Government of the United States of America, the Government of the Commonwealth of Australia has agreed to provide military assistance to the Government of the Republic of Vietnam to defeat Communist inspired insurgency [i.e. southern insurgents] and aggression [i.e. the presence of the North Vietnamese Army, in regiments and as individuals in the South] in order to restore peace and security."[112]

After stating that the general mission of the force would be to carry out operations in coordination with and in support of operations of American and Vietnamese forces, the directive enumerated tasks that the task force could be assigned:

> a. To secure and dominate the assigned Tactical Area of Responsibility in Phuoc Tuy Province [operations against the main forces].
> b. To conduct operations related to the security of Highway 15, as required [strategic highway from Vung Tau to Saigon, much of which ran through Phuoc Tuy province].
> c. To conduct other operations in Phuoc Tuy province as required [operations in support of pacification].
> d. To conduct operations anywhere in the Army of the Republic of Vietnam (ARVN) III Corps Tactical Zone (CTZ) and subsequently in the area of the adjacent province of Binh Thuan in the ARVN II CTZ as agreed between yourself and COMUSMACV.[113]

Lieutenant General Daly, then serving as chief of the General Staff, expanded on the role: "The military reason for the deployment of the Australian Task Force in Phuoc Tuy province under national command was to improve the military situation so that Route 15 from Vung Tau to Bien Hoa can be used for major military movement. This is required to allow the development of the port of Vung Tau in order to relieve the congestion of military shipping in the Saigon area. The political reason, of course, is to assist in providing the security necessary for the Vietnamese Government to proceed with its Revolutionary Development Programme in this Province."[114]

The general nature of the directive, supplemented by another directive and tactical missions allotted from time to time by II FFV, was welcomed by the commanders who sought as much independence as possible. "I was quite happy with the broad directive given me as the Task Force Commander," recalled Pearson. "It gave plenty of scope and flexibility provided of course the American Commanders were satisfied with the operation and gave necessary support."[115] Satisfaction with their operational flexibility is apparent amongst all task force commanders, in deed as much as in pronouncements.

Wilton was formerly the chief military planning officer in SEATO. As Chief of the General Staff before becoming chairman of the Chiefs of Staff Committee, he had orchestrated the deployment of the 1st Battalion, RAR, and then the 1st Australian Task Force to Vietnam. The rules, priorities, and policies of the force in Vietnam were shaped principally by his judgment. The task force represented almost the whole strength that the army could commit and maintain in war, and he was determined to keep it intact.[116]

The keynotes of Wilton's philosophy toward the Vietnam force were steadiness, caution, and confidence in the commanders chosen for the task. He never appeared to pressure them, or the COMAFVs, into greater and quicker results. He himself was a man of rare patience, and he projected this quality, which harmonized with the methods of the soldiers. Task force commanders were not hassled into too rapid expansion of the controlled area around their base, or into conducting operations in depth before they were ready—no matter how much Westmoreland might have fumed at a lack of set-piece battles.[117]

Wilton was a cautious man.[118] He shared a concern with most officers that the Australians should never be caught in such devastating ambushes and traps, as were the French Union forces in the First Indochina War. He could entertain forces being pushed to the limits of their endurance, but not to the limits of their safety. He was cautious also about what he believed to be an American tendency for the "big battalion," "slog-it-out," direct frontal battle with plenty of firepower and plenty of losses. He had served close to the Americans as the senior staff officer in the 3rd Division in New Guinea in 1943 and again as commander of the 28th Commonwealth Brigade in Korea. He had witnessed what he thought was unnecessary loss of life. This was enough for him to try and keep the Australians as separate as he could. Wilton had initially curtailed the role of the 1st Battalion, RAR, with the 173rd Airborne Brigade, and refused Westmoreland's request for it to become part of the U.S. general reserve (available to troubleshoot throughout Vietnam).

He applied similar considerations to the task force that he had to the

1st Battalion. The following extract of an interview relates to the possibility of the task force specializing in the depth role against North Vietnamese and Vietcong main-force units: "To have done that we would have had to be integrated as part of a US division. Quite frankly, those US divisions were flung around the place with great abandon and their operations became a bit of a meat grinder—they had tremendous casualties. Our Task Force was so good that I think we were tempted to put it into every crisis. If we hadn't been assigned an area of responsibility [deliberately sought by Wilton] we would have been in the mobile reserve being shuttled all over Vietnam at a moment's notice. My God, we would have had lots of casualties."[119]

The allocation of a regional task in Phuoc Tuy at once ensured the relative independence of the force and indicated a greater understanding of the fundamentals of counterinsurgency. It was a move that received the approval of one of America's leading soldiers, Lt. Gen. Frederick C. Weyand, who commanded II FFV in 1967. In a conversation with Maj. Gen. D. Vincent, then COMAFV, Weyand voiced his belief that a regional responsibility on the lines of the task force paid better dividends. Local commanders had the chance to know their areas and could pursue the task of eradicating a dispersed enemy. Going off on big operations, Weyand believed, only denuded areas of troops and was uneconomical. At the same time, security was blown because of the preoperational logistical preparations.[120]

Wilton had faith in the integrity of his commanders: "They had their directive, and it was the kind of war that having set down the policy and the tasks which could be done the local man on the spot should be allowed to get on with it. It's not the kind of war which you can run even at battalion level let alone company level from Canberra. This is ridiculous, you would get nowhere. . . . You can give them the mission and task and restrictions and all the other support you've got but you let the man on the spot make his own judgement. And remember we had three lots of judgement there: we had an experienced COMAFV, we had experienced brigadiers (the Task Force commanders), we had good battalion commanders and good company commanders."[121]

The task force commander was under the control of the II FFV commander for operations. He was responsible to COMAFV for matters of Australian national interest. He had an area of operations allocated within Phuoc Tuy Province. When assisting the Vietnamese province chief with restoring control in the villages he acted in collaboration with local authorities. The parameters of his role thus were clearly established and agreed upon with the Americans and Vietnamese. These tasks, carefully conceived, enabled the force to retain a degree of independence as it pursued a course aimed at the heart of the insurgents operating in the region.

Within the considerable latitude he was given, the commander had to choose between operations against the main force, pacification operations, or if the conditions were propitious, a combination of both tasks. It devolved upon the task force commander to establish his priorities without interference from his national headquarters in Saigon or from Canberra. The sole exception to this was when the II FFV commander ordered the force to conduct specific operations outside the province.

The Final Results

The deployment of Australian combat forces to Vietnam in 1965 and 1966 marked the culmination of Australian defense and foreign policies that had been developed over a period of almost twenty years. The adoption of a strategy of forward defense in Southeast Asia resulted in the creation of a standing army that could take its place in regional alliances. It was the first time such a force had been formed in peacetime. Hard-hitting, mobile, and well-equipped battalions of the small standing army received their initiation in jungle warfare during the Malayan Emergency. By 1962, the whole army had been given over to training in communist counterinsurgency.

The 1st Battalion, RAR, established the high reputation of Australian combat troops in Vietnam, but its techniques differed markedly from those of the American brigade to which it was attached. The Australian propensity for painstaking searches and careful efforts to separate the guerrilla forces from the population met with impatience from the American command. The Americans followed a pattern of airmobile operations in strength against scattered targets throughout the country, designed to put the enemy off balance and stop the losing trend. With the enemy offensive successfully stalled, the 1st Australian Task Force entered Vietnam in Westmoreland's planned second phase: the destruction of the Vietcong and the restoration of government control in selected important areas.

Frost's final pronouncement, that the Australian effort to support the Republic of Vietnam was "ultimately futile," has been measured against the outcome of the war.[122] The Australian contribution to Vietnam was too small to effect greatly the result. Moreover, the ultimate fate of Phuoc Tuy was in the main determined by forces from outside the province. Frost's judgment of the task force thus is being made based on factors beyond its control, and adds little to our understanding of any distinctive part it might have played. Australia's entry into the Vietnam War was an integral part of the Cold War. The final events of this historical period are still running their course and definitive judgments are premature.

An assessment of the contribution made by the force can only be made in relation to the tasks it was given. Its first responsibility was to secure and dominate its TAOR in Phuoc Tuy Province. This task was accomplished with twelve months and was never relinquished. Resounding victories such as those at Long Tan and Binh Ba forced the enemy away from the battlefield and rarely after that did he show himself in large numbers. This affected the degree to which the enemy could exercise control over the population. After the battle of Long Tan in the task force's first year of operations, its presence was never deliberately challenged. By the end, enemy forces in the area had been so reduced that the original two main-force Vietcong regiments consisted of northerners. Even as the task force withdrew it inflicted one final defeat on a North Vietnamese regiment that ventured into the province. Enemy recruiting within the province became difficult as government control was extended. The provincial mobile battalion, D445, which fought hard and well and relied on recruits from the villages, was reduced to less than one-third its normal size as it tried to support weakened district units. Communist accounts of the war in Phuoc Tuy are filled with examples of the difficulties caused in base areas, with lines of communication, and with logistical support and recruitment caused by the task force's operations.

Its second responsibility was to secure Highway 15 from the port of Vung Tau. In 1966 it required a major combined force of Australians and Americans to secure the highway for the newly arrived U.S. 9th Infantry Division. By 1971, Saigonese and diplomatic families were driving down Route 15 without fear just to reach the holiday port of Vung Tau.[123] The opening of Highway 15 became a notable feature of the security of Phuoc Tuy.

A further responsibility was the conduct of operations outside Phuoc Tuy Province when ordered by the II FFV commander. Such operations were conducted during the 1968 Tet Offensive and throughout 1968 and into early 1969. It was in this role that the task force had consistently spectacular success as it displayed its capabilities to best advantage. The last task, that of operating generally in Phuoc Tuy, relates to the aim of assisting with providing the security necessary for the government to exert control over the province. The task force provided this security in the districts. As Frost has shown, it could in no measure eradicate communist influence altogether, and units had the capacity to leave the province and return, albeit filled with northerners.[124] The Vietcong cadre in the villages, although reduced, had not been eradicated and had the capacity to regenerate when the task force departed.

By 1971, however, the roads were open, markets were flourishing, enemy tax collection was all but removed, and government control was restored. So much had been accomplished that the last COMAFV, Maj. Gen. D. B. Dunstan, thought that the task force's last two years of operations had been almost a waste of time—that the enemy had been neutralized to the extent that seeking him was like looking for a needle in a haystack. Dunstan had served as deputy force commander in 1968 and quickly noted the difference on his return in early 1971. "Undoubtedly we had achieved a great deal," he said, "and undoubtedly we made a major contribution to the security of the people in Phuoc Tuy."[125] In Dunstan's opinion, the task force could have left the province to the Vietnamese in 1970.[126]

The task force had been successful in restoring government control, but it did not last. As stated by Lt. Col. Nguyen Duc Thu, commander of the D445 Battalion after 1969 and in 1988 head of the Fatherland Front in Long Dat District: "With the presence of Australian troops and American troops in Phuoc Tuy, the Government of South Vietnam in Phuoc Tuy province managed to control the population. But after the withdrawal of the American troops and the Australian troops we turned the tables."[127]

Turning the tables had to wait, however. Eight NVA divisions made the first attempt by launching a massive invasion into South Vietnam in 1972 that was repulsed. The 33rd NVA Regiment went on the offensive in Phuoc Tuy Province with Vietcong forces, but it too was beaten back. It marked the last time that government forces had the support of U.S. airpower. The cease-fire was signed on 23 January 1973 and the last Americans withdrew.

Australian soldiers who fought in Vietnam were imbued with the notion of serving an honorable cause at the nation's behest. For most, this ethos seems not to have changed.[128] In Vietnam, the task force had no sense of defeat. The final collapse, four years after the task force's withdrawal and at the hands of the North Vietnamese Army, exemplified the tragedy but seemed remote from the experience of the men and their leaders.

Addendum: Australian Air and Naval Involvement in the Vietnam War

Australia's principal involvement in Vietnam was on the ground, and the major focus for the Australian public throughout the war was Phuoc Tuy Province and the operations of the 1st Australian Task Force. Units of the RAAF and Royal Australian Navy (RAN) were also committed and served around and over South Vietnam, and some naval elements operated off the coast of North Vietnam in 1967–68. The three Australian services did not function as part of a single force, and Australian aircraft and ships operated as part of higher-echelon U.S. units and formations. The deployments were relatively small, and neither service utilized conscripts. For all these reasons, their activities occasioned much less interest in Australia.

In the mid-1960s the RAAF and RAN were both in the middle of major capital equipment acquisition programs, orienting them away from Britain as the primary source of supply and increasingly toward the United States. For most of its history, the RAN had been structured as a component of the Royal Navy, to whose command it had reverted automatically at the outbreak of both world wars. Its ships were of British design, although some were built under license in Australian shipyards, and its officers had overwhelmingly received a substantial part of their training in British ships and shore establishments. In contrast, the RAAF, created in 1921, was one of the oldest independent air forces in the world, and from the end of the Second World War had looked as much to the United States as the United Kingdom for developments in airpower practice and theory. Australian airmen had already operated as part of a higher-level U.S. formation during the Korean War, and the RAAF had been acquiring U.S. aircraft since the 1950s.

The Australian forces were committed independently of each other to Vietnam. In the 1960s, decisions governing the three services were made with little reference to each other, and such coordination of strategic policy as there was occurred at the highest levels of the services, principally on the Chiefs of Staff and Defence Committees. Air and naval operations made relatively little public impact at the time, and the involvement of the RAN and, to a slightly lesser extent, the RAAF, was even more peripheral to the major currents of the war than was that of Australian involvement overall.

The RAAF in Vietnam

Units of the RAAF had been deployed to Southeast Asia since 1950, first in Malaya as part of the counterinsurgency efforts against the Malayan Communist Party, which ended in 1960, then at Ubon in Thailand from 1962 as part of a SEATO force intended to guarantee the air defense of Thailand from any possible spillover of the war in Indochina. Royal Australian Air Force units continued to be based in Malaysia through the 1960s, although they took no active part in the confrontation with Indonesia between 1963 and 1966. In Thailand, they worked alongside American squadrons and ground personnel while in Malaya/Malaysia the context continued to be a British Commonwealth one. In none of these areas did they have much direct operational involvement with the other two Australian services.

In early 1963, American officials had suggested a possible role for Australian air units in South Vietnam to match the ground advisory tasks then being undertaken by the AATTV, but nothing came of this initially. In May, 1964, however, the cabinet approved the deployment of a flight of twin-engine Caribou tactical transport aircraft despite the fact that the aircraft were only just coming into Australian service and no survey of facilities or flying conditions in South Vietnam had been conducted. The new aircraft and their crews hurriedly prepared to deploy from the RAAF base at Butterworth in Malaysia (which potentially at least compromised Malaysian neutrality) and arrived at Vung Tau in August. The RAAF Transport Flight Vietnam (RTFV) was placed under the operational control of MACV, which delegated authority to a U.S. Air Force wing. The base at Vung Tau was host to the U.S. Army's own Caribou operations at that stage, greatly easing maintenance and other logistics considerations for the small Australian subunit. Redesignated No. 35 Squadron in June, 1966, and known colloquially as "Wallaby Airlines" after its radio call sign, the unit mostly carried supplies and passengers across the length of the country and regularly engaged in airdropping to isolated positions and units. The tasks undertaken were not especially difficult for well-trained personnel, but notwithstanding this the Australian flight and ground crews regularly attained high standards of performance throughout the unit's seven and one-half years in country. A number of men were wounded (none were killed), and aircrew often flew punishing numbers of hours that in turn put a further onus of performance on the ground staff. The squadron remained fully integrated into the U.S. airlift system in South Vietnam for the whole of its wartime service.

The deployment of No. 2 Squadron with its aging Canberra bombers to Phan Rang Air Base in April, 1967, was a response to the pressure exerted by the Johnson administration for further force contributions from America's allies. There had been initial reluctance to send the Canberras on active service, based on doubts about their usefulness in the operational environment of Vietnam and on misconceptions about the nature of air operations there. These views were revised as a result of suggestions from the U.S. Air Force and a desire on the part of the Australian government to acquire further credit with Washington and to do so by contributing forces that were available and could be spared from other tasks, or for whom no other pressing tasks then existed. The decision to dispatch the unit was announced in late December, 1966.

The Canberra squadron was placed under the command of the U.S. Seventh Air Force and was incorporated into the 35th Tactical Fighter Wing. Its operations were restricted to South Vietnam, both because of doubts about its survivability in the intense air defense zones of North Vietnam and because of Australian political sensitivity to the bombing campaign. The Australians thus flew relatively safe missions by comparison with many of their American counterparts, sparing the Australian government the consequences of Australian airmen becoming prisoners of war. Initially confined largely to high-altitude night missions that made few demands of the flight crews, after September, 1967, the squadron switched to low-level daylight missions in close support of ground forces, a role for which the Canberra proved itself unusually well suited. Two aircraft were lost during the squadron's commitment to Vietnam, one shot down by a surface-to-air missile near the DMZ in March, 1971. Small numbers of Australian airmen also flew combat missions as forward air controllers with U.S. Air Force units, and a few flew F-4 Phantoms while attached to American squadrons. Although it was expressly against Australian government instructions, on at least two occasions Australian flight crews flew operations into North Vietnamese airspace.

All of these efforts were part of the wider American air war in Vietnam. The Iroquois helicopters of No. 9 Squadron were sent to Vung Tau in June, 1966, to support the 1st Australian Task Force and as an integral part of the AFV. During the squadron's overall six-year deployment, the Australian helicopters provided essential support to the ground units in a variety of combat missions, but initial reactions to their operational use on the part of senior (and some junior) army officers were highly negative. Although the Iroquois had been acquired in 1962 for the purpose of army support, the Chief of the Air Staff had assigned little priority to this function and the senior ranks of the service appeared to have little interest in helicopter operations at all. There had been little, if any, joint training with the army before the first Australian battalion was sent to Vietnam in 1965, and the air force had refused to deploy No. 5 Squadron from northern Malaya to Borneo during the Indonesian Confrontation, despite direct British requests to do so. The belief in some army circles that the army needed to own these assets if they were to be of any use was strongly reinforced by this attitude and by subsequent developments.

When the 1st Australian Task Force was committed to South Vietnam in mid-1966, the helicopters of No. 9 Squadron went with them. They were not ready. Most aircraft lacked armored seats for the pilots, none had door-gun mounts, and the crews lacked basic personal equipment. The directives that had been issued and which were to govern operational flying reflected both peacetime assumptions and a seeming lack of awareness that the Australian soldiers on the ground in South Vietnam were fighting a war, not staging an exercise. Concern for the vulnerability of aircraft and the safety of flight crews was apparently placed ahead of support of units and subunits engaged on the ground. Aircrew endurance limits (the number of hours crews were to remain on duty, whether flying or not) were set at ridiculously low levels. Stories circulated of soldiers being left stranded in the field because the RAAF had simply "gone home" at the end of the flying day. There was also personal friction between senior army and air force officers at AFV headquarters, which did nothing to ameliorate the difficulties.

Relations between the two sides were improved by revisions to various air force procedures, and by the exemplary assistance provided by No. 9 Squadron aircraft to an army company cut off and under heavy attack in atrocious weather conditions at Long Tan in August, 1966. Pressure on the limited number of helicopter pilots available in the RAAF was eased when both the RAN and the Royal New Zealand Air Force began assigning limited numbers of pilots to No. 9 Squadron in mid-1968. The importance of helicopter gunships to assist in securing landing zones was recognized, and some of the Australian troop-carrying Iroquois were modified to perform that role in 1969. However, the suggestion that the RAAF acquire purpose-built gunships was rejected out of hand by the air force hierarchy despite its advocacy by the Chief of the General Staff. Earlier suspicions within army circles about the RAAF's lack of concern for ground-support missions thus were reinforced further. Not until 1986 did Minister for Defence Kim Beazley agree to transfer the Australian Defence Force's battlefield helicopter assets from air force to army control, a final round in the dispute between the two services that had begun in the early 1960s. When the task force withdrew from Phuoc Tuy Province in November, 1971, No. 9 Squadron departed with it.

The RAN in Vietnam

The Royal Australian Navy had a role in support of the Australian commitment to Vietnam beginning with the deployment of the first battalion group in mid-1965. The HMAS *Sydney,* a converted light fleet carrier, acted as a fast troop transport between Australia and the port of Vung Tau until the final withdrawal of remaining Australian military personnel in the course of 1972. Nicknamed "the Vung Tau ferry," this relatively routine but very important role made the *Sydney* the most widely known of the RAN's various commitments to the war.

Other than logistical support, the navy made three major contributions to Australia's Vietnam War: with surface combatants on the gun line, with clearance diving teams in the explosive ordnance demolition role, and through the provision of pilots and ground crew to both the RAAF's No. 9 Squadron and to the U.S. Army's 135th Assault Helicopter Company.

The commitment of the RAN's recently acquired U.S. *Charles F. Adams*–class destroyers reflected that service's gradual reorientation away from the Royal Navy. These were the first major ships acquired from the United States, and they fit easily into the logistics and command and control structures of the U.S. Seventh Fleet, with which they operated. The RAN destroyers served six-month rotations, and the cycle of commitment and relief was interrupted only once, in 1969–70, when an older, British-pattern destroyer, HMAS *Vendetta*, served a tour in Vietnamese waters. Although equally successful in its missions, the ship suffered some problems because its equipment and machinery were not standardized with the U.S. system. Australian destroyers served on Operation Sea Dragon missions in 1967–68, engaged in the interdiction of North Vietnamese supply craft and attacking shore defenses from positions in the Gulf of Tonkin. Although brought under enemy shore fire on various occasions, the only fatalities suffered in these operations occurred as a result of friendly fire from U.S. Air Force planes in an attack on HMAS *Hobart* in June, 1968. After Sea Dragon was suspended, Australian ships joined their American counterparts in patrol of the "Market Time" maritime control zone around the coast of South Vietnam, and in regular naval gunfire support missions for soldiers ashore.

The clearance diving team was maintained in South Vietnam continuously from February, 1967, to April, 1971, with its members relieved as a group every six months. Until 1970, the Australians operated from Vung Tau and were responsible for explosive ordnance demolition tasks throughout the Mekong Delta area, as well as port security tasks within Vung Tau itself. Thereafter, they moved north to Da Nang until withdrawn to Australia. They often worked in conjunction with American units, including U.S. Navy SEALs, and on one or two occasions took part in operations in areas from which they were restricted by Australian government directive.

The RAN had been keen to find a role for the navy's flagship, the obsolete British-built light fleet carrier HMAS *Melbourne*, but its small size and incompatibility of systems and logistic requirements meant that no role could be found. However, the members of the carrier's helicopter squadron, trained and equipped for an antisubmarine warfare role, were retrained to fly the Iroquois helicopter and from October, 1967, flew as part of a composite Australian-American unit, the U.S. Army's 135th Assault Helicopter Company. Flying from the base at Black Horse, they ranged all over southern and central South Vietnam, flying troop transport and helicopter gunship missions in support of ARVN, South Korean, Thai, Australian, and U.S. ground units. In the process, they took more casualties than any other section of the RAN fighting in Vietnam. In February, 1971, they had to be placed on mission restrictions because Australian government directives prevented them from flying in support of the ARVN's incursion into Laos. They were returned to Australia in May of that year as part of the gradual reduction in the Australian presence. A small number of RAN pilots flew in direct support of the 1st Australian Task Force while posted to the RAAF's No. 9 Squadron.

Conclusions

The roles of the RAN and the RAAF were minor, each a small part of the limited national commitment that fought Australia's Vietnam War. Casualties were light: for the RAAF, four killed in action, two missing and presumed dead, and thirty wounded; for the RAN, eight killed (one by accident), and eighteen wounded. The professional opportunities provided through active service were numerous, but were unevenly spread through the services, unlike the situation with the army because of its much greater numerical and proportional involvement. Neither the navy nor the air force came much into the public view during the course of the war because neither service utilized national servicemen, again unlike the army. Finally, while the opportunities to work with the Americans were important to the development of the two services in the post-Vietnam era, the small and scattered nature of their involvement meant that there were few opportunities for more senior command and staff experience.[129]

JEFFREY GREY

3 Protest and Dissent
Anti–Vietnam War Activism in Australia

Popular responses to war and military activity in Australia took a variety of forms during the twentieth century. The periods of greatest antiwar agitation, with profound effects upon the nation's social and political fabric, occurred during the First World War, especially between 1916 and 1918, and during the war in Vietnam. A key influence on political dissent on both occasions was the issue of conscription for overseas service, and it is tempting to see this as the dominant issue. But while it explains the political galvanization of many, especially those in the middle classes with no previous personal history of political and social activism, it does not by itself explain the form of anti–Vietnam War protest in Australia, nor solely define the course such political agitation took, especially in the late 1960s and early 1970s.

Several issues, and their history, need to be disentangled in considering anti-Vietnam, anticonscription and antiwar activism in Australia in this period. Protest in the 1960s was remarkable for the ways in which it brought together various strands of sociopolitical thought and behavior in a manner not seen since the First World War. We need to understand traditions of pacifism and antimilitarism in Australia, the history of the Left, both communist and noncommunist, the development of views on conscription, especially when intended for overseas service, and the growth of youth culture and the universities. In Australia, the latter was very much a feature of the 1960s with the number of tertiary education institutions nearly doubling between 1958 and 1966. As in the United States, protest, resistance, and dissent in their various forms did not suddenly appear out of nowhere.

Traditions of formal pacifist, antiwar and antimilitarist action are the easiest to identify, and their historical development is fairly well documented.[1] In the colonial era there was both parliamentary and some limited popular opposition to the commitment of colonial contingents to Britain's imperial wars in the Sudan in 1885, and in South Africa between 1899 and 1902. In neither case was opposition large or conspicuously successful. Some individuals—such as the Challis Professor of History at the University of Sydney, G. Arnold Wood—took considerable personal risks in asserting their dissent from mainstream opinion. With the advent in 1911 of compulsory military training in peacetime for Australian boys aged twelve to eighteen, questions of conscientious objection and refusal to serve became public and political issues. Although theological students were granted exemptions, no provision was made at this stage for objection on grounds of conscience (although, in the interests of practicality and economy, those living in sparsely populated areas were excused duty). Noncompliance was punishable with fines and detention, and refusal to register or to undertake or complete training presented a problem for military authorities. During the period 1911–15 (when the scheme was suspended owing to the exigencies of the war), there were thirty-four thousand prosecutions under the legislation, but this was from a total enlistment of 636,000, and many of the prosecutions were directed at multiple offenders. Most of those arraigned pleaded guilty or else attempted to argue circumstance; few dissented from the requirements of the Defence Act on grounds of conscience.

The Australian population greeted the First World War with a unity of purpose that proved impossible to sustain much beyond the end of 1915. Some on the Left shared the apprehension of their political comrades in Europe, but the Labor Party had been a strong proponent of compulsory military training before 1914, and a strong advocate of an Australia capable of defending itself against possible Japanese aggression. Moreover, initially at least, there was little or no dissent against the war in the mainstream. This changed in the course of 1916. Australian prime minister William Morris Hughes returned from Britain in midyear an enthusiastic supporter of conscription for overseas military service, and the first conscription campaign, which culminated in a national plebiscite on the issue in October, 1916, split the government, the labor movement, and the country. Hughes won a national election in May, 1917, with a resounding majority, and attempted to persuade the country of the merits of conscription in a second campaign that resulted in another, more decisive, rejection of the measure in December of the same year.[2] The bitterness engendered by the conscription issue in 1916–17 lasted into the Second World War, and the opposition to conscription for overseas service mounted by some members of that generation of Australians was invoked by their grandchildren in the 1960s and 1970s.

The reintroduction of compulsory training after the end of the First World War did not result in similar levels of opposition or refusal to serve, largely because the scheme was much more half-hearted than its prewar equivalent, and because it was soon severely reduced in scope. Rather, the interwar years, especially the 1930s, saw various ideological battles fought out in Australian political and public life of a kind entirely familiar to observers elsewhere in the western democracies. Those on the Left who moved into the Communist Party of Australia (CPA) in the 1920s mounted various, entirely ineffectual, political offensives against capitalism, militarism, and other foes of the international working classes and on behalf of the Soviet Union.[3] The rise of fascism and the surge of Japanese militarism, coupled with wars and crises in China, Spain, and Abyssinia met with differing responses from the political Left, fellow-traveling, and religious pacifist groups. The membership of such groups was neither large nor influential beyond their own ranks, while the war in Spain produced in Australia, as elsewhere, a more militant response with small groups of the politically committed volunteering to fight in Republican ranks. When war broke out in 1939, the CPA agitated against participation in a war against Nazi Germany on orders from Moscow, and was proscribed in June, 1940. The provisions of the Defence Act that enabled the compulsory call-up of men of military age for the defense of Australian territory were utilized from the beginning, and in February, 1943, the area in which conscripts might be deployed was extended a little to encompass territory beyond Australia's coastline. Prime Minister John Curtin, a prominent anticonscriptionist in 1916–17 who was jailed for his activities, had a political pedigree that undoubtedly helped him to persuade his own Labor Party to accept a measure about which many still harbored deep suspicions and strong convictions. There was some dissent from the provisions of the call-up in the wider population, but with Australia's own territory directly threatened in 1942–43, and with the menace of fascism and the Japanese clear to all, it was miniscule in number and insignificant in its impact on the war effort. Some provision was made for conscientious objection.

The revived national service scheme of the 1950s also failed to engender much opposition. The absence of any requirement to serve outside Australia was an obvious factor in this, as were the minimal demands the scheme made on the young men called up for service. A further factor, undoubtedly, was the very recent memory of the Second World War, with its apparent threat of Japanese invasion, and the climate of Cold War opinion, which the Menzies government exploited successfully during the first half of the decade for domestic political advantage. Australia's forces served overseas during the Korean War and from 1955 in Malaya fighting communist insurgents during the Emergency, but these commitments aroused little opposition, either popular or parliamentary. Members of the Communist Party and their fellow travelers protested against Australian involvement in Korea, and attempted to stimulate criticism of the United States with allegations of "germ warfare," but the United Nations' sanction and bipartisan political support in Canberra were sufficient to persuade most Australians of the merit of the case. Moreover, the membership of the CPA had tumbled dramatically from its high-water mark in the mid-1940s, and was never to recover from the revelations of the twentieth Party Congress in Moscow or the Soviet invasion of Hungary in 1956. There was some opposition to Australian deployment to Malaya from within the Labor Party, concerned at the image of neocolonialism that a troop commitment might represent and underpinned by a naive assertion of the supposedly noncommunist nature of the insurgency. The complete internal disarray of the Australian Labor Party (ALP) by the mid-1950s blunted any effect that this critique might otherwise have had, while public statements by Malayan prime minister Tunku Abdul Rahman welcoming the Australian commitment undercut suggestions that an Australian presence was resented by the local people. Peter Edwards, the official historian, has suggested that Menzies's reading of the Malaya situation in the 1950s and the ease with which he disarmed criticism within Australia was to have an unfortunate influence on his analysis of Vietnam in different circumstances in the mid-1960s.[4]

Anti-Vietnam activism was not confined to those countries with troops committed to the war. There were large anti-American demonstrations in Britain and West Germany that had no connection with Vietnam, and in France, where direct involvement had ceased more than a decade previously. In the Eastern bloc, demonstrations opposing U.S. policy and expressing "solidarity" with the North Vietnamese formed part of the Soviet Union's diplomatic offensive against the United States in the period before detente. The context in which anti-Vietnam demonstrations took place was also important.[5] In both Australia and the United States there was a generalized questioning of existing social and political assumptions, represented by "the Establishment," especially amongst the young. When Pres. Dwight D. Eisenhower left office in the United States in 1960, and Prime Minister Menzies stepped down in Australia in 1966, it seemed to suggest a generational change in national leadership. The political Left had fared badly in the United States during the 1940s and 1950s, hammered by McCarthyism and struggling to find a role in a political culture which was generally "right of center." In Australia, while communism was largely discredited, political activity of a radical or "social democratic" nature still had a natural place within the left wing of the Labor Party and amongst some of the trade unions. Conversely, the issues were more clearly defined in the United

States, especially in terms of the fight for civil rights, which had been gathering momentum since the early 1950s. Racial issues had a centrality in American radicalism that they almost entirely lacked in Australia, at least until the 1970s. In comparing the development of radical and single-issue political activity in the two countries, it is more accurate to see the struggle for Aboriginal rights as being on a par with the rise of the Native American movement, just as the growth of women's and gender issues in mainstream politics emerges from the experience of anti-Vietnam activism and, in Australia at least, takes much of its initial theoretical underpinning from overseas.

Opposition to American policy in Southeast Asia predates the major troop commitments of 1965–66, and in both Australia and the United States was located originally in traditional sources of dissent: the Old Left and religious pacifism. Protests outside the U.S. consulates in Sydney and Melbourne in the second half of 1964 were organized by the Eureka Youth League, the communist youth wing. Fellow-traveling organizations like the Australian Congress for International Cooperation and Disarmament and the Women's International League for Peace and Freedom passed resolutions of support for the National Liberation Front and in condemnation of the Saigon government and U.S. policy. None of this would have meant very much had not the Liberal-Country Party coalition government (within a year of its reelection) revived the national service system in late November, 1964, with an additional provision for active service overseas.

There is a pervasive belief that the government introduced conscription specifically for Vietnam. This is simply not true, but the close timing of the sequence of subsequent events convinced many at the time that it was so, and the notion is now firmly rooted in the popular memory of the times. In late 1964 no decision had been made regarding a possible troop commitment to Vietnam, and the government was, in fact, much more exercised by the threat to regional stability posed by the Indonesian confrontation of Malaysia, with its potential to spill over the shared border into Papua New Guinea, for which Australia had defense responsibility. Very small numbers of national servicemen served in Sarawak in early 1966 in the last stages of the Confrontation, by which time a regular infantry battalion was fighting alongside U.S. units in Bien Hoa Province. The first national servicemen did not go to Vietnam until mid-1966. The fact of their being sent was to give a significant impetus to the antiwar movements within Australia, but it is worth remembering that the combination of unpopular war and unpopular manpower policy were not automatically linked. Had national service been reinstituted for service in Australia and Papua New Guinea only, with regulars sent to Vietnam, there is some reason to think that the antiwar movements would never have moved beyond their traditional isolated and largely irrelevant position. That this was not to be was illustrated with the formation of the Youth Campaign Against Conscription at the end of 1964 and, more tellingly, of Save Our Sons within a few weeks of Menzies's April, 1965 announcement that Australian troops would be sent to Vietnam.

Anti-Vietnam activism can be divided into three chronological periods: that before April, 1965; from then to the massive rejection of the ALP in the federal election of November, 1966; and the gradual resurgence of activity and organization that culminated in the 1970–71 Moratoriums.[6] The first period, as we have seen, was low-key until galvanized by the reintroduction of conscription. The second saw the emergence of activism in the universities, really for the first time. However, opposition to Australian involvement lacked focus, whereas the advantages the government enjoyed, symbolized by President Johnson's visit, were too great for an unreformed Labor Party to counter electorally. The return of the government jolted the complacency of many of those who had assumed, despite evidence to the contrary, that the electorate would reject government policy, and a slow but steady growth in the organization of anti-Vietnam activity was reflected in the result of the 1969 federal election, which saw the coalition government returned by a much narrower margin. At the same time, the antiwar forces in Australia were able to take succor and ideas from their equivalents overseas, especially in the United States, while the twists and turns in Australian and American policy after 1968 seemed to validate the antiwar position, especially with the advent of "Vietnamization" in 1969.[7] Accurate figures on levels of participation in the major demonstrations of 1970–71 are notoriously difficult to establish, but it is clear that the Moratorium was strongest in Victoria with seventy thousand people turning out in Melbourne for the first protest in May, 1970, and perhaps fifty thousand for the second one that September. These estimates are smaller than the Sydney figures, but measured against the relative population sizes of the two leading cities, Melbourne was by ratio more opposed than Sydney. Nonetheless, the link between involvement in a street protest and a commitment to political activism is impossible to establish through quantification.

Opposition in the United States was fueled to some extent by the gradually increasing media awareness of American casualties. No one should underestimate the impact of Walter Cronkite's famous broadcast in which the names and pictures of that week's American casualties were screened in prime time.[8] Dissent in the United States was also driven by America's status as a great power and by ideas about American particularism and its "civilizing mission," which many liberal Americans believed in, sometimes passionately. These notions meant little to Australians, most of whom had yet to engage with Southeast Asia in any meaningful manner, and for many of whom the health of the security relationship with the United States was of paramount importance. Nor did "ordinary" Australians generally welcome or approve of politics in the streets. The Morgan Gallup Poll and other surveys conducted throughout the period 1965–72 demonstrate a gradual evolution of opposition to the war, and little fervor for the public demonstrations. These considerations hamstrung the antiwar movement initially, with demonstrators seeking to keep protests nonviolent in the lead-up to the 1966 election so as not to hurt the image of the ALP, and violent outbursts against President Johnson's 1966 visit certainly did Labor no electoral favors. Labor itself was in a difficult position. It was concerned not to appear anti-American in its platform, yet the leader of the federal parliamentary party in 1966, Arthur Calwell, was a passionate anticonscriptionist who avowedly fought the election that year on the Vietnam issue; the defeat ended his leadership. Even with the elevation of the younger and intensely able E. G. "Gough" Whitlam to leader of the opposition in February, 1967, and the growing involvement in street protests by senior members of the Left of the party, especially Jim Cairns, change came slowly. Whitlam proved to be a sharp critic of government policy in the 1969 election, but the ALP continued to tread a fine line on the issue because of the wider implications for Australian defense and foreign policy. As a subsequent ALP leader, Kim Beazley, has noted, the public perception of a Labor Party in unqualified opposition to government policy on Vietnam, at least before 1970, is wide of the mark.[9] Adam Garfinkle has noted that Pres. Richard M. Nixon, and to a lesser extent President Johnson, both faced considerable difficulties with antiwar activism in the Congress.[10] Although leading antiwar figures like Cairns held senior positions within the parliamentary Labor Party, their opposition to government policy was expressed more effectively *outside* parliament than in it, reflecting the very different nature of the congressional and Westminster systems of representative politics.

Involvement in the antiwar movements proved a radicalizing experience, at least for some. The arrest of respectable middle-class women members of Save Our Sons for protesting peacefully outside national service induction centers helped start some on a move to the political left that was to continue well after the end of Australian involvement and the fall of Saigon.[11] At least in the short term, a similar phenomenon was observable in student politics. The mid-1967 effort by the

Monash University Labor Club (a far left group with no ties to the ALP, despite its name) to raise funds for the Vietcong was more extreme than most, but it was symptomatic of more widespread shifts within the anti–Vietnam War movement. The prominent role of some trade unions, especially those with communist or left-wing leadership, provided both disciplined numbers and resources, as well as experience in organizing and mobilizing. As in the United States, however, organized labor was divided over the issue, mirroring the division of views in society more generally. It was not until February, 1970, that the Australian Council of Trade Unions, organized labor's peak body, endorsed the Moratorium, by which time it was reflecting a trend rather than providing a lead.

The role and importance of the various communist groupings needs to be considered as well. Government ministers and other conservative commentators were prone to depicting the antiwar movements as communist-dominated which, if true, would have suggested a far more powerful political entity than was actually the case. The Old Left was clearly important in the early years, before the Moratoriums and a mass base of antiwar activism, but its influence was gradually supplanted by newer, younger, and more violently radical groups within the New Left, which was mostly based in the universities and which had a strong Trotskyite element.[12] Those seeking to rewrite the history of the Moratorium from the inside have sought to downplay the role of communist groups within its ranks, and to stress instead the diversity of membership the movement undoubtedly reflected by 1970–71. In the absence of any extended work on the subject—a curious gap after thirty years—it is difficult to be sure where the balance lay, but it is probably fair to say that whatever equivocation over CPA involvement may be expressed now was not reflected at the time.

In both the United States and Australia, the antiwar movement convinced itself, and in many cases remains convinced today, that it "stopped the war"—or at least ended its own nation's involvement. Evidence in support of this proposition is mixed at best.[13] It seems unlikely that the Australian government made any decision affecting involvement in the war in response to the activities of the antiwar movement. Put simply, Australian policy was tied to and predicated upon American policy. Australia's commitment of forces in 1965, and incremental force increases in 1966–67, came at the behest of the United States. Equally, the gradual disengagement of Australian forces reflected President Nixon's policies, and marched in step with them. National servicemen were withdrawn from Vietnam because the force as a whole was withdrawn, not because the government recognized that sending regulars alone would be more viable domestic politics. In fact, national service was not suspended entirely until Whitlam came to office in December, 1972, by which time Australian forces had long since vacated Phuoc Tuy Province.

In seeking to gauge the impact of the anti–Vietnam War movements it is better to take a medium-term perspective. While the 1970–71 Moratoriums certainly made the government uncomfortable, they reflected wider changes under way in Australian society, not all of which reflected the evolving impact of the 1968 scene in Europe or the campus revolutions breeding in the United States. The protest marches were not the impetus for those changes, whatever the undergraduate revolutionaries on Australian campuses fondly believed.[14] It is equally important not to overstate the impact of participation in anti-Vietnam activism; protest was not necessarily a "fad," but neither was it a form of Damascene conversion.[15] The most important consequence of this period for Australian society was the growth of the women's movement in the 1970s, heavily peopled with former antiwar protesters who had discovered that the male leadership of the Moratorium was as sexist and exploitative as its opponents (arguably more so).[16] The grassroots, single-issue politics of the 1980s and 1990s, whether concerned with radical environmentalism, homosexual rights, or animal rights calls on the methods, and sometimes the personnel, of the 1960s.[17] The fracturing of the conservative sociopolitical consensus that Menzies forged in the 1950s owed something to the Vietnam War, and to opposition to it. But it owed more to the climate of change that fundamentally challenged all such positions in the West, and from which Australia could scarcely stay aloof whether it wanted to or not.

If our understanding of the movements that opposed involvement in Vietnam is imperfect and still full of gaps, we know next to nothing about those who took the opposite position and supported the Vietnam commitment. This is equally true for Australian domestic politics in the First World War, or the war in South Africa at the century's beginning. The extensive treatment given to the antiwar movement in historical writing belies the claim by some former protesters that they have been written out of the war's history, and suggests something about the maintenance within the universities of the left-liberal consensus that emerged from that period. The antiwar activism of the 1960s and early 1970s is seen by some as part of a continuum within our modern history, stretching back to the First World War, if not before. But the antiwar position was a reactive one, one that was reacted against in its turn. If we are better to understand the actions of the period, and to assess their significance, we need a more fully rounded understanding of the various and conflicting positions to which involvement in Vietnam gave rise. Not to do so is to leave us deficient in our knowledge of ourselves.

PETER PIERCE

4 "Never Glad Confident Morning Again" *Australia, the Sixties, and the Vietnam War*

For one who first attended university in Australia in 1968, full of grand and not easily quenchable expectations, this could indeed seem in retrospect to be an *annus mirabilis*. Beginning with the Tet Offensive in the Vietnam War, events exhilaratingly tumbled upon one another. Lyndon Johnson decided not to seek renomination as president of the United States. Martin Luther King was assassinated. The musical *Hair* opened on Broadway. Student-worker protests (an alliance never comfortable) in Paris and elsewhere in France hinted for tantalizing days at the overthrow of Pres. Charles de Gaulle. Nor was this all. Presidential heir and candidate Robert F. Kennedy was assassinated. The Russian invasion of Czechoslovakia withered the Prague Spring. Richard Nixon was elected president. In Australia, a mineral boom on a scale unknown since the gold rushes of the 1850s appeared to take place. Near the end of 1968, an Apollo spacecraft made a voyage around the moon. The signature tune of this period was the rhythmic thump of helicopters in Vietnam, a noise whose eerily similar counterpart was provided by the hundreds of Gestetner machines running off leaflets for the antiwar protest movement. These were times that contradictorily shocked, aroused, and satisfied the desires of spectators and participants. The world, and not only the United States, impinged on Australian cultural life with a pungency and directness that memory does not altogether falsify.

In his study *Sixty-Eight: The Year of the Barricades*, David Caute reckoned that year "the most turbulent since the end of World War II," although he lamented that in "a chain of insurrections," nowhere was "the challenge" (presumably to regimes of very different political persuasions) successful. Caute argued, as have many others, for years within the sixties—if not for the whole decade—to be regarded as representing historical fissures: "The revolutionary movements of 1968–9 marked, in one respect at least, a break with history: in a period of unprecedented material prosperity and cultural tolerance, the sons and daughters of the most privileged sections of the population rebelled. It was a moral revolt generated by 'alienation' from dominant values, but it did not, on the whole, extend to the working class. The iconoclasm and mounting violence of the New Left outraged the mass of citizens, reinforcing the paternalistic values of 'law and order.'"[1]

That revolt was milder in all its forms in Australia, as befits not only a process of imitation, but also a more homogenous, less riven political culture. Nevertheless, the reverberations of the events of 1968 and the foreign war that was their principal cause have been seminal in political history and nascent myth in Australia ever since.

But where in the sixties does 1968 belong? Is it near the middle or the end of this now much-exploited and popularized decade? Further, where in the process of historical mythmaking in Australia is the decade beginning to fit? Answers to these questions require some concession to the belatedness of happenings in Australia, such as the anti–Vietnam War protests. These took their methods and inspiration largely from American examples. Any response to questions about the 1960s must also reckon with how that chronology is complicated by the Vietnam War. Australian involvement did not end until 1972. It was three more years until the fall of Saigon. There is a paucity of memoirs of this time, whether from veterans of the war or of home front confrontations. Mike Hyde, Michael Hamel-Green, and Francis Perry have offered fragmented accounts of their role in the antiwar protest.[2] Unit histories and individual reminiscences are regularly published. Works such as Bob Buick's *All Guts, No Glory: The Story of a Long Tan Warrior* (2000), continue to give some formulaic versions of the experiences of Australian soldiers in Vietnam.[3]

In spite of this paucity of material, the decade of the 1960s is coming to endure the legendary shaping that only the 1890s has previously enjoyed in the short history of European Australia. That earlier decade of supposed radical, proto-nationalist stirring has been conveniently extended to 1903 to include the publication of Joseph Furphy's experimental novel *Such is Life.* Sometimes called "the Age of Lawson and Furphy," the 1890s can appear to be no longer a mere decade at all, rather passing into the shady purlieu of cultural icon, where the 1960s may also be fated to rest. Remembered in that manner, each period's radicalism loses its pungency.

It is likely that the sixties, as concept or decade, will prove as elastic as the 1890s have. If measurable indices of the spirit of this "Golden Age of glorious caprice and possibility" (as Robin Gerster and Jan Bassett describe the period in *Seizures of Youth: "The Sixties" and Australia*) are taken into account, then a significant portion of the social history of 1960s

Australia will be seen to be more properly located in the 1970s.[4] The first anti–Vietnam War Moratorium was held on 8 May 1970. Two others were subsequently mounted. Far from dying away when Australian troops were withdrawn from Vietnam, tertiary student protests (influenced by the wider agenda of the New Left in the United States and in Europe) remained intense until the mid-1970s. There were occupations of university buildings at Monash in Melbourne, Flinders in Adelaide and the Australian National University in Canberra as late as 1974. In terms of days lost through strike action, the 1970s was a period of much greater industrial militancy than the 1960s had been. In the peak year of 1974, 6.3 million days were lost through strikes.[5] The Left in Australia continued to set the political and industrial agenda, for instance through the successful Green Bans campaign against the redevelopment of historic areas of inner Sydney, at least until the defeat of the Medibank strike in 1976. That followed soon after the dismissal of the Whitlam-led Labor government on 11 November 1975 (the first leftist government in Australia since 1949).

At the beginning of both 1991 and 1992, the 1960s (or more specifically the old anti–Vietnam War protest movement) spluttered uncomfortably to life again in Australia. The occasions that brought now grizzled veterans of earlier street marches and their less numerous youthful acolytes out to demonstrate again were the Gulf War and the short visit of U.S. president George Bush, respectively. In the main uncertain of any motive apart from a visceral anti-Americanism, these manifestations were the last gasp of the halcyon radical days of the late 1960s and early 1970s. When, in January, 1992, the protesters had run out of American targets and decided to attack Myer and David Jones department stores, the intellectual legacy of the sixties looked threadbare.

How should the decade in Australia be represented, not from mythology's vantage in hindsight, but—as it were—from its own time? The 1960s (taken for the moment as that literal span of years) was a period of economic advances in Australia, ample enough to foster the illusion of illimitable future prosperity. There were gas and oil discoveries in Bass Strait of a magnitude that allowed politicians to dream of self-sufficiency in fuel resources. Great quantities of iron ore began to be mined in the Pilbara region of Western Australia. Mineral stocks and shares soared grandiosely. And, in 1965, the Menzies government (a conservative alliance of the Liberal and Country Parties) rejected the dutiful one million words of the Vernon Report on economic planning for Australia.

The conservative parties won the four federal elections held during the 1960s, under three Liberal prime ministers: Sir Robert Menzies in 1961 and 1963, Harold Holt in 1966, and John Gorton in 1969. The first and last of these were narrow victories, and the beginnings of the revival of the fortunes of the Australian Labor Party (which had suffered since its split in the mid-1950s when the Democratic Labor Party was formed) were evident before the 1970s. Because of their support for the increasingly discredited participation of Australia in the Vietnam War, the Liberal and Country Parties steadily forfeited the political cum moral authority that they had enjoyed since Labor lost power at the end of 1949.

An important educational and social adjunct to this gradual shift in political fortunes was the radicalization of Australian university campuses from the late 1960s through the following decade and beyond. The results of this process (which was not, of course, uniform or uncontested) continue to be notable in the syllabuses, ethos, and demography of humanities and education faculties in particular. They can be seen in the 1970s vogue for sociology, in the popularity of notions of "deschooling" with newly and improbably radicalized education bureaucrats, and in the suspicion and decay of "traditional" disciplines. The further politicization of curricula, under the influence of feminism and ideas of "political correctness," while never taking hold as strongly in Australia as in the United States, belonged to the mid to late 1980s. The earlier tendencies—although increasingly resisted in the 1990s (the decade that so far has mostly fondly remembered the 1960s)—have not yet been reversed. It was possible, if distressing to see, in the early 1990s, members of the Australian Defence Force described in a Victorian secondary school textbook as "harm-workers." This unlovely, disingenuous jargon has its ancestry in some soured memory of the intellectual fashions and foes of the sixties.

The pursuit of political aims outside formal party structures (however flexible and opportunistic, especially within the Australian Labor Party, these would prove themselves to be) was also in significant measure a consequence of the anti–Vietnam War protest movements of the 1960s and early 1970s. Radical supporters of the extension of civil and political rights for Aborigines organized Freedom Rides along American lines. Aborigines eventually gained the right to be regarded as Australian citizens after a referendum in 1967, although there were restrictions on their voting rights until 1984. Advocates for women's liberties (broadly and shiftingly conceived), for the abolition of nuclear weapons, and for ecological issues all, to some extent, found suitable tactics in the experience and then in the memory of the antiwar movement. The ironic aspect of these appropriations was that the anti-American animus in several of these causes did not at all prevent the wholesale borrowing of the methods and rhetoric of American protesters.

In qualification, it is necessary also to stress the indigenous origins of the various protest movements in Australia during and since the 1960s. The role of church groups and of individual clerics was important not only in the Australian Moratoria, but much earlier, in the demonstrations against the White Australia Policy in the 1950s and in the Campaign for Nuclear Disarmament (where the instructive model was British rather than American) in the same decade. Campaigns against literary censorship took place in print and in courtrooms in the 1950s and 1960s, as Geoffrey Dutton illustrated in *Australia's Censorship Crisis.*[6] Here the issue might be the continued banning of D. H. Lawrence's novel *Lady Chatterley's Lover* or the attempt—as late as 1970—to prosecute the editors of the Tasmanian University students' paper *Togatus* for printing an extract and a review of Philip Roth's preposterously banned novel, *Portnoy's Complaint.* A protest movement, which in the heterogeneous nature of its social composition foreshadowed the campaign against the Vietnam War, formed in Victoria to oppose the hanging of Ronald Ryan for the murder of a prison warder. It was unavailing, although Ryan was the last man to be hanged (on 3 February 1967) in Australia. More violent than these demonstrations, or the Moratorium marches, were the protests in both Australia and New Zealand against the South African Springboks Rugby Union tours in the early 1970s.

The consequences of antiwar protests for the foreign policies of the antipodean allies of the United States in the Vietnam War are harder to assess. The American withdrawal from that country, which the Australian Labor Party could readily have seen as evidence of the rectitude of its opposition to the war, may have prepared the way for a renewal of bipartisanship over foreign policy issues in Australian politics. The visits to China of Richard Nixon, and soon afterward Gough Whitlam, were crucial complementary events in this process. In an instructive comparison, Roberto Rabel has argued that—influenced as were antiwar protests in New Zealand by American examples—the movement there "had an enduring effect on New Zealand thinking about foreign policy and carried significant long-term implications for the alliance with the United States."[7] Arguably it was more decisive—in terms of the articulation of independent foreign policy objectives—than in Australia. The most notable difference was the decision by the New Zealand government to refuse further visits of nuclear-powered American vessels, which led to the fracturing of the ANZUS alliance in the mid-1980s.

What were the effects of these economic, political and diplomatic changes on Australian culture during the 1960s and 1970s? Initial, apparently simple soundings of literary production in Australia in the first of those decades (as distinct from the mythologizing of the period in fiction and television miniseries two decades later) provide teasing bases for conjecture as to how the practitioners of high culture were reacting, or declining to respond, to the upheavals of these years. Some literary careers began in the 1960s. Expatriate Australian Peter Porter's first volume of verse, *Once Bitten, Twice Bitten,* appeared in 1961. Among novelists who were first published in this decade, none has had a more enduring and successful career than Thomas Keneally, whose first book, *The Fear* (1964) set in Sydney during the Second World War, was followed only two novels later by *Bring Larks and Heroes,* winner of the Miles Franklin Award for the best Australian novel of 1967. No other mainstream writer has paid so much attention to Australia's Asian wars. There are brilliant vignettes of the Malayan Emergency and of Vietnam in Keneally's *Passenger* (1979).

A younger generation of poets was also urging its claims to renown. Foremost among the so-called Generation of '68 was the poet Michael Dransfield, who died of problems related to drug addiction in April, 1973, before he was twenty-five. In his introduction to *Australian Poetry Now* (1970), Thomas Shapcott, another Australian poet—albeit a generation older—had perhaps doomed Dransfield by describing him as "terrifyingly close to genius." Dransfield's biographer, Patricia Dobrez, author of *Michael Dransfield's Lives: A Sixties Biography* (1999), is as intent on characterizing a decade as a poet. Speaking of Dransfield's place in a reckoning of the sixties she observes how "[t]he idea of a personal myth points to a key feature of that peculiar sixties cocktail of illusion and utopian desire which affected every aspect of culture from politics to poetry."[8] There is a signal ambivalence in the career that she traces. While Dransfield was arrested on 4 July 1966 for leading an all-night antimilitarist vigil at the U.S. consulate in Sydney, and on 5 September 1969 would compose an elegy for Ho Chi Minh, who had died two days before, in the same year he wrote "Last Post," a poem dedicated to his paternal grandfather, who had served with the Australian forces at Gallipoli in 1915. Such a tormenting division of spirit was more often masked in the polemical verse that the Vietnam War inspired in Australia.

The careers of some long-established poets appeared to change direction in the 1960s. David Campbell, Royal Australian Air Force veteran of the Second World War, was one of the few whose poetry tried to accommodate opposition to the war in Vietnam, notwithstanding his earlier conservative allegiances. Another veteran of the Pacific conflict, James McAuley, who served briefly in New Guinea, responded in ways that were unexpected in light of his previous work, yet were characteristic of the introspective temper that much of 1960s Australian literature reveals. McAuley's not quite "confessional" collection of autobiographical verse, *Surprises of the Sun* (1967), seemed to belong to the Romantic rather than the Classical tradition to which he had usually been assigned. Seen in a wider context, McAuley's book is part of one of the two most notable literary phenomena of the sixties in Australia: the burgeoning of works of autobiography (whether this was their professed genre, or they were fiction or poetry) and the publication of an increasing number of works of social and cultural diagnosis. These two fields of endeavor are related, insofar as each attests to a faith—never so confidently or copiously asserted before—that Australia at last provided a sufficiently rich body of material to be exploited for analysis or reminiscence. In fact, the combination of the two was typical of the decade, and of the empirical temper that preferred to rely on individual memory and speculation, rather than theory, in intellectual debate in Australia.

The 1950s had seen vital stirrings of analytical attention, especially to cultural history, and again extending from subjective witness. Significant works in this mode included Vance Palmer's *The Legend of Australia* (1954), Russel Ward's *The Australian Legend* (1958), A. A. Phillips's *The Australian Tradition* (1958) and John Douglas Pringle's *Australian Accent* (1959). More various in the objects of their scrutiny, the diagnostic works of the 1960s included Robin Boyd's philippic against the facades and structures of urban life in *The Australian Ugliness* (1960); Bernard Smith's (1960); H. M. Green's *A History of Australian Literature* (1961), a very long conspectus that had been promised for two decades earlier; the first of the six volumes of Manning Clark's *A History of Australia* (1962; the final volume appeared in 1987); *The Literature of Australia* (1964), a compendium of essays edited by Geoffrey Dutton that met such a need that its two editions sold more than sixty thousand copies; Donald Horne's *The Lucky Country* (1964); Judith Wright's *Preoccupations in Australian Poetry* (1965); Geoffrey Blainey's interpretation of Australian history, *The Tyranny of Distance* (1966); and Alan Moorehead's account of the consequences for its indigenous people of European penetration of the Pacific, *The Fatal Impact* (1966). In the same year, Dutton edited *Australia and the Monarchy,* which politely addressed a connection beginning to weaken. This was the decade in which Menzies lost the battle to have the unit of Australia's decimal currency called the "royal." Other works of interpretative and retrospective bent, contributions to a Romantic investigation of Australian cultural history, were John Manifold's *Who Wrote the Ballads?* (1964), and *Folk Songs of Australia* (1968), edited by Hugh Anderson and John Meredith.

The history and art of Europeans in the Pacific and in Australia, the translation of demotic forms of song from the old to a new world, the physical and political environments constructed in Australia, and the literary history that had been made were among the subjects of this impressively wide-ranging and adventurous collection of books. Their complement was the body of personal and domestic explorations conducted in the first and finest flowering of Australian autobiographical writing that took place in the 1960s. Again a list is necessary to take some measure of this achievement, one the more remarkable because the genre had such a scanty previous history in Australia. Miles Franklin's *Childhood at Brindabella* appeared posthumously in 1963. Hal Porter's *The Watcher on the Cast-Iron Balcony,* the first installment of an autobiographical trilogy, and Katharine Susannah Prichard's *Child of the Hurricane* were published in the same year. All three were primarily novelists. George Johnston's semiautobiographical novel (and the start of another trilogy) *My Brother Jack* was published in 1964 (and made into a television miniseries broadcast in 2001). There followed Rose Lindsay's *Ma and Pa* (1964); Martin Boyd's *Day of My Delight* (1965) and Donald Horne's *The Education of Young Donald* (1967). There are two subsequent parts to Horne's saga of self and society as well.

In *The Penguin New Literary History of Australia* (1988), Brian Kiernan argued for another likeness between the diagnostic and the autobiographical works of the 1960s. Comparing Boyd's *The Australian Ugliness* to Johnston's *My Brother Jack,* Kiernan found in both "nostalgia for the values (and associated material trappings) of a more 'authentically' Australian working class life which had been overtaken by events: the war, steadily rising affluence during Menzies's unprecedentedly long reign, and the ambivalently resisted processes of Americanization. There was conflict between the values of this older, more authentic Australia and the brashly new, between a guilty recall of the previous half century of war and depression and the seductive opportunities and consumer satisfactions of postwar Australia."[9] In their particular dramatic setting, these are also the conflicts that animate the most notable play of the early 1960s: Alan Seymour's *The One Day of the Year* (first performed in 1961 and published the next year).

The history of theatrical writing in Australia has been distinguished by many false dawns and by renaissances too quickly proclaimed, as Donald Horne has commented.[10] Seymour's play (a hit on a scale that he never managed again; later in the decade he would settle permanently in England) was apparently so successful a piece of naturalism that it was refused performance at the first Adelaide Festival of the Arts in 1960. Evidently some committee members feared the Returned Servicemen's League (RSL, now known as the Returned and Services League) would be offended. In enlightening respects, *The One Day of the Year* is a proto-Vietnam play dramatizing a conflict between generations, expressed in their antagonistic allegiances and pieties, by concentrating on a son's skepticism toward the tales and remembrances of the previous wars in which Australians (such as his father, grandfather, and their friend, Wacka Dawson) had fought. These would be staple aspects of American and Australian literature of the Vietnam War. When Seymour wrote his play, that war was for both countries still in the near future. The truce between father and son with which *The One Day of the Year* uneasily concludes might not have been manageable if arguments over Australian involvement in Vietnam, rather than the observance of Anzac Day, had been the issue of contention.

By the end of the 1960s, Seymour's play was looking antediluvian to the experimental playwrights in Melbourne who were associated first with the Union Theatre at the University of Melbourne, then with the Australian Performing Group and La Mama, companies situated in the inner suburb of Carlton. Most durable of the dramatists whose careers began in the 1960s were Jack Hibberd, David Williamson, Alex Buzo, and John Romeril. Influenced by Samuel Beckett, but also by the political plays of Brecht, Hibberd was the most ideologically driven of these writers. Introducing *Three Popular Plays* (1976), Hibberd articulated a concept of "popular theatre": "a theatre of accessibility that is above all Australian in theme and substance, a theatre of the populace that deals with legendary figures and events, perennial and idiosyncratic rituals, mythically implanted in the nation's consciousness. It is a form of folk theatre, without being folksy."[11]

In his dramatic practice, by contrast, Hibberd intensified the curious blend of nostalgic analysis of Australia that distinguished many of the autobiographical and diagnostic works considered above. "The matter of Australia" was the business of his famous monodrama *A Stretch of the Imagination* (1972, 1973). Boxer Les Darcy and opera singer Nellie Melba were national celebrities whose partly tarnished legends he reconsidered and renovated in *The Les Darcy Show* (1974, 1976) and *A Toast to Melba* (1976), respectively. For all the professed socially and politically reformist intentions of his plays, there is a sentimentality and a quietism implicit in the retrospective orientation of Hibberd's drama.[12] Here, another comment from Kiernan's essay appears apt, if not committed to causal explanation: "postwar Australia up to the mid-1960s seems to have gone through a self-reflexive phase during which a sense of independent national identity that necessitated appraisals of its nature, extent and worth was more widespread than ever before, even in the 1890s."[13]

It is hard to detect such self-consciousness in the Australian novels of the 1960s and early 1970s that dealt directly with the war in Vietnam.

Admittedly, there were few. First of the books that treated the conflict, and still one of the most controversial, was John Rowe's *Count Your Dead* (1968). Written against the grain of Australian war literature, with an American officer as its protagonist and some unflatteringly direct criticism of Australia ventilated in the course of the story, the novel's reception within the Australian Army led Rowe to resign his commission. He went on to a second career as the author of paranoid thrillers that imagined, variously, war between India and China and the destruction of the Aswan Dam. Rhys Pollard's *The Cream Machine* (1972) set an unfortunate precedent. His was one of several first novels set in Vietnam written by Australian authors who dried up thereafter. For the professional writer Kenneth Cook, who wrote the portentously titled *The Wine of God's Anger* (1968), the war was another fictional opportunity in much the same fashion that brutalized outback towns and tuna fishing were also.

There was a deal of protest poetry cum polemic written in Australia, as in the United States, at the end of the 1960s. Some of this verse was collected in a special issue of *Overland* magazine called "Vietnam Voices." More appeared in the anthology *We Took Their Orders and are Dead* (1971), edited by Shirley Cass, Michael Wilding, and others. This book co-opted miscellaneous material and unlikely contributors with which to thicken itself: Seymour offered an anti-American diatribe; Keneally permitted the inclusion of an extract from his novel of Australia's first settlement, *Bring Larks and Heroes;* and A. D. Hope's noble threnody for any war gave this compendium some dignity as well as its title. In the United States, several novelists' careers began with Vietnam books (Robert Stone's and Tim O'Brien's among them), and poets' careers changed with them (consider Denise Levertov or Robert Bly). This did not happen in Australia, either in the 1960s or subsequently, with the possible exception—noted above—of the change in direction caused by his response to Vietnam in the career of David Campbell.

Both the Vietnam War and the sixties received belated and oblique literary treatments in Australia. The nation's cultural dependence agitated characters in Frank Moorhouse's "discontinuous narrative" *The Americans, Baby* (1972), which was later made into the movie *The Coca-Cola Kid.* Novelists and poets in the 1970s would revisit and revise legends and events of the First World War, seeking—by indirection perhaps—to understand the Vietnam War, which was another domestically divisive conflict, the cause of another supposed historical fissure between an innocent era and a subsequent betrayed and disillusioned one in Australian history. Writers would also turn to Asia for literary subject matter and for moral inspiration and mentorship, in part—it might be conjectured—in assuagement of the presumed national guilt over Vietnam.

Christopher Koch's novel *Across the Sea Wall* (1965) is one of the earliest fictions in which ingenuous Australians are confronted with Asia. Three decades later, Koch dealt explicitly with Vietnam in *Highways to a War* (1995). Many others followed his first venture, an output and exploration that was remarkable not least for how rarely Vietnam or the Indochinese wars figured at all in them. After 1972 it seemed that the Vietnam War was consigned swiftly into silence by an act of historical amnesia that Australian writers largely abetted.

Oddly, the situation in respect of Australian popular music went against this trend. The heyday of Australian rock music was the 1970s, rather than the 1960s. This was a development that paralleled and interacted with the revival of the local film industry and the boom in Australian theater in the 1970s.[14] In the previous decade, few protest songs were written in Australia. Ronnie Burns's "Smiley," about a young man "off to the Asian war," carefully avoided giving opinions about either conscription or the war. There were folk protest songs by Gary Shearston and Don Henderson, but nothing comparable in urgency or force to the work of Phil Ochs, Tom Paxton, Pete Seeger, and Malvina Reynolds in the United States. However, Australia produced distinguished songs about the problems of its Vietnam veterans. Notable among these was "I was only 19" by the group Redgum. Three of its early members and songwriters—Michael Atkinson, John Schumann, and Verity Truman—had studied at Flinders University under Brian Medlin, then the highest-profile Australian academic recruit to Maoism. Another group, Cold Chisel, produced the song "Khe Sanh," which addressed the disorientation of a Vietnam veteran and asserted that only "other vets" could hope to understand the "Vietnam cold turkey."[15]

Those "other vets" began to be appreciated and considered afresh in Australia near the end of the 1980s. The Vietnam War reemerged, refurbished in Australian consciousness with two television miniseries and a march by veterans in 1987 that gestured at reconciliation and homecoming (and again aped its American model, the Chicago march of the previous year). In October, 1992, a Vietnam War monument (also encouraged by an American example) was unveiled in Canberra. In fashion, the hippie wave of the 1960s was awkwardly reinstated. Police remarked upon a new wave of popularity for the favored sixties hallucinogenic drug LSD. In 1991 the rock musical *Hair* was revived at the same time as the Gulf War resuscitated old protesters. Mythologizing the 1960s had earnestly begun. Thomas Pynchon traversed the decade in the United States through the memories of such survivors as Zoyd Wheeler and Frenesi Gates in *Vineland* (1990), his first novel in seventeen years. The blurb was more than usually informative, relating that in 1984 in northern California "a group of Americans was struggling with the consequences of their lives in the sixties, still run by the passions of those times, sexual and political, which have refused to die."[16]

For the ingenuous Jack Rudd, the protagonist in Victor Kelleher's novel *Wintering* (1991), the sixties—"the Vietnam War thing"—seem an epoch of intrepid self-adventuring by comparison to Sydney in 1988. Aging veterans of that past decade are still objects of veneration for him. Alan Gould took a more skeptical view of the days of righteous protest in one of the novellas, "Decency and Honour," in his book *The Enduring Disguises* (1988). Gould had been part of those days as an antiwar, anti–Springbok Tour demonstrator and as one who refused to register for National Service. Nevertheless, in the first lines of "Decency and Honour," he had taken a sardonic backward glance, though not a repentant one, at his radical activities: "it became customary for us to speak of ourselves as the generation of '68. Wicke and I both belonged to this generation by virtue of the fact that it was in that year of turmoil on the streets of Paris and the campuses of America that we went up to the small and sylvan university in Canberra."[17] The sixties, in such a view as this, was a time of imitation, rather than of initiation.

So, too, have been the pop-culture-sponsored sixties revival and the rosy renewal of interest in the war in Vietnam and its veterans in Australia. Since the end of the 1980s, Australian society has been involved in a decade-long manufacture of another, pseudo-historical period of exhilaration, risk, and promise betrayed. That such a fashion of recollecting the 1960s and Australia's part in Vietnam is largely undiscriminating and exploitative betokens the bad habits of mind of a country that prefers the solace of popular myths to the agonies of exacting remembrance.

JEFF DOYLE

5 Other Contingents

Australian Veterans Beyond Vietnam

Bringing up the rear of the thirty thousand odd men and women marching on 3 October 1992 at the dedication ceremony of the Australian Vietnam Forces National Memorial on Anzac Parade in Canberra was a small group of serving personnel, civilians, and others (some foreign nationals, or from other military units) not numerous enough or for other reasons not able to march under any of the other regimental flags, guidons, and so forth. Instead, they had only the official label or banner signaling "Other Contingents." It is perhaps ironic that within those ranks were a number of American, Korean, and Thai nationals celebrating the rehabilitation of Australian Vietnam veterans, just as the United States had celebrated its veterans' rehabilitation a few years earlier, after Pres. Ronald Reagan reennobled the war. This time, however, the Australians were the largest force, and the United States was reduced to participating as the "other." It had not been so during the war. Then, Australians were just one small unit of the foreign or "other" contingents allied to the United States (no more than eight thousand personnel at any one time), "invited" by the South Vietnamese to enhance the political appearance of unity within the designated Free World Military Assistance Forces. Looking at what the Australians achieved militarily—even on a pro rata basis of troop numbers versus area contained, or cadres killed in Phuoc Tuy Province—over eleven years, it would be hard to see Australia's participation, on a world scale, as more than contingently useful to the allies. Yet on every other basis of estimation, the troops did what was asked of them (despite General Westmoreland's often heard demands to increase kill ratios). Indeed, Vietnam was the biggest military enterprise for Australia since the Second World War. Nevertheless, during the war Australian troops were no more than "other contingents" for their allies, and, on the world news front, hardly recognized at all. Once they returned home, that "otherness" continued in a number of ways.

Anecdote and oral history make the following points relentlessly.[1] Few if any Australian veterans were recognized as honorable soldiers on their return from their one-year tours. Most were allegedly smuggled singly into their local airports at midnight and given taxi fare home. No one was honored with a "welcome home" march during the war years from 1962 to 1973. The one exception to this oral history rule is that the one unit given such a parade was shamed when an antiwar protester ran from the crowd covered with fake blood and smeared herself on the leading officer. Almost all veterans were tagged as "baby killers" and spat on or refused service sometime in the next decade or so. Even their fathers' generation at the RSL (Returned Services League) clubs, treated their veteran sons with disdain since they did not win the war, and there had been no major battles reportedly full of Kokoda Trail victories or Gallipoli-like sacrifice and valor. This erasure of the veterans' memories into a collective "myth" of betrayal by allies, government, and friends and families, then took on a few other features. Most veterans can recall being near Agent Orange and other defoliants at base camps and so forth, or rained upon by U.S. defoliant-spraying aircraft. Contentiously, Australian official documentation has failed to support this evidence or even acknowledge these memories as having some of the status of "facts." The most famous of Australian Vietnam pop songs, "I Was Only 19" by the folk band Redgum, virtually catalogues the series of popular oral myths, or "histories," of the veteran—from mines to Agent Orange to Post-Traumatic Stress Disorder (PTSD). However, for a long while the Australian populace and its government did not want to know about any aspect of this popular veteran "history." While the veterans' groups began their various struggles to gain political and medical recognition from 1975 until about 1987, the general Australian public turned away from matters military. At the same time, at least one kind of "formal" history, which some call official or state history, was seen by some to neglect the veterans.[2]

Earlier in 1992 in the Anzac Day Parades around the nation on 25 April, for what seemed like the first time, the Australian Vietnam Forces had been allowed to lead many of the big-city marches. To the contrary, many Vietnam veterans had led marches in the early 1970s, but their collective memory recalled otherwise, and for many years this gap in the memory, a kind of "daze," became *the* popular memory. In this narrative, in 1992 the "other contingents" had been recognized at home, at last. Indeed they were, by all accounts, rapturously well received by some of the largest crowds in living memory. Not only was the Anzac spirit revived, but the Vietnam veterans also had been taken back into the fold in large measure. For many, if not most, of the men and women designated in the mid-1960s as the "third wave of Diggers," their treatment as serving personnel and for a longer time as returned service people or veterans by their military peers, by the wider society, by historians, and lastly by the government, had in their view always made them an "other contingent"—at best marginal to the society they felt they had dutifully served, at worst an embarrassment that could not be ignored swiftly enough. Indeed, to reassign and reinterpret that banner one more way, the Australian veteran's status as a genuine veteran, an authentic "digger," had been made contingent on the way the nation had come to view the "history" of its engagement in Vietnam after the fact. For many in the veterans' community, the antiwar movement's version of history, allied to the failure of political will of both the American and the Australian governments, had won the war—or, rather more psychologically correctly, this "history" had robbed them of their rightful place as validated third-wave Anzacs by rewriting the "facts" of the war in such a way that their honest, dutiful service was spent for naught.

For many veterans, worse was to come. As time unfolded, many felt that their treatment by government and other institutional or semi-institutional bodies was a sign that they were to be ignored or even punished for what they had done. Ignorance and evasion of responsibility took the form of government failure to honor debts of service as many veterans fell "prematurely" ill and died, while a large number succumbed to psychological traumas, PTSD, and/or suicide—all due, they argued, as individuals and then as organized groups, to the effects of war service, especially the medical conditions, which can be neatly summarized under the rubric of Agent Orange.

Here, too, "history" has allegedly been rewritten. Official histories, medical reports on mortality effects, and royal commissions appeared at various times over the last fifteen to twenty-five years and were, for the most part, received well within the scholarly and professional ranks, while being dismissed and derided by the veterans as inadequately researched and logically flawed. At least two kinds of history were at work. Some in the academic ranks tried to explain, but most often the veterans' communities asked one seemingly unanswered (possibly unanswerable) question: Why do you never ask *us* about Vietnam? How was scholarly "history" to answer when this kind of contingent gap lies in the very nature of the historiographic practices under contention? It is worth noting here one more contingent "otherness" about the Australian Vietnam veteran image. At least since the Second World War, Australia has been undergoing a fascinating shift of cultural emphasis—one might even say loyalty—from being cultural inheritors of the major British-European traditions to being a cultural consumer of American-

European traditions. In many ways, Australia has resisted this influx of American culture, products, and values with some success. However, during the Vietnam War, as a prime location for American rest-and-recuperation activities, Australia succumbed largely to a kind of U.S. commercial fast-food entertainment and street-life culture that still dominates large sectors of the lifestyles of Australians under age forty or thereabouts.[3]

It thus is perhaps curious, but not totally surprising, that many in the Australian Vietnam veterans' communities set about rehabilitating the veteran by following U.S. models, although the local Australian timing seems to enjoy a lag of some five years.[4] This parallelism includes the timing and designs of the Welcome Home March, the National Memorial, and the continuing processes and litigation focused on Agent Orange and other matters associated with the Department of Veterans' Affairs. Parallels might even be drawn within the cultural and entertainment worlds where the representations of the Australian veteran have paralleled that of his U.S. counterpart, from the *Rambo* films of the 1980s to *Born on the Fourth of July.* But there is difference, too, at least notionally so, in the transmission of history. The U.S. veterans' groups in the late 1990s seem to have established their centrality within mainstream American politics. As a result, in large part the veteran community now has control of the "history" of the war, including the aftermath. Following the continued chemico-military interventions of the Gulf War, the American veteran does not seem now to have to continue to win the fight about due recompense, at least not at the group level.[5] The Agent Orange syndrome has largely been subsumed by Gulf War syndrome, and all parties accept that chemical warfare was undertaken in Vietnam while equally admitting the misjudgment of the preventative chemico-medical intervention in the Gulf.

Perhaps the sheer size of the Vietnam cohort in the United States means that their political power base is substantial and continues to be influential. This would not appear to be the case in Australia. There have been large gains made by the various Australian veterans' groups in matters such as compensation for permanent or semipermanent incapacity due to exposure to chemicals or other medical and psychological conditions. Yet paralleling those gains has been the fragmentation of the groups into a relatively small number of separate interest groups whose foci are various and which, in effect, disperse any political force they might collectively manifest. These groups, even in total numbers, represent only a small part of the total Vietnam veteran community that might be concerned. Moreover, within the wider population, the Vietnam veteran community can hardly match the proportions of its U.S.

equivalents. The effective community is simply not big enough, or so it seems, to attain substantial political status.

The Vietnam Veterans' Association of Australia

The Vietnam Veterans' Association of Australia (VVAA; originally the Vietnam Veterans' Action Association) was begun in 1980 by a number of concerned veterans who felt that the Department of Veterans' Affairs was failing to act in their best interests.[6] Recourse to other interested groups, such as the RSL, also resulted in dissatisfaction. Initially, the VVAA undertook two tasks: first, a program of crisis counseling and intervention, a kind of forerunner to the Vietnam Veterans' Counseling Service; and second, to lobby government for recognition of Agent Orange syndrome. At first the RSL did not support the VVAA's claims, sharing the popular view that Vietnam veterans had not had such a hard time of it compared to earlier generations of soldiers. Later, in the 1980s, some elements of the RSL, by then with many Vietnam veteran members in positions of influence if not power, did support some aspects of the Vietnam veterans' groups, most notably the group that pushed for and eventually succeeded in getting the National Memorial built in Canberra.

From its inception to the present, the VVAA represents only a fraction of veterans. It claimed 15,000 members at its peak, but the most usually cited figure is between 5,000 and 7,000. In addition, there are a number of small and fragmented splinter groups, often representing quite specific local and factional needs. There are also unit associations and other welfare groups, and Vietnam veterans increasingly are running local RSL groups independent of the VVAA. Some organizations are "political," whereas others are decidedly not, continuing a trend from the earliest days of veteran response in which political affiliation was suspected of alliance with the authorities responsible for sending Australians to the war in the first place. Many do not accept the VVAA's portrayal of the veteran as in need, sick, or damaged by an external agency in the form of chemical intervention. For others, their identity is seemingly tightly allied to their war service and its "correct" representation in both history and in their day-to-day lives. As one might expect, all this results in a complex of responses with little chance of coherent focus into a single pattern of either "history" or myth.

In 1990, Jane Ross observed: "the two issues central in defining *the* Australian veteran [were] Agent Orange and the problem of homecoming and the need for a welcome home march."[7] However, both problems derived from confusing the American experience with that of Australians. There *was* a Welcome Home March—in October, 1987—

and the Agent Orange issue has been partially resolved. I say "partially," because the questions surrounding Agent Orange and posed by some veterans have broadened. Ross could not have foreseen that there would be a National Memorial as well as a Welcome Home March, but elsewhere she presciently observes a tendency to "Australianise" the war:

> The 50,000 veterans deal with their memories of the war in many different ways. For some, the full-time veterans, it is the defining element of their identity. Some are damaged beyond cure either physically or mentally, while others lead productive lives untroubled by their experiences. For some, the war is with them constantly, while others left it behind. . . . It is difficult to say to what extent "the veterans" do indeed form any sort of coherent group: and it is also difficult even as late as the end of 1990 to see whether the experiences of Vietnam have stabilised into coherent cultural forms. It does seem, however, that both the Vietnam veterans as a whole and their memories are progressively being absorbed into the mainstream community of returned servicemen, and into its official ideology, the Anzac tradition. In this sense, the war is at last being Australianised.[8]

As late as 2001, the reception of the war by veterans is still synchronous with Ross's first paragraph. Reactions to the war vary, although there is some evidence that more of the nonconscript veterans are turning to the veterans' associations for help as they leave the services or are finding their health in premature decline. The second paragraph is more contentious now. It does seem that by 1990 both the veterans and the wider community were "normalizing" the war, accepting these veterans into the Anzac fold. These rehabilitative gestures reached their Vietnam-focused climax in the celebrations surrounding the National Memorial dedication and march in October, 1992. In the years following, all things Anzac in popular press and visual media were steadily on the incline in popularity, reaching a plateau of national favor throughout the whole of the 1995 "Australia Remembers" celebrations marking the end of the Second World War. There has been no large scale or noticeable decline since, and Anzac Day Parades in 1998 and 1999 were again well attended—due in part to the sense that many of the First World War diggers, including the few living Gallipoli survivors, were unlikely to see many more such marches, and as well not a little to millennial celebrations allied to more national festivities, such as the 2001 Centenary of Federation and the holding of the 2000 Olympic games in Sydney. In all of these events the status of the Australian military was high and more than nationally visible. Another and major factor was the high profile of the Australian Defence Forces' participation and leadership of the forces in East Timor.[9]

However, the general increase in Anzac's popularity is not the same as specific awareness of and care for the Vietnam veteran. In fact, the presumption of having been attended to reads as neglect for others. Ross's two poles, "parade" and "Agent Orange," however narrow they look in 2001, are still present: the parade group arguing for more service medals and recognition; the others still seeking full recognition, as they see it, for the "complete" Agent Orange package.[10] In that sense, the Vietnam War *has been* Australianized, since the Agent Orange issue no longer parallels its U.S. predecessor, while the politically minded groups have yet to succeed in gaining strong political representation through their Vietnam veteran electoral base (and would seem unlikely to be able to do so), in contrast with experience in the United States.[11]

Agent Orange in Australia

The early stages of the Agent Orange legal cases in Australia are largely derivative of American initiatives and data.[12] At first, the Australian government denied any Australian exposure. Retraction followed, but the government then insisted that established channels could handle these matters, and did not acknowledge a separate or distinct problem. But the VVAA declined to use these channels and continued lobbying, though not through established political means such as the RSL, relying instead on media pressure and direct contacts. They supplied, widely and without discrimination, at times anecdotal evidence of both physical and mental ill health among veterans, and of a high incidence of birth abnormalities among their children. The sorts of symptoms they reported cover a wide range and were published as an "Agent Orange Questionnaire of possible allergic symptoms" in the journal *Debrief* in October, 1982. The list is comprehensive—every part of the body is represented under headings of skin, ENT, eyes, respiratory, cardiovascular, gastrointestinal, gastro-urinary, muscular, and nervous system. Few people could fail to find some kind of symptom, even healthy people. Repatriation clinics reported higher than usual incidences of the presentation of such symptoms just after the list's publication.

When the VVAA also demanded a judicial rather than scientific inquiry, the government referred the matter to the Senate Standing Committee on Science and the Environment. This resulted in 1982 in the publication of *Pesticides and the Health of Australian Vietnam Veterans,* and the promise of a comprehensive study into the health of veterans and their offspring—the so-called morbidity survey, which never appeared.

Other completed studies were unacceptable to the VVAA on the grounds that they failed to survey all veterans, but used samples instead. The VVAA continued its push for a royal commission, the best means, it felt, to avoid government interference and get all the required criteria in place. The royal commission was established in turn under Justice Philip Evatt in 1983, and presented a nine-volume report in July, 1985, after hearing evidence from many veterans and experts. The royal commissioner announced his verdict in extravagant language, which demonstrated that the trial was, in effect, a question of "for" and "against" Agent Orange:

> So Agent Orange is Not Guilty and the chemical agents used to defoliate battle zones in Vietnam and to protect Australians from malaria are not to blame.
>
> No one lost.
>
> This is not a matter for regret but for rejoicing. Veterans and their wives are no more at risk of having abnormal offspring than anyone else. Veterans have not been poisoned. The number with general health problems is small, probably much smaller than amongst their peers in the community. The few that have psychological stress disorders can seek help freely and without shame and above all with hope of early relief and in the sure knowledge that no poisoning of their minds has occurred.[13]

This was not the end of the matter, however. The VVAA believed in effect that it had to act as prosecution, proving Agent Orange guilty, not as in the past in such matters, simply demonstrating the effects on their constituency. The proof was now to be more forensic, proving not merely that illness and exposure occurred but that they were linked in a clear causal manner. The commission admitted the existence of health problems but it declined to see the connection between herbicides and poor health. Indeed, it denied the proof of sufficient exposure, finding the problems linked to the more widespread (and less defined) PTSD, and to social abuse of other drugs (tobacco and alcohol) enhanced by service in the war zone. The possible carcinogenic effects of antimalarial drugs were also acknowledged, as well as a cautious link between some cancers and chemicals: "[The Commission] regards the suggestion of Soft Tissue Sarcoma and Lymphoma (non-Hodgkins) induction by exposure to TCDD in 2, 4, 5-T (in Agent Orange) as unlikely but not fanciful. A Determining Authority might well be reasonably satisfied that a reasonable hypothesis linking incapacity following such inductions with service in Vietnam exists."[14]

But the VVAA found no satisfaction in this, either. Instead of accepting the report and its implication that incapacity could be happily related to other causes within the ambit of Vietnam service, the VVAA chose to pursue the Agent Orange issue as if it felt that any other grounds, such as PTSD, diminished the veteran's self-image.[15]

In the next few years, reports from the United States such as the 1987 judgment in Illinois against Monsanto, cast doubt on studies that found in favor of Agent Orange, and also highlighted positive linkages between cancer and the herbicide in the work of the Independent Agent Orange Task Force. By 1990, Evatt still remained firm, even though the press was beginning to take an oppositional stance.[16] In a landmark case in the Repatriation system in 1990,[17] a link was declared between a soft-tissue sarcoma and chemical exposure in Vietnam.[18]

Finally, the government was persuaded to commission a report from the Australian Veterans Health Studies (AVHS) group. Known as the "Birth Defects Study," the group published its findings in 1983, reporting that it found "there is no evidence that Army service in Vietnam relates to the risk of fathering a child with an anomaly."[19] It is this result that is still the focus of most disagreement, since no subsequent research has overturned it (although the veterans' groups in question do not accept this view). The AVHS undertook a second study, a pilot morbidity study, which showed no discernible pattern of poor health among veterans. The royal commission supported the larger study, but the government declined funding. A third study—*The Mortality Report*—was also completed.[20] It compared the patterns of life and death, as opposed to ill health, of conscript and nonconscript servicemen who served up to 1982. The conclusions on mortality mirrored American studies on Second World War and Korean War veterans, proving that they all exhibited the "healthy soldier syndrome." True, many American veterans died of alcohol or tobacco-related sicknesses, but on the whole they were fitter than the average citizen of their cohort. The same was true of the Australian conscripts. This is hardly surprising, as the conscripts were chosen with a higher level of fitness than their cohort's average. What the study concluded was that wherever a higher incidence of illness was presented, it was attributable to easy access to, and increased consumption of, nicotine and alcohol. The Australian Repatriation system accepts both these social drugs as being implicated in incapacities presented by veterans of all wars.

PTSD and Mental Health

The royal commission also considered mental stress and illness, most notably adopting the definitions and many of the figures of the incidence of PTSD from United States sources. The commissioner concluded: "There is a Vietnam veterans' syndrome, broadly corresponding to PTSD. At this time about 25% of Vietnam veterans will have psychological symptoms requiring treatment, and this number may be expected to peak in 1988–89 and then gradually but steadily decline."[21]

Once again, the linkages between Agent Orange and the incidence of PTSD are impossible to determine precisely. Indeed, the figure of 25 percent is in line with what one might see as "normal" incidences of PTSD under combat conditions. That all of these people might actually present in a clinical environment is equally unlikely. As much as the commission's findings seem guesswork, the VVAA responses are again evidence of what could be seen as an obsession with Agent Orange as the principal and only cause—the source of all Vietnam effects. Nothing less, it seems, would or will do.

Despite a series of negative results in the various commissions and inquiries, the VVAA achieved a substantial coup in 1982 when the Vietnam Veterans Counseling Service was set up as a result of its lobbying. In the early 1990s it still had over twenty-three thousand contacts per year with more than five thousand clients. These figures have not declined in the late 1990s. Many contacts are only about minor problems, but a large number of veterans have been diagnosed with PTSD.

The Welcome Home Marches

One aspect of the Australian collective veteran memory of Vietnam is that early "welcome home" marches have been comprehensively forgotten.[22] On the contrary, all battalions marched in capital cities upon return to their home bases. There were sixteen marches in all. Most were in Sydney and Brisbane, but there were some in Adelaide and Townsville (a town in North Queensland, situated near an army base). The first march was in Sydney in June, 1966, and the last in Townsville on 18 December 1971. By that time, popular support had allegedly swung away from Australian involvement. Yet as the *Townsville Bulletin* reported on 18 December 1971: "Thousands of Townsville people turned on a rousing heroes' welcome. Cheering drowned the sound of marching feet for three city blocks as Townsville made the most of the last major parade by troops from Vietnam. The marchers were swamped with streamers and ticker-tape thrown from balconies and roadside vantage points. The crowd which packed the Flinders Street footpaths to capacity has been described as the largest ever to turn out and welcome troops returning from the war zone."

Of course Townsville is an army town, but in the early 1970s Anzac Day parades elsewhere were not, as popular memory suggests, unsympathetic to Vietnam veterans. Indeed, in a number of marches the veterans' battalions led the parades.

In Washington, D.C., in 1986, the Americans staged the biggest of many of their "Welcome Home" marches. The effect was electric and Australian veterans in Sydney almost immediately set up a committee, supported by various veterans' groups, the state branch of the RSL (not the national body), and some local government representatives. The organization was not easy because many others opposed a march. All the old prejudices surfaced again, pro- and antiwar voices fought over the same old grounds, seeking to control the existence of a celebration, seeking to control the "history" associated with having such a celebration. Such a march some argued (on both sides) might be construed as validating ex post facto the war itself.[23]

The Welcome Home March was held on the morning of Saturday, 4 October 1987, in Sydney, followed by further ceremonies and a concert. Local regional marches and celebrations were subsequently held all over Australia. A *Sydney Morning Herald* editorial anticipated the potential for the Welcome Home March to be seen as a ritual reintegration of veterans into the community, a sign that the nation had "begun to gain a sense of historical perspective on the profound conflicts which the Vietnam War aroused."[24]

The contingent histories were not so easily resolved. For the veterans, the march was a great success—some twenty-two thousand took part, including ARVN veterans marching under the old flag of the Republic of Vietnam. The enthusiastic crowds lining the streets cheered the veterans profusely. Most of the signs, crowd comments, and the commentary on the documentary broadcast nationally a year or so later were decidedly "prowar."[25]

As an organization, the most striking success for the VVAA has been its capacity to define the image of "the veteran" through the media. Ever since the fall of Saigon, this has been an overwhelmingly negative image defined in the media, often without recourse to more formal proof, as one of a man exposed to toxic chemicals or suffering from his treatment on return from the war—images probably drawn more from American than Australian experiences. But the Australian popular media helped with this gradual "imaginary traumatization" of the veteran.

The Veteran in the Popular Media

In both Australia and the United States, the Vietnam War challenged the traditions of their fighting men. Considerable gestures toward recuperation, revaluation, and rehabilitation of the military culture in the United States have been made, especially during the 1980s. In the 1990s it seemed likely that, in the light of the Gulf War, some would determine that these processes of cultural reinvestment in the American military ethos had once again achieved the status associated with the icons of pre-Vietnam soldiery. The same reinvestment of the military ethos within the culture, or of the culture's reinvestment in the military ethos, was not true of Australia until the late 1980s and early 1990s. Australian involvement in the Gulf War was slight, but the eagerness with which Prime Minister R. J. L. "Bob" Hawke offered Australian support for Operations Desert Shield and Desert Storm was matched by his rehabilitation of the rhetoric of the digger and his assurances that it would not be another Vietnam. In the United States, Vietnam has also loomed large, also as the negative example, a pattern that the Gulf War did not emulate. References to Vietnam may prove for the Australian case a more divisive *aide-mémoire*. Evidence of changing attitudes within Australia to the military ethos before the Gulf War began implies a perceived recuperation in Australia's military ethos that sees Australia's Vietnam involvement redrawn from the marginal to the mainstream. Significant gestures toward a restructuring, if not a rehabilitation, of the Anzac mythology reached peaks in the celebrations surrounding the seventy-fifth anniversary of the Gallipoli landing in 1990 and in the fifteenth and twentieth anniversaries, respectively, of the fall of Saigon and the 1970 Australian Moratorium marches, which were celebrated in the following two weeks. All were marked by a flood of publications and broadcasts devoted to those events and their reassessment. On several occasions the Anzac legend was restructured to incorporate the Vietnam material.

As this popular media rewriting of both Gallipoli and Vietnam at once created and enhanced the sense of a newly all-embracing Anzac legend, it also served to construct within popular culture another location for a new nationalistic history. The Labor government orchestrated a media-vaunted return to Gallipoli of fifty-eight original Anzacs. The speech given there by Bob Hawke exhorted Australians to remember their earlier wars and the sacrifices made on their behalf, and urged them to follow the Anzac soldiers' model of sacrifice, courage, and mateship. The speech refocused these Anzac commonplaces as the means of carrying the nation through to the next century. Indeed, Hawke urged the nation to face the new current enemy—Australia's version of the West's continuing economic adversity—with a spirit emulating that of the original Anzacs. Moreover, he urged this economic warrior spirit as a means of refounding the nation as it neared its second federated century. The logic that appeared to be operating in Hawke's speech is well known: "national character," and hence the nation's cultural integrity, were bequeathed to the future not so much by the founding of Australia as a federation of six states in 1901, but through the "blooding" of the nation at Gallipoli in 1915. In appealing to the infusion of a newly invigorated Anzac spirit, Hawke's speech seemed to argue that this spirit would ensure the nation's economic integrity in the next century. In the weeks following Anzac celebrations, the media conflated the sentiments of that seventy-fifth anniversary with a celebratory reassessment of Australia's involvement in Vietnam, and rewrote that involvement into a revalued and "remembered" nationalist myth that praised the soldiers' courage, sacrifices, and "mateship." Simple acknowledgment of the effects of Vietnam upon the soldiery, let alone integration of their war into the myth, had not always been so straightforward, as we have seen already.

Diggers in Vietnam

Australian popular representations of Vietnam have displayed a considerable appropriation of the American imaginings of the war, consciously or otherwise. In certain areas, such as Australia's Welcome Home March in October, 1987, this appropriation has extended to the returned servicemen themselves—for whom there seems to be an uneasy psychological conflation of fragments of the Anzac tradition, often brought together with elements derived from the American military and media imagery. In the weeks surrounding the seventy-fifth Anzac celebrations there were many other confirmations that Australian society had reassessed the popular iconography of the military and its practical effects, and in this process had begun to restructure its responses to the Vietnam War in particular. But unlike the acceptable face of Vietnam now propagated by the American cultural industries, with Hollywood at the forefront, the Australian responses evident in those celebratory weeks in April and May, 1990, did not find a resolution. Rather, the various debates that ensued were suggestive of a continuing and politically active irresolute stance within Australian culture, seemingly wishing to dismember some aspects of the Anzac legend. That inconclusiveness was evident until 1999, when the East Timor crisis pointed, some might say forced, Prime Minister John Howard's Liberal government to see the need for reassessment of its own foreign affairs and defense policies. With that came a renewed interest in matters military at least in the popular media. However, while the operations in East Timor are still unfinished, it is best not to venture too far into the long-term effects on Anzac. So far, the veterans have not been treated to responses approaching the Vietnam veterans' sense of betrayal and indifference. But there are no substantial artifacts beyond the immediate roll of current-affairs media documentaries and human-interest stories. In any case, it is difficult to say with any certainty what effect the Timor events will have on the status of the Vietnam veteran after the fact.

In the 1980s and 1990s, Australian popular cinema and television charted a course similar to, but of a far smaller scale in comparison with, Hollywood. Major Australian representations of Vietnam are relatively few in number. Where the U.S. film industry's original evasion of direct comment and confrontation with Vietnam found expression in the appropriation of other genres, notably in the western, the smaller but burgeoning Australian film industry, and its television counterparts, emphasized Australian society at the turn of the century, that is, it focused upon an Australian equivalent of the western and upon the originating contexts of Anzac itself. Films such as *Breaker Morant* (1980), *Gallipoli* (1981), and *The Man From Snowy River* (1981); miniseries such as *A Town Like Alice* (1981), *1915* (1983), *Against the Wind* (1978), *The Cowra Breakout* (1984), and *Anzacs* (1985); and the Second World War soap opera *The Sullivans* (whose more than five hundred episodes were still being replayed in 2001) explored the territory of the Anzac legend or its components, such as the alleged bush or outback (frontier) origin of the Australian national character. But these dealt with the active soldier, not the veteran.

Australia has so far produced three large-scale popular movie "texts" on Vietnam. The earliest, Tom Jeffrey's *The Odd Angry Shot* (1979), a combat film adapted from William Nagle's novel of the same name, belongs to the tradition of Erich Maria Remarque's *All Quiet on the Western Front* and Norman Mailer's *The Naked and the Dead,* focusing relentlessly on the ever-decreasing squad or platoon. The difference lies in the way Jeffrey's film, following Nagle's novel, introduces overt political comment in a manner not found in most Hollywood "frontline" films. Jeffrey's film gives to the senior member of the squad, Harry, a series of statements that define the political locus of the fighting man as the "sticky fingered politicians' playthings." In this film, the class system and its correlative exploitation of the lower orders are exposed not just as the symptom of the Vietnam War's wrongs, but almost as if it were the root cause of the war. Jeffrey's and Nagle's attacks are not simply directed at the failures of political will, neither those of the United States nor Australia's; it is not a variation on the betrayal myth. It falls more strongly upon the whole political and social structure of Australia, a nation in which the egalitarian appeal of Anzac to the "fair go" holds sway. Harry's speeches expose the fact that the "fair go" is a myth observed more in the breach. When a young soldier named Bung asks, "Why are we here [in Vietnam] then?" Harry replies: "You're a soldier, the same as every other silly prick in this tossed-up fucked-up never-come down land, and that's why you're here, because there's no one else and everyone's gotta be somewhere and you're here, so get used to it."

The Odd Angry Shot is significant in marking the early phase of the Australian interpretation of the war as different to America's. Harry's reasons for Australians being in Vietnam pose the Australian version of the surreal no-place: Indian country, 'Nam, the "funny place"—"the tossed-up fucked-up never-come down land"—that was Australia's Vietnam.[26] The war is being fought by the lower classes: "not too many silvertails here." While this is a combat film, its political stance and its release date of 1979 mark it as a film touching on the disenchanted attitudes of the veteran community. Harry, as the film's mouthpiece, speaks with knowledge of the war's aftermath from within its bounds.

In the late 1980s, Australian culture had begun the processes of rewriting Vietnam as a more positive account of the experience of war, and even as a means of reconciling Australia within Southeast Asia. Two television miniseries appeared in 1987, Simpson-LeMesurier's *Sword of Honour* and Kennedy-Miller's *Vietnam.* Both present a set of "representative" Australian families, and both map a route of redemptive loss and reintegration via the varied experiences of the Vietnam War.[27]

In *Vietnam,* the microcosm of Australian society is the Goddard family, their concerns reflecting precisely the pattern of divisive reactions to Australia's place within the larger contexts of Southeast Asian and American politics and culture. The historically divided sectors of Australian society are drawn almost allegorically in the figures of the family. The father, Douglas, is a senior public servant for the Liberal government. Initially in favor of the war, his development to a position of political opposition schematizes the development of political awareness in Australian society throughout the war. Mother Evelyn's development from house-bound and suppressed wife to liberated and mature femininity is suggestive of the pattern of social and political empowerment some strands of the 1970s women's movement may have located in opposition to the Vietnam War. Megan, the daughter, "drops out of school, joins moratorium marches, experiments with sex and 'life-styles' and acts as the protector for her sometime boyfriend Serge—a draft dodger."[28] Lastly, the son, Phil, is conscripted and sent to Vietnam, where he comes to believe in the necessity of the war. On his return to Australia he is alienated from the newly "aware" and antiwar nation, and suffers from PTSD.

Vietnam explores all of the familiar Hollywood tropes, but in an Australian setting. Phil's alienation from his family manifests a mild form of PTSD and mirrors the larger disaffection of many of his veteran colleagues from the whole society. Phil's mental damage is reflected in the physical damage of his mate, Laurie, whose sexual dysfunction symbolizes the failure of the masculine image to find its complete resolution.

The miniseries ends with a tentative reconciliation in which the lost son, Phil, arrives at his mother's flat. His plaintive greeting, "It's me—sort of," sums up the dual impetus of the series toward a hopeful reunification of the family and, by inference, of the nation. The hesitancy suggests the residual trauma, refracting the hope that Australia had reached a point at which the healing process might begin in earnest.[29] The war is condemned but the soldiers are exonerated, the nation at last wishing to absolve them from guilt and return them to the fold.

Sword of Honour is less complex, but its choice of characters is similarly schematic. Tony Lawrence, who comes from a wealthy rural background, is the recipient of the "Sword of Honour" as the number one cadet in his year at the army's officer training institution, Duntroon, with a brilliant military career awaiting him. Both his career and personal life are blighted by Vietnam. His girlfriend, Esse Rogers, is enlisted in the peace movement at her university and their relationship falls apart, signaled by her letter telling Tony that she has aborted their child. On his return, unable to face the changed attitudes in Australia, Tony flees to Thailand with a Vietnamese refugee, Tam, from Phuoc Tuy. They have a child, Kim. Esse searches for Tony and discovers that Tam has conveniently died of tuberculosis, leaving Tony and Kim ripe for the return. Their reconciliation at the Lawrences' farm is far less equivocal than that of the Goddards' in *Vietnam,* and confirms a hopeful reconciliation of the disputing factions within Australian society, here allegorically welded by the presence of the Asian son. However, both miniseries suggest that the reshaping of the national identity has been forged via an incursion into an Asian setting at the behest of the American ally.

Other exemplary "texts" of the popular Vietnam imagery have largely followed the desire for closure, and yet have also maintained the nation's apparent inability to effect a reintegration of the legend. The large and well-attended march of the veterans' community on 4 October 1987 was for many held to be the Welcome Home March, the moment from which this reintegration could begin. And indeed it initiated a public process of recognition and healing of the psychological wounds. But the march was also released in 1988 as a TV documentary made by Martyn Goddard. It demonstrates that the incorporation of Vietnam into Anzac was still incomplete in 1987. On the contrary, the continued exclusion of Vietnam veterans from the full tradition of Anzac is enforced very noticeably in the Goddard documentary and in the numerous photographs reproduced in the media. How? Through the corporeal intrusion of the veterans themselves. The camera lingered on disabled, wheelchair-bound veterans, seemingly ignoring the able-bodied marchers. The concentration on those whose bodies bear explicit evidence of wounds denied an easy incorporation of Vietnam within Anzac. The documentary presents an extremely moving, even excessively moving, lingering on the grief of the nurses and former patients, most especially veteran Graham Edwards, a double amputee who is now a Labor member of federal Parliament. In this lingering on excessive bouts of shared grief, the documentary is at odds with the stoic tradition of Anzac's "Lest We Forget," and is consequently very disturbing in its, until recently un-Australian, focus on emotional release. The strongest image of this grief was provided by several men who, as that popular song by political folk-rock band Redgum says, "kicked mines" and consequently lost limbs. Two such amputees are interviewed throughout the thirty-minute program. The last scene of the documentary shows Redgum leader John Schumann singing "I Was Only 19," while to his right on the stage is the veteran—Frankie—who is the subject of the song. An amputee, he sits in his wheelchair surrounded by family and, as the song continues, by more and more friends. At the song's conclusion Schuman shouts out, "Welcome Home."

The Australian image is ambiguous, an uneasy acceptance of futility and mutilation. The Australian Welcome Home March film did not avert its gaze from the implications of combat, but in presenting an unblinking gaze on the "history" of war as mutilation, both physical and mental, it ran the risk of presenting all veterans as victims. In subsequent public spectacles and their documentaries, such as the 1990 Anzac Day celebrations, the 1995 "Australia Remembers," or the 1992 memorial dedication ceremony, the public gaze on dismemberment was averted. The central focus of the media orchestras that accompanied these spectacles was upon more traditional Anzac values: sacrifice and endurance replaced lost limbs, and death, if it occurred, was clean and "elsewhere." The country had fought for well-known and clear-cut values and triumphed. Among the First and Second World War reminiscences, Vietnam veterans were rarely remembered, but when they were included, it was as true sons (and daughters) of the digger heritage. The contingent history of dismemberment and PTSD was scurrying backward into the past as all good Australians remembered only the best aspects of the nation's military involvement in the twentieth century.

The Australian Vietnam Forces National Memorial

Just as the 1987 Welcome Home March had followed rapidly on the heels of its American prototypes in 1986, some of Australia's veterans groups looked at the model established by veterans in the United States when they built the Vietnam Memorial in Washington, D.C.'s,

Mall.[30] Another committee was set up, and soon after the Welcome Home March, a steering committee began lobbying the federal government for access to a site along Anzac Parade in Canberra, Australia's capital city. By 1990 the competition had been announced and then won by a Sydney-based group led by artist Ken Unsworth and architect Peter Tonkin. The first sod was turned on 3 October 1990, and the dedication ceremony was held on 3 October 1992. A number of things are worth noting about the National Memorial. It is at once clearly different and meant to be different from the American "wall," and at the same time, since the committee took such pains not to emulate the American model, the Australian product is a kind of negative after-image of its Washington counterpart. Additionally, the committee, as final builders of the memorial, modified the original design so as to ameliorate its political impact. Meant to "explain" in sufficient detail the Australian experience of Vietnam and to last for two hundred years, the final message of the National Memorial presents a blandly conservative Anzac reincorporation. Much like the Welcome Home March, the building and dedication of the Memorial promised to be a move in the reconciliation of the veterans with the wider community. Certainly this was the atmosphere surrounding the thirty thousand marchers and an almost equivalent number of cheering onlookers. And, once again, the live television coverage promised much patriotic message making. However, just like the Welcome Home Marches. this did not satisfy everyone in the veteran community. For many in the VVAA and related groups, the Memorial was part of the changing of the guard at the RSL—more about medals, national honors, and other paraphernalia of glorification, and less about solving the ongoing dilemmas of the veteran community. Not only did some of them stay away, they saw the event as counterproductive. Some of these veterans continued with their work for the VVAA, and some merely kept their distance from all groups. Others sought to bring the wider public's attention to the continuing and, in their view, perilous situation of the veterans. In particular, a group of veterans who had trained as artists sought to use their talents to focus on the effects and aftermath of the war.

The Vietnam Veteran as Artist

As early as 1986–87 a number of Vietnam veterans who were also artists—among them Peter Daly and Ken Wilhite, as well as those both professionally trained and untrained—brought together in venues in Sydney, Brisbane, and Canberra for the first time on any large scale works devoted to the Vietnam War and its aftermath. These were the "Dog Tags" exhibitions, and they were collectively another cultural marker of Australia's willingness to accommodate the veteran, to return the veteran into the wider community. The resulting audiences at each venue were remarkable, and the comments made in visitors' books tell just how ready most of Australia was to make renewed contact with some of its lost children. In subsequent years other, smaller solo shows were mounted, but the return of the veteran artist to a large gallery had to wait until the 1997 "Vietnam Voices" exhibition curated by Con Gouriotis at the Casula Power House Arts Centre in Liverpool on the southern fringes of Sydney. More than two hundred works were on display for months, and the event featured a large three-day conference with over twenty-five speakers. The show covered a wide range of topics and artists, and various nationalities were represented, including both Vietnamese sides. Certain aspects of the conference provided an uneasy proof of the exhibition's title: There were many competing "voices" vying to establish the dominant "history" of Vietnam for the show, something the paintings managed much more completely to avoid by showing that there was no simple resolution of the issue. Once again the show's popularity was considerable, and the large audience response pointed to how importantly the subject was still seen to be within Australian society. So much so that a second and traveling exhibition, "Vietnam Voices II," also curated by Casula staff, opened in Melbourne in January, 2001, featuring some works from the "Vietnam Voices I" (1997) and Australian Art of the Vietnam Experience (1999) shows, as well as many new works or works not seen widely before.

Late 1998–early 1999 saw veteran artist Terry Eichler mount a show in Geelong, adopting as its title "Vietnam: War Myth and Memory" (knowingly echoing the title of the 1992 academic study of Australia's Vietnam War, Jeffrey Grey's and Jeff Doyle's *Vietnam: War Myth and Memory*). In mid-1999, in association with the Australian War Memorial (AWM), Bundaberg Regional Art Gallery mounted some interrelated exhibitions. One, devoted to the letters of wives and families of veterans, was titled "Treading on Eggshells," while the other, "The Threads that Bind," curated by Jennifer MacDuff, consisted of waxed-paper moulds of clothing worn by veterans, friends, and family, and presented a feminist response to war. Another feminist response was seen in the 1998 group show, "Shields," convened by Veronica Calarco and others, held in Canberra. From August through October, 1999, Jeff Doyle curated "Australian Art of the Vietnam Experience" at the Defence Force Academy Library in Canberra, hanging over a hundred works by veterans, family members, and friends who had experienced Vietnam and its aftermath.[31]

By contrast, the AWM, the official collector of Australian war art, souvenirs, archives, and memorabilia, has held only a few limited shows of Vietnam art since 1972. In the main, though not always, these shows were drawn from the AWM's collection of "official art"—art commissioned by the armed forces from designated official war artists who were sanctioned to go into the combat theater. At this stage of its collecting policy, due in large part, it ought to be pointed out, to the economics of both funds and space, the AWM is not, it seems, housing material outside this narrow brief. Nor, one might add, are many of the other government-funded galleries—national, state, or regional (Bundaberg and Casula are atypical). In this light, the "official" exhibitions and those listed above are presenting different and oft-times strongly competing "image histories" of Australia's Vietnam War. In a limited sense, these visual contingents mirror the competing claims of the VVAA oral histories and the academic histories. At present there seems little chance of resolution within the visual world, either.

Indeed, as late as August, 1999, an artistic work surfaced that demonstrates how resilient the veteran's nexus of myth and memory proves to be. The nationally broadcast Australian Broadcasting Corporation current-affairs program *The 7:30 Report* of 3 September reported that a veteran and commercial artist, Derek Walsh from Adelaide, had painted a twelve-panel mural depicting the "history" of Australia's Vietnam experience, allegedly because it had not yet been done. The mural included portraits of the five hundred or so Australian dead, as well as key images and events (helicopters featured largely in the sweeping television coverage). During the report, other veterans commented that the mural met the desires of many of their number in ways until now not touched upon by anyone in Australia. Anchor Kerrie O'Brien's introduction unquestioningly rehearsed all of the Agent Orange syndrome statistics of early deaths, deformities, and so forth, while a veteran interviewed about the panel observed how his own memory of his midnight return was typical: he had been "king hit" from behind (assaulted with a fist), and knocked unconscious when he arrived at the airport. So, he alleged, had others.

The painting, destined to become an "emotional touchstone," went on a national tour in late 1999 to help raise money to bury indigent veterans, assist others, and generally to raise national consciousness about the ongoing plight of the veterans. Worthy causes to be sure, and the painting is impressive despite some of the more extreme claims. For one thing, artist Dennis Trew had produced an enormous work of some five hundred panels depicting all of the dead and others several years earlier that was featured in the "Vietnam Voices I" exhibition. Such still is the tyranny of Australian distance—some parts of the country do not know of events elsewhere. Also curious was a veteran's insistence that the National Memorial in Canberra was not for "all of us," and that it failed since it functioned inadequately by not listing the names of the dead. (Those names are publicly listed at the nearby Australian War Memorial, one of the reasons why the National Memorial designers chose not to relist them visibly. But critical reassessment of the Memorial has always been an option.) The report was riven by its contradictory evidence, as well as by the desire of the veterans to transcend and yet be bound by their self-image—a self-created image—of veteran-as-victim.

Contingent Historiographies

Throughout the 1990s the VVAA continued its fight, lobbying governments, institutions, and academics alike to support its causes. It increasingly mustered large amounts of scientific evidence, largely gleaned from U.S. sources, but with increasing amounts of European material. Cases in the United States and governmental decisions there following the Gulf War also meant that the VVAA felt it had all but won its arguments. Concessions were forthcoming, but for some elements of the VVAA there was an ultimate area that remained in dispute: the problem of birth defects and early deaths presenting among the children of Vietnam veterans. Undeterred by the steady refusal to negotiate this material, the VVAA constantly urged people of all persuasions to read its documentation, and at the same time continued its appeals for the authorities to consult not only the VVAA and its masses of documents but to interview the veterans themselves.[32] Praise was leveled on historian Stephen Garton when, in his *The Cost of War: Australians Return* (1996), he made it clear that he had read through much of the VVAA material and thought it rewarding and worthy of consideration. Less happily for the VVAA's account of him was his judicious stance about the status of the veteran, a view in which he echoed much that was written by others in the late 1980s and early 1990s. Garton asserted that care was needed to discern just how representative the angry and betrayed veteran—implicitly an image of the VVAA constituency—was, and furthermore just how much of that image was derived from an imported American model, one with limited applicability to Australian experience.[33]

When the volume of the official history dealing with the Agent Orange issue was published in 1994, the VVAA was outraged that Barry Smith's essay resiled to the standard and, in its view, wholly discredited position that denied any negative effects from herbicide exposure.[34] So strong was the response that well-known veteran activist Graham Walker wrote, as he had to Garton earlier, a very passionate reply published in *Debrief* and circulated widely among the community and its associates. Walker's case is yet again a strong plea for the need to consult with the veterans themselves, to consider that official documentation is not the only source of truth—by which he means, by implication, "history." Everywhere within the paper he demonstrates the difference between professional "history" and what he is seeking. The problem for the VVAA is that only one version of "history" is acceptable. The most recent book on the subject, Ambrose Crowe's *The Battle After the War* (1999), is a worthy volume, and its author, a veteran, has searched through all of the relevant literature, especially the VVAA archives and documents. Yet, as its rather selective bibliography demonstrates, it is not a complete history. Rather, it is a contingent history—contingent on believing the VVAA case—which still asserts that veterans are the focus of government and bureaucratic neglect as its concluding chapters argue, if at times with a shrill voice where calm passion would have done. Indeed, Crowe's rhetoric extends to calling government the "foe" pitted against the veterans, seen again as they were in Vietnam, "outgunned and outnumbered."[35] Such are the rhetorical habits of a siege mentality; they argue against the likelihood of any kind of reconciliation of the competing histories within the next few years. Thus, the Vietnam veteran, as historicized in Australia, is likely to consist of a split or torn image within two widely diverse sections of the community. The larger group will continue to accept that a kind of reconciliation has been made, that the community has largely now paid or will pay its major debts to the veterans. It is a community that can accept slightly imperfect versions of its histories and accommodate dissenting views as long as it does not have to pay them too much attention too often. The other contingent is composed of those members of the veteran community who can only maintain their historicized veteran as the truth, the whole truth, and nothing more or less than the truth. For them there is no semiperfect version of Vietnam history—only theirs is free of distortion and conspiracy. Certainly one should wish that these "other contingents" might someday fully return home.

JEFFREY GREY

6 Getting into the Books

Vietnam as History in Australia

In 1982, distinguished American Vietnam scholar Douglas Pike divided writing on the war into three phases. The first or wartime stage produced the work of participants and observers, long on description but often lacking in analysis. This was followed by an incipient stage of scholarship proper in which passions had subsided somewhat but "objectivity" remained elusive—an "Apocalypse Now" school, if you will. The third phase, still to come at the time of his writing, would see broad agreement reached and the "historical truth" established. In this latter stage, he foresaw the work produced falling into two further categories: postmortems on what really happened and why, and studies of the residual effects of the war in which the war is featured not as history but as a contemporary influence that shaped and continues to shape the societies involved.[1]

Pike's belief in ultimate truth aside, American writing on the Vietnam War has generally followed his prescription and has entered his third phase, as the numerous fine and detailed monographic treatments of the American experience make clear. The situation in Australia and New Zealand defies such strict, and easy, categorization. The flow of work on Vietnam in the United States now rivals that on the American Civil War, easily the most written about topic in American history. The historiography of much smaller countries, for which involvement in the war was a much less central issue, cannot hope, and has no need, to match this flow in size, richness, or variety.

There is a long tradition of writing on the Australian experience of war, and like any tradition it has a number of distinguishing features. One of these is that until recently it has been carried on largely outside the universities. This is not only because the academic study of Australian history itself is a relatively recent phenomenon, but equally because many academic historians (and not in Australia alone) regard war and the military with incomprehension if not distaste. This latter facet is given added impetus by the leading role in the Moratorium movement played by some university academics, and the movement into the humanities and social sciences subsequently by former members of the "protest generation."

Australian military history (broadly defined) draws heavily on the tradition established by C. E. W. Bean, the official historian of Australia's involvement in the First World War, whose monumental work is frequently cited while much less frequently read. His concentration upon individual experience in war marked a significant departure from the usual style of official histories, which were influenced heavily by their respective general staffs, although the technique itself was not a new one. Bean believed that the war's significance lay in what it revealed about the Australian character, and that Australia's impressive military performance was a function of its democratic social and political system and the influence of "bush values." While some at least of this is arguable, the influence it exerted cannot be doubted. Both Gavin Long's official history of the Second World War and the operational volume of R. J. O'Neill's Korean War official history followed this model, as have many of the most popular historical treatments of the Australian experience of war by, for example, Bill Gammage or Patsy Adam-Smith, and film and television products such as *Gallipoli* (1981), *1915* (1983), and *Anzacs* (1985).[2]

An additional limiting factor in any consideration of Vietnam history in Australia has been the operation of the relevant archival legislation, the "thirty-year rule," which restricts public access to government documents. While some operational material was released in 1985 in consequence of being tabled before the Evatt Royal Commission during its study of the use of chemical agents, and the open period is now moving through the years of Australian operational deployment, many of the records remain closed to all but official researchers. Unlike in the United States, the provisions of Australia's Freedom of Information Act do not apply to material generated before the legislation was enacted. We thus are dealing with a disparate group of published works, some of it academic (which is not a value judgment), some of it firmly in the Bean tradition of concentrating on the private soldier and individual experience, and some falling into neither category. The official history of the war, published under the editorship of Peter Edwards, is in a category of its own.

Pike's chronological categorization will not suit a discussion of Australian writing on the war; additionally, there is less to discuss. Most of the contemporary debate was ephemeral, either in its methodology or even, indeed, in its physical production. Most of the material generated by the antiwar movement, for example, took the form of posters, pamphlets, and handbills, and has not survived outside specialist collections in libraries and archives—where it has survived at all. Several journalists attached to the Australian forces wrote books on their return to Australia, and some of these repay reading now, but their value, like that of contemporary American work, is principally descriptive, not analytical.[3] Following the withdrawal of the last Australian troops at the beginning of 1973, and after the fall of Saigon in 1975, the Vietnam War largely dropped from sight in Australia. Prime Minister E. G. Whitlam tabled a report ("the Neale Report") in the House of Representatives in May, 1975, that detailed the manner in which Australia had become involved in the war,[4] and journalist Evan Whitton published several articles in the *National Times* that covered much the same ground,[5] but for nearly a decade after Australia's commitment ended Vietnam did not feature in Australian historical and political discourse.

The work that began to appear in the early 1980s was usually critical of Australian involvement and often emphasized the foreign policy dimension. Given the existence of the Neale Report and a traditional view of Australian foreign policy on the Left, in particular, which assumed Australian subservience to British and American interests (a view much admired in antiwar circles in the late 1960s), this was not surprising. During the war itself, the critics had always been more voluble than the supporters of Australian and American policy. Indeed, it can be argued that the Australian government never really enunciated its policy aims clearly and unambiguously and never took the electorate into its confidence. It is also notable that few if any of those who supported involvement in Vietnam at the time have done so subsequently, and that there have been no studies of those who, if not exactly "pro-war," might be described as "anti the antis."

The first of the substantive critiques of Australian involvement proved largely abortive. Michael Sexton's *War for the Asking* argued for a crucial Australian role in American policy and decision making, an argument that both ignored the domestic and wider international contexts surrounding President Johnson's decision over Vietnam and which proceeded from virtually no evidence.[6] More scholarly in general, though equally critical and occasionally strident, was the collection of essays gathered by Peter King, *Australia's Vietnam.*[7] Appearing at a time when the Vietnam publishing industry in the United States was beginning to thrive, this volume effectively turned Australians' attention back onto their own involvement and opened up discussion of some topics for the first time. Although the chapters by Labor politician Kim Beazley, on the parliamentary Labor Party and the Vietnam issue, and Frank Frost, on the operations of the task force, in particular, made notable first contributions to the debate, the volume overall was uneven, in places even slightly defensive in tone. Perhaps characteristically in a society that seems to value informed public debate of historical issues hardly at all, it was not followed by vigorous public dispute.

By the mid-1980s, however, interest in Vietnam had revived sufficiently to generate a small but consistent flow of books, although it was still too early to speak seriously of a debate on the subject. In addition, the official historian for the series dealing with Australian involvement in postwar Southeast Asian conflicts was appointed in 1983, although it was a decade before the volumes themselves began to appear. Until recently, writers tended to perceive the central issues of Australian involvement in a fairly uniform manner: the decision to commit Australia to the war was generally deplored, the soldiers were held to have performed a difficult task well, the claims of the antiwar oppositional groupings were accepted largely at face value, Vietnam veterans were portrayed as having suffered immoderately as a consequence of their service, and so on. This is changing, however, as both writers and readers perceive how pervasive have been the American images that dominated much of the Australian argument over the war at the time and subsequently, and have returned to issues previously thought settled in order to extract an Australian story.

Much of the scholarly attention has focused on domestic issues during the war and on policy developments in Australia. This is not coincidental, and mirrors the newfound interest in the 1916–17 conscription referenda during the First World War that emerged in the late 1960s, often among university historians who were themselves involved in protest against conscription for service in Vietnam.[8] For some reason, although a sizable number of graduate and other theses have been written in this area, very little of the resultant work has appeared in print, and almost none in book form. While it is quite untrue, therefore, that the protest movement in Australia has been "written out" of our history, as a few have suggested, it remains the case that the work that has been done has not received a high level of public exposure.

A number of those who have written on anti–Vietnam War activism were themselves active participants in the events with which they have dealt as historians or political scientists: Barry York, Michael Hamel-Green, Charlotte Clutterbuck, Kenneth Maddock, Ann Curthoys, and Ralph Summy all have produced theses and articles in this area.[9] The most significant single body of work here has been produced by Malcolm Saunders, who has written widely on the role and development of peace movements in Australian history generally.[10] The broader issues of social and political context in which opposition developed and played itself out attract less attention on the whole, although there have been two quite good assessments of the 1960s in Australia that have sought to relate the antiwar movement to developments around it.[11] The publication of Greg Langley's *A Decade of Dissent* suggests that this field has now moved into the mainstream, at least in publishing terms. Its attempt, largely successful, to integrate the broader context of events with consideration of the antiwar opposition is to be welcomed, although like most previous writers on the subject he continues to accept the movement's claims at face value. Moreover, his assertion that the antiwar movement "has been largely sympathetic to the plight of the [returned] soldiers" would be contested by many of those concerned.[12]

Work on government policy has been constrained by the "thirty-year rule," referred to earlier. We thus have very little outside the official histories on the workings of government in reaction to the antiwar movement, or on the mechanisms of conscription.[13] Foreign policy has attracted its students, however, and some of the work concerned has shown itself markedly more sophisticated than the arguments marshaled at the time. In particular, the central role played by concern over Indonesian expansion in the late 1950s and early 1960s, never mentioned publicly at the time, can be shown to have influenced Robert Menzies and his cabinet in powerful ways. On the whole, though, the diplomatic history of this period seems concerned still to portray Australian governments as often uncritical servants of American interests, and allows less scope for an interpretation that might stress involvement in Vietnam as being central to Australian interests.[14] Nonetheless, this places it well within the mainstream of the left-liberal critique of Australia's external policies this century.

The study of battle has never been of much interest in the universities, and so this aspect of Australian involvement in Vietnam has been dealt with more often by nonacademic historians.[15] The results have been mixed. On one hand, these books have helped to bring the experiences of Australian soldiers back into the public eye, and have presented them always in a sympathetic manner, although also in a manner not always or necessarily flattering to the army. On the other hand, they generally lack rigor and rarely analyze the events with which they deal; they thus add little to our overall understanding of complex events. There are significant exceptions to this generalization that, for a variety of reasons, offer much more sophisticated treatments of the subject at, for example, the level of individual Australian units.[16] It is probably no coincidence that these authors might accurately be typified as "soldier-scholars." R. J. O'Neill, who served as intelligence officer with the 5th Battalion, Royal Australian Regiment (RAR), had been a Rhodes scholar and had completed a doctorate. He went on to become director of the International Institute for Strategic Studies in London and then Chichele Professor of the History of War at Oxford, and his subsequent academic prowess is reflected in his study of his battalion's first operational tour. Michael O'Brien, a thirty-year career army officer, also served as intelligence officer in his unit, and his study of the 7th Battalion, RAR, is particularly valuable because it examines two operational tours by the same battalion, several years apart, to illustrate changes in the nature of the Australian war in Phuoc Tuy Province and in the army. Some academic historians have also dealt with the "sharp end" details of our involvement, most notably Frank Frost.[17] The problems with this work are often the opposite of those that characterize the popularizers: strongly analytical but sometimes demonstrating insufficient appreciation of the realities of operations in war. They have been sharply criticized by Ian McNeill, author of the official history volumes dealing with the ground force commitment in Vietnam.[18]

At the generic level there is a greater spread of good work on a variety of subjects, although much of this is the work of a single individual, David Horner. Like O'Neill and O'Brien, Horner served as a junior officer with an infantry battalion in Phuoc Tuy Province, in his case toward the end of the Australian commitment. He went on to study under O'Neill at the Australian National University, publishing widely in the field of Australian higher command and strategy during the Second World War. A prolific writer, he has also produced a number of major histories of the combat arms of the Australian Regular Army that contain significant amounts of material on the Australian approach to and experience of operations in South Vietnam.[19] Ian McNeill's earlier history of the Australian Army's advisory effort with the ARVN falls into a similar category and McNeill, too, had active service during the war, in his case as an adviser in the northern provinces.[20] A further example of what can be done through painstaking scholarly analysis of particular aspects of Australian operational experience is provided by Richard Bushby in *Educating an Army,* which examines the interplay between the formal tactical doctrine with which the army went to war in 1965 and the tactical modifications that real war prompted.[21]

The Official History of Australia's Involvement in Southeast Asian Conflicts, 1948–1975, to give it its full and formal title, has much in common with earlier official histories and builds on a tradition created by them. At the same time, it differs from them in crucial respects.

Since C.E.W. Bean's time it has been the proud claim of Australian official historians that they have written with full access to all official sources and without interference. In intelligence matters this was not quite true for either of the histories of the world wars (Bean was constrained by the Admiralty from commenting on certain aspects of naval intelligence that might have been useful to the Japanese, while Long and his authors, like most others, were ignorant of the existence of ULTRA), but the general claim held true. Robert O'Neill's history of the Korean War likewise benefited from this openhanded policy.

Bean's history concentrated at overwhelming length on the wartime expeditionary force, the Australian Imperial Force, especially in France from 1916 through 1918. The home front was treated in a single volume, and there was little or no discussion of the higher direction of the war since Australia had little or no involvement in it. Long's history likewise devoted the great majority of its twenty-two volumes to operations, although this time the RAAF received much more treatment in recognition of the greatly increased role of air power in that war. The home front was allocated five volumes, but the intention to devote a volume to strategy and foreign policy was not realized. By the time O'Neill came to write the history of the Korean War, however, the balance had begun to shift. One volume was devoted to "strategy and diplomacy," resulting in the best and most detailed analysis of the origins of the ANZUS treaty yet published, while the operations of the three services were combined into a single, albeit weighty, volume.[22]

In the postwar era, the diplomatic ends of military involvement assumed an importance out of proportion to the size of the commitments, which in truth was often small. This was reflected in the composition and balance of the Korean War history, and is also true for the history of involvement in Southeast Asian conflicts. Unlike the Korean War, the other postwar conflicts, especially Vietnam, had a domestic dimension that was both influenced by and brought influence to bear upon the other spheres of government policy. The structure of the present official history reflects this, with two volumes out of a total of eight dealing with "politics and diplomacy."[23] Unlike American practice, in which official histories are sponsored and published on an individual agency basis (the Joint Chiefs of Staff, the Department of the Army, the U.S. Marine Corps, the State Department, etc.), Australian official histories are written on an integrated basis sponsored by a single agency, in this case the Australian War Memorial. Although individual volumes will deal with a single function (the medical history of the war or diplomacy, for example) or an individual service (separate volumes are devoted to the air force and navy), the volumes are expected to treat the interaction of politics and higher policy with operational and organizational imperatives. The other distinguishing feature of this series is that it deals with Australian military, strategic, and diplomatic involvement in postwar conflicts in Southeast Asia as a whole, including Malaya and Borneo, of which the commitment to the Vietnam War is the centerpiece. Just as it may be argued that American involvement in Indochina came by way of concern over developments in the Cold War in Europe, so Australian involvement was a reflection of developments in the region more generally, especially as these concerned Indonesia and the emergent Federation of Malaysia. The result again is a much less compartmentalized treatment of the various facets of Australian involvement. Edwards's first volume concludes with the decision to commit forces alongside the Americans, while the volumes on the RAAF and RAN and the first volume on ground force experience devote considerable space to the ways in which earlier counterinsurgencies in Malaya in the 1950s and against Indonesia between 1963 and 1966 shaped Australian thinking on low-intensity conflict and counterrevolutionary warfare.[24] There is, in addition, a separate volume dealing with operational aspects of Australia's contributions to the conduct of the Malayan Emergency (1948–60) and the Indonesia Confrontation (1962–66).[25]

It would be wrong to characterize the official history merely as a conservative response to an earlier corpus of work, a simple restating of a position, although some early critics of the series claimed just that. The volumes by Edwards and McNeill in particular substantially modify, where they do not correct, previous interpretations of the early diplomatic and operational involvement in the war, and make clear once again the pitfalls of attempting to write on matters of government policy from public sources only, or as reflected through the archives of other nations, in this case principally the United States.[26] As with earlier series, the volumes on the individual services would probably not have been undertaken at that length or with that thoroughness if left to commercial consideration alone. The volume dealing with the Malayan Emergency and Confrontation is a major addition to the literature of those conflicts, not least because the British have not produced equivalent treatments and show little sign of doing so. What is generally lacking in the Australian writing on the war is the synoptic overview of the kind that both Bean and Long provided after their main official series had been completed, although Murphy's *Harvest of Fear* is a worthy first attempt at such a task.[27]

English historian A. J. P. Taylor asserted once that the function of official history was to set the record, to establish what happened and why, and American historian Robin Higham has suggested that they constitute the first word, not the last, on a given subject. Rarely have official histories concerned themselves with the long-term consequences of the wars they analyze. On the other hand, Douglas Pike pointed to writings that treated the war not as history, but as contemporary influence and cultural and social force. This has manifested itself in several treatments of the 1960s as a decade, noted already; it also has resulted in studies of the veteran population and, to a lesser extent, the impact of Vietnamese migration on the Australian community.

The issues surrounding the treatment of Vietnam veterans are complex and emotive. There is considerable disagreement on the long-term consequences of Vietnam service, and no decent studies of the Vietnam veteran cohort as a whole. Nor have comparisons been drawn between Vietnam veterans and their coequals in the nonveteran community, from which sensible extrapolations might be made.[28] Some of the work that presents what we might characterize as the "veteran-as-time-bomb" school is simply thoroughly bad, sloppy in its methodology and intended to prove a predetermined thesis.[29] Personal accounts of service and its consequences are in serious conflict with each other, as one might expect, and often assume an outcome without feeling the need to prove a connection between service in Vietnam and perceived disadvantage in postservice life.[30] Those reminiscences that suggest the problem lies less with the returned serviceman than with the society to which he returned, in short, which decline to portray the veteran as victim, were not initially as successful commercially, although there are signs that this is changing.[31] Analyses of Vietnam veterans that attempt to counter some of the more prevalent public myths are not generally well received by the Vietnam Veterans' Association of Australia (VVAA) either, although there is anecdotal evidence to suggest that many other Vietnam veterans are out of sympathy with the VVAA's position.[32] Some of the earlier heat has gone out of Vietnam veterans' issues in the late 1990s, a reflection of the greater willingness of successive governments to extend compensation and other benefits in recognition of service, while the reintegration of those veterans into the national military myth of Anzac has reduced the sense of isolation and exclusion alleged by some in the course of the 1980s.

Antiwar protest and postwar veterans' issues provide two strong themes for conservative commentators in the United States; the third is the role and conduct of the media. Assertions concerning a media hostile to American aims in Vietnam, the impact of a so-called television war and coverage of the Tet Offensive in 1968 that supposedly portrayed the campaign as a Communist victory when it was, in fact, a major battlefield reversal for the Vietcong and North Vietnamese, are familiar themes in the American literature of the war. Careful work on the American media and its relationship with the American military, for example, has qualified many of the claims advanced during the war and its immediate aftermath, while the notion of an oppositional media at variance with successive administrations is a facile generalization. Yet for a number of reasons there has been relatively little study of the role of the Australian media during the Vietnam War. The Australian media was to some extent less influential in shaping public opinion on the course and conduct of the war since much of what it reported came from overseas news agencies via syndication and reflected American views and experiences. Television had only reached Australia in 1956, and in the mid-1960s was still relatively unsophisticated, while color was not to arrive until 1974. The government broadcast network, the Australian Broadcasting Commission (ABC), moved heavily into current affairs and news commentary, especially on television, in the early 1960s, and by the late 1960s was airing views critical of or in opposition to government policy. However, the commercial networks took much less interest, while the ABC attracted a distinct minority of viewers. Rupert Murdoch, then a relatively small player in the national media, established the first truly national newspaper, the *Australian,* in 1964. Although there were some correspondents based in Southeast Asia for both the ABC and some of the major metropolitan newspapers, their brief usually included more than just Vietnam, and certainly more than just the activities of the Australians there. Because of the strict oversight the Australian Army imposed on journalists in the Australian area of operations, many preferred to work with the Americans, whose supervision was much more lax.

For a variety of reasons, then, Australian reportage of Australian activities in Vietnam was limited and episodic. Rodney Tiffen has analyzed the print media while Lyn Gorman discusses the treatment of Vietnam issues on one of the ABC's flagship news-analysis programs of the period.[33] The ABC experienced significant internal challenges, like most established organizations at that time, and some of this is discussed in Ken Inglis's standard history of the ABC.[34] The leading Australian correspondent in Southeast Asia, with extensive experience in Indochina, Denis Warner, has written his memoirs and there is some generally anecdotal coverage of other Australian correspondents, but there has been little attempt to analyze Australian media coverage of the war in an institutional or systemic context, which perhaps indicates how marginal it was to shaping public opinion and government policy at the time.[35]

The greatest single legacy of the war in Australia will prove to be the Vietnamese who have settled in this country, whether as refugees or under more orderly migration schemes. In the aftermath of the fall of Saigon there was little public or official sympathy evinced for the plight of the Vietnamese. Their willingness to risk an appalling fate at sea rather than remain where they were was a standing refutation to those who had portrayed Ho Chi Minh and the communists as simple nationalists leading an essentially popular movement for the benign reunification of their country. (Labor politician Clyde Cameron's version of an alleged remark of Whitlam's when it was suggested by his foreign minister that Australia should evacuate South Vietnamese citizens—"he didn't want any 'f****** Vietnamese Balts coming into Australia'"—was representative of this attitude.[36] Australia did nothing for those Vietnamese who had worked for us in whatever capacity during the war, and almost all of these people and their families were left behind. The Americans, on the other hand, managed to evacuate over 130,000 people in the weeks before the final collapse.) Some work has been done on this influx of population from a previously "nontraditional" source.[37] Most of it is concerned with multicultural issues and questions of refugees, migration, and foreign policy; in a sense, it is another story in a different book.

Australians generally take New Zealand for granted. A brief discussion of New Zealand's historiography of the war is warranted here because the two ANZUS partners served closely together in South Vietnam itself, while New Zealand attitudes and experience provide a sometimes subtle counter to established Australian views of the war. As Roberto Rabel has shown,[38] New Zealand's involvement in Vietnam sprang from different considerations to those in Australia, but the detail of New Zealand's commitment has yet to be charted at any length. Many of the same strictures regarding the study of war at an academic level in Australia apply equally, if not more so, in New Zealand, but the consuming interest in the existence, or otherwise, of a recognizably Australian foreign policy in the course of the twentieth century has little counterpart across the Tasman. Considerations of scale also play a part: If the size of the Australian literature on the war vis-à-vis the United States is a reflection of the disparity between their respective commitments, so much more is this the case with New Zealand. Until the appearance of the two volumes of New Zealand's official history, the interested reader may refer to several articles on government policy, a short overview of the New Zealand Army's involvement originally published as a classified, in-house document, and a glossy regimental history of the artillery battery that served with the Australian Task Force.[39] There are one or two short participant-memoirs from the ranks, and a variable oral history of New Zealand soldiers' experiences together with a short article that provides an overview of the New Zealand effort, but the most recent general history of New Zealand, drawing on contributions from some of the country's leading academic historians, devotes only a page and a half to Vietnam and does not bother to index it.[40] The neglect is exemplary.

Interest in Vietnam, both as academic history and at the nonspecialist level, is growing. More than 45 percent of the Australian population is under thirty years of age, born after the first Australian advisers were committed to Vietnam in 1962. For them, Vietnam is truly history, as remote in most cases as the Peloponnesian Wars. For a comparably large slice of the nation, Vietnam is part of their own lived experience, and the only war in our history of which the great majority now have any experience, however far removed in personal terms. Its fascination as past event is matched by its continuing relevance to current and future concerns. Veterans' benefits remain a "big ticket" item in federal budgets, while in early 1999 the first Australian defense attaché in twenty-five years was posted to Vietnam, although his office now is in Hanoi rather than Saigon.

The poet and veteran of the American Civil War, Walt Whitman, believed "the real war will never get into the books." In the sense that the combat experience is essentially unknowable to those who have not been through it, he was right. In most other respects, the problem in the Australian case is not to try to understand the war at the level of individual experience (since we have plenty of that), but to continue to direct the focus of writers and readers toward those aspects of our involvement without which a fully rounded understanding is impossible.

PETER PIERCE

7 Australian and American Literature of the Vietnam War

Australian and American imaginative writing about the Vietnam War is instinct with the memories, symbols, and fashions of telling of earlier wars in which each nation had fought. At the same time, people who wrote of Vietnam were as keen to insist on its difference from all previous wars as the trench poets and novelists of the First World War had been. By taking backward glances toward previous literary models for dealing with the experiences of war, writers opened up ambivalent views on the martial and domestic past and present circumstances of their nations. There is nostalgia for the heroic and legendary moments of old wars, for what can be construed as less complex, morally unambiguous times, for the past as a secure base to which retreat may be possible. Yet this sentiment consorts uneasily with an ironical, incredulously scornful attitude toward such times and certitudes, with mockery of the pious regard in which they are held by the generation of the soldiers' parents. This is one of the literary equivalents of the political and social rebellions of the Vietnam days.

Writers in Australia and the United States, seeking sometimes in similar and at other times in instructively different ways to work themselves out of this contradiction and confusion, found that they were trapped in the narratives that they were telling; were uncertain of what national legends could replace those that had been unfrocked and dethroned; were intensely suspicious of the efficacy, either moral or literary, of metaphorical language; and were enticed by, although wary of, the temptations to begin or renew their literary careers. The artistic choices that they made and the dilemmas they experienced can focus the cultural anxieties of these two of the combatant countries in Vietnam. Among much else that troubled these authors were the Americans' need to confront a dire challenge to their presumed special destiny among nations, and the Australians' need to discover if their country had a separate identity that could still be expressed in battle, as martial legends forged in the First World War suggested it once had been.

The conditions of combat in Vietnam differed significantly from those of the two world wars, although public understanding that this was so, and the literary reflections of the differences, were alike belated. When authors began to insist upon the nature of those differences—for instance the collective sense that fighting men from Australia and the United States were abandoned to die in a cause that was increasingly unpopular and futile, the distrust felt for allies, the often intense practical difficulty of discriminating between friend and enemy (and sometimes the convenient failure to do so)—it was often as a means of repudiating the authorities—political, cultural and familial—who sent soldiers to Vietnam. In *The Face of Battle* (1976), John Keegan wrote that "war itself, rather than its institutions, does not seem to have shocked the American psyche as the Great War did the British. The occasion for that shock lay in the future, during the Vietnam War, when a war that was not a success story, fought for reasons that muddled rather than united the American electorate, prompted its veterans—notably Herr and Caputo—to a violence of protest that, in intensity if not in quality of language, recalls the outpourings of the British trench veterans of the 1920s and 1930s."[1]

For Australian writers, a curdling resentment rather than a shock (that might exhilarate as well as terrify) was explored as the emotional legacy of the Vietnam War. The origins of this resentment lay in the role that Australian, as compared with American, forces played in Vietnam. The most important and irksome aspect of the Australian role was its dependence on the American military command, with consequent restrictions and compromises at the tactical and operational levels. These differences notably affected the temper of Australian literature about the conflict. The antagonisms that a wider cultural dependence can generate were canvassed in a spirit of acrid comedy in Frank Moorhouse's *The Americans, Baby* (1972), in which one of the characters exclaims: "We have nothing of our own to do. I contemplate, nothing. We are culturally incapacitated and dependent. Everyone has known this in his heart and for some time. Actually we're Anglo-American. A composite mimic culture. Miserable shits."[2]

One alternative to such a resigned lament was offered by Lex McAulay, writing as "David Alexander" in *When the Buffalo Fight* (1980), a novel whose purpose was to defend the martial legend of Anzac.[3] McAulay also wrote conventional battle histories of Vietnam concerning the Australian actions at Long Tan (subtitled "The Legend of Anzac Upheld") and at Firebases Coral and Balmoral. Writing fiction as "Alexander," he averred that his book "is inspired by the Australian soldier, by his matter-of-fact day-to-day courage, his sense of humour and his sense of comradeship." This typical soldier exhibits "the dry Australian sense of humour and the inborn independence of the Australian male." The fighting skills of the small Australian contingent in Vietnam are insistently contrasted with the bungling of their American allies. The crudity of this procedure signals "Alexander's" despair at Australia's reliance upon the United States military, hence the undermining—through no fault of their own—of the reputation of Anzac soldiers. The legend of Anzac has been an agreed piety of Australian life. "Alexander" appeals to it nostalgically and misleadingly as if there had ever truly been a time when Australians controlled and expressed their national identity in battle.

There are many enemies in *When the Buffalo Fight,* which is appropriate to the angry defensiveness of its tone, but this also suggests an important contrast between Australian and American fictions of Vietnam. The ostensible enemy in "Alexander's" novel—the Vietcong—is worthy of the Australians' steel. The Vietcong are cunning, dogged, and brave adversaries. "Alexander" awkwardly gives them not only the dignity of individual names, but a common, binding ideology: "Hoa has laid down his life for the Revolution." These Vietcong find the Australians to be fit opponents. The ARVN and the Americans are not capable of mastering them. For "Alexander," the worth of the enemy justifies the Australian military involvement in Vietnam. For home front opponents of the war, such worth—conceived more broadly and for different ideological purposes—was the warrant of their opposition. These people, antiwar demonstrators, cowardly "creatures" who prey on servicemen's wives, as "Alexander" presents them, are among the many enemies in his novel. The incompetent allies who endanger the safety and morale of Australian troops are others. *When the Buffalo Fight* is imbued with a melodramatic perception of ubiquitous threat.

Americans figure prominently in Australian narratives of the Vietnam War. There are teasing moments, although fewer, when Australians are featured in novels and memoirs by Americans. Although his name is appropriated by good, bad, and amnesiac guys in Robert Ludlum's trilogy, it is explained in *The Bourne Ultimatum* (1990) that "the original Jason Bourne was garbage, a paranoid drifter from Tasmania who found his way into the Vietnam War as part of an operation no-one wants to acknowledge."[4] In that bestseller, Vietnam—specifically the damage its moral consequences does to individuals—has become a miasmic, all-encompassing, potentially all-explaining metaphor—one that is the more sinister because it is so comprehensive.

In John Rowe's novel *Count Your Dead* (1968), the author—an Australian regular army officer who served in Vietnam—uses an American as his central character in order to ventilate an outsider's view of the Australian military performance. Sometimes this is genially expressed: "great guys . . . and did they zap some Cong. Boy!" Australian perceptions of their American ally derive in large part from the hostility generated by the presence of hundreds of thousands of American troops in their country from 1942–45. They are "the bloody big-time, interfering, busy-body bloody Yanks." They are also ruminated upon more complexly, as in the remarks of the conciliatory Australian major who speaks of American reasonableness as one of "your nicest national failings," argues that at all levels and at every opportunity Vietnamese will exploit Americans, and reflects upon an Australian defense policy wherein "dead diggers" are seen as a down payment for the shelter provided by the military power of the United States.[5]

This set piece of debate is upturned by the surprising speech from ambush by an all-American boy called Kurt, who refers to the hatred its allies and enemies sometimes feel for the United States. Says Kurt: "Not much of that hatred is based on fear; but do you know what boy? It ought to be!" Kurt concludes with an observation on Australia, whose iconoclasm is emphasized because this Australian novel has an American protagonist. Of Australia, Kurt remarks, "You're not a country, you're a tennis court." Rowe uses this novel, which ended his career in the army and started him on another as an author of popular fiction, as he used his subsequent authoritarian fantasy novels: to condemn the vacillations and complacencies of Australian politics and foreign relations, in particular the shaming habit of dependence on "great and powerful friends" who are resented just because of that dependence.[6]

A sense of reliant, hampered status feeds satirical and ironical notions of any experience of war, although these may be exaggerated by the legacy of colonial experience in such a country as Australia. Most war stories, of course, purport to render individuals' rather than nations' responses to conflict. Typically these stories, which in effect are indistinguishable whether cast as nonfictional memoirs or as novels, tell—as Paul Fussell wrote in *The Great War and Modern Memory* (1975)—of their protagonists' removal "from pre-war freedom to wartime bondage, frustration and absurdity . . . from the low mimetic of the plausible and the social to the ironic of the outrageous, the ridiculous and the murderous."[7] This predictable core of narrative can be found at large in the fictions of the war in Vietnam.

Somewhat unjustly, the conventional, formally noninnovative character of much American (and it can also be said, Australian) fiction of that war has attracted disparaging comment. In a review of American Vietnam War fiction appearing in *Harper's,* veteran-turned-novelist C. D. B. Bryan, parodies the "Generic Vietnam War narrative":

> He is sent to Vietnam by commercial jet complete with attractive stewardesses. . . . In his platoon our young man meets Day-Tripper, who is stoned all the time; Rebel, the crazy white guy who loves killing; Juice, the cool black dude who can smell ambushes and booby traps. . . . There is the first patrol. . . . There is the atrocity scene, to demonstrate that My Lai was not an isolated incident. . . . There are dope scenes. . . . There are helicopter assaults into hot LZs. . . . There is R and R in Saigon with Susie the bar-girl. . . . The Generic Vietnam War narrative charts the gradual deterioration of order, the disintegration of idealism, the breakdown of character, the alienation from those at home, and finally, the loss of all sensibility save the will to survive.[8]

Returning home to "the World," the hero will torment himself with the unavailing attempt to make sense of his experience. This will be the more difficult because, in several of the now numerous Vietnam War novels and films that follow the soldier's or marine's progress this far, the veteran is identified within his own country as the most unwelcome of revenants, the truest enemy. This was the suggestion of David Morrell's *First Blood* (1972; sire of the *Rambo* movies), Robert Stone's *Dog Soldiers* (1975; filmed in 1978 as *Who'll Stop the Rain*), Newton Thornburg's *Cutter and Bone* (1976; filmed in 1981 as *Cutter's Way*), James Webb's *Fields of Fire* (1978), Peter Straub's *Koko* (1988)—in which Vietnam is a persistent nightmare, endlessly revisited by a group of men who served there—and Michael Connelly's series of novels that feature the veteran cum Los Angeles detective, Hieronymous "Harry" Bosch that began with the *Black Echo* (1993).[9] American ambivalence toward Vietnam veterans, both in imaginative treatments of their lot and in the political uses to which they have been put, is ably analyzed by Keith Beattie in *The Scar That Binds* (1998). The Australian veteran (an American term that displaced "returned serviceman" in common usage after the Vietnam War) has had a slighter literary role, and usually figures as psychopathically harmed, as in David Williamson's play *Jugglers Three* (first performed in 1972, published in 1974, and heavily revised and remounted for the stage in 1997 as *Third World Blues*), C. J. Cairncross's novel *The Unforgiven* (1977), and Gabrielle Lord's thriller *The Sharp End* (1998).[10]

In his essay "Novelists and Vietnam: The War Goes On" in the *New York Times Review of Books,* Michiko Kakutani wrote: "A flaw shared by many Vietnam novels . . . is that they do not become works of the imagination; rather they retain the predictable shape and grainy texture of personal history. In novel after novel, a variation of the following true to life sequence occurs: the naive or gung-ho hero's initiation into military life at boot camp; his arrival in Southeast Asia; his encounters with suffering, pain and death; his attempts to escape the realities of war by drinking, whoring and fantasizing; and his return to an indifferent America."[11] Bryan and Kakutani at least obviate the need for much plot summary of the American (and Australian) fictions of the war.

Kakutani wanted a "large novel" of the war, but few have met this demand. One that might be so reckoned is Michael Peterson's *A Time of War* (1990). John M. Del Vecchio's *The 13th Valley* (1982) is another.[12] Rather than being cast as a war memoir, Del Vecchio's novel is a fictionalized account of the battle at Khe Te Laou in August, 1970, replete with maps and daily casualty lists. Its conventional elements—the lengthy detailing of the class backgrounds and personal histories of the members of a platoon, for example—owe much to Norman Mailer's Second World War novel *The Naked and the Dead* (1948), which told of the U.S. attack on the Pacific island of Anopopei. Other novelists have parodied this formulaic material. When the platoon is complemented by the "new guy" in Stephen Wright's *Meditations in Green* (1983): "Griffin experienced a dreary film buff's satisfaction. The single character lacking from their B-war had finally arrived: The Kid."[13] There is no parody from Del Vecchio, however, whose debts to Mailer are also revealed by the discursive, philosophizing interludes with which his book abounds.

Pining, perhaps, for a latter-day *War and Peace,* Kakutani could be instructed by Keegan, who wrote that "nothing in their national experience has prescribed" that either Britain or the United States could produce such a novel as Tolstoy's: "In France, Russia and the lands of central Europe, countries many times invaded, in which the army is a major national institution, and military service an almost universal obligation, the literary convention is to portray war as a corporate experience, affecting the life of the nation and of all who belong to it. The Anglo-Saxon convention, on the other hand, is intensely individualistic and reportorial, for the good reason that it is as reporters of distant events that most Anglo-Saxons have written."

Kakutani also overlooked how Tolstoy ironically contrasted ways of representing the experiences of battle by setting historians' versions of Napoleon's tactics (clinical, ex post facto material such as Del Vecchio provides: "with Alpha safely atop 848 and Recon on a lower peak 900 meters due north the command decision was made to insert all other units as planned") against the sensations of the individual (for example,

Rostov's during the French cavalry charge) who can only register the immediate, horrifying, incongruous, inexplicable, and physical aspects of the situation of which he is part. That the individual's thoughts may be capable of a detachment approaching reverie at the same time is another of Tolstoy's intuitions concerning war (fruit, no doubt, of his experience as well) that Tim O'Brien confirms in *Going After Cacciato* (1978).[14]

The 13th Valley is told in the third person and speaks of battle experience collectively—"the patrol froze"—rather than in the first person, through the atomized consciousness of a survivor remembering the events. Most Vietnam fiction, seeking to keep faith with what the individual endured, is related in the first person. These narratives are ostensibly as predictable as Bryan and Kakutani reckoned them to be. Australian Rhys Pollard's novel *The Cream Machine* (1972) begins with the narrator's departure from home, introduces his comrades in arms, has some intimations of the life left behind, and continues with the ritual induction into war: being posted to the battalion, meeting its men, hearing its legends, and learning its acronyms. Many Vietnam novels, both Australian and American, come with glossaries of the words coined to abbreviate and familiarize the items of an alien and barbarous experience. In the course of Pollard's novel, the first patrol, the first corpse, and the first matter of conscience routinely follow. In *The Cream Machine,* the latter involves the arrest of an old Vietnamese woman. In the testimony of one of the "Australian Voices" in Stuart Rintoul's *Ashes of Vietnam* (1987) it is an accidental atrocity. Such a narrative pattern as Pollard's novel shows is substantially repeated in William Nagle's *The Odd Angry Shot* (1975; filmed under the same name in 1979). This book opens with embarkation for Vietnam and proceeds speedily with the conventional sequence of first things: corpses, an Australian casualty, the purchase of "Saigon tea," and hence of a prostitute. The indispensable moment in such sequences is the initial sight of a combat victim. The body is the talisman that unlocks the right to report.

These fictionalized memories of war sometimes begin at the end and circle back in an attempt to explain how the breakdown and alienation of which Bryan speaks were reached. Kenneth Cook's Australian soldier is AWOL in Bangkok when *The Wine of God's Anger* (1968) begins. He has fled the war in self-loathing. The structure of *Fragments* (1984), by American Jack Fuller, is similar because that novel commences with a U.S. Army inquiry into the killing of civilians by the idealistic soldier Jack Neumann.[15] There is an acquittal, but in order to explain the deed the narrator leads us back to his and Neumann's induction at Fort Bragg, then on to the war. In the context of Vietnam War fiction, we are told nothing new. The horrors of this war are predictable and unavoidable.

They cannot be transcended by any belief in the heroic character of the national or the individual's involvement. Nor does the vernacular language soldiers resort to in order to countenance these horrors eliminate or ameliorate them.

Vietnam War fiction, a large percentage of which has been written by former combatants (though the percentage is certainly higher in the United States than in Australia), was less occupied in scrutinizing the motives for participation than was contemporary poetry about the war. Most of the poetry was written by noncombatants and in protest against the war. When those motives, or war aims, were mentioned in fiction, the tenor of reference was usually derisory and resigned. As the protagonist of Australian Michael Frazer's *Nasho* (1984) is informed: "It's not called the funny place because Bob Hope does a concert there every year. It's really a strange war. It's a politicians' war, not a soldiers' war. If the Americans declared war on the Antarctic penguins, Australia would have a battalion there."[16]

The focus on individual survival in Australian and American Vietnam fiction had as its corollary a tendency to blame the governments that sent troops there, for whatever reason. The same focus encouraged a cynical or incredulous view of personal risk taking that in earlier wars might have been designated as heroic. Any publicity for the heroic, for instance through army or press promotions, was a particular object of scorn. Graham Greene's seminally anti-American novel *The Quiet American* (1955) established important terms of perception of the conflict in Vietnam. A notable villain of this moralizing tale of the French war in Indochina is American war correspondent Bill Granger. When the U.S. economic attaché compliments him on "that account of Road 66—what did you call it? Highway to Hell—that was worthy of the Pulitzer," Granger disabuses him: "Do you think I'd really go near their stinking highway? Stephen Crane could describe a war without seeing one. Why shouldn't I? It's only a damned colonial war anyway. Get me another drink. And then let's go and find a girl."[17]

For the manufacture of the speciously heroic, cliché ("Highway to Hell") and classic war fiction (Crane's novel of the American Civil War, *The Red Badge of Courage* [1895]) serve much better than reporting at firsthand. Equally, such clichés and fictions in prose and film were by comparison the surest proof to Australian and American soldiers in Vietnam of the unheroic nature of their activities. *Token Soldiers* (1983), by Australian author John Carroll, describes a graveyard that reminds a soldier of "those old war pictures where truckloads of prisoners are driven to the countryside and slaughtered wholesale."[18] This seems to recall the 1963 film *The Great Escape*, but in American fiction the reference is usually still more specific. John Wayne is the ironic counterpart of Greene as a tutelary presence for those who want to comprehend Vietnam. The expectation that the events and surroundings of this war will resemble cinematic portrayals of the Second World War is one of the first casualties Americans suffer. Michael Herr is an exception. In *Dispatches* (1977) the Vietnam War came increasingly to resemble for him a film of itself.[19] Since writing that book, Herr has collaborated on the scripts of three films about the war: *Apocalypse Now* (1979), *Platoon* (1986), and *Full Metal Jacket* (1987). More typical is the reaction of the recruit Chellini ("Cherry"), who in his first days in country in *The 13th Valley*" imagined himself as part of the liberating armies coming across France or Belgium in an old World War II movie." Later, he becomes more contemplative: "We're the kids who've dreamed of far lands and exotic places, of the lands and wars of Hemingway and Mailer. Kids dreaming of seeing hobo jungles and shanties and of jumping off a Steinbeck freight and of seeing America and the world."[20] Forgetting this dream of literary tourism, Chellini later fights with a mad, homicidal intensity.

Australians managed to sustain the illusion that Vietnam was a conflict such as the Second World War had been much longer. Evidence of this can be found in anachronistic early photographs of the Vietnam War that set craggy-faced, old-fashioned-looking Australian troops in jungle surroundings more suggestive of the war in New Guinea and a good cause than the ambiguities of Vietnam two decades later.

Not only "old war pictures," but also old war stories—embellished tales of the endurance of survivors—are handled skeptically in American and Australian war fiction. For Morgan, in Stephen Phillip Smith's *American Boys* (1975), "his father's old World War II stories" are incongruous beside "the war stories of the last six days."[21] Jack Fuller's *Fragments* includes an epigraph from *The Red Badge of Courage*. In Fuller's book, another soldier called Morgan muses how it is that "they say that in other wars, men went off to battle with visions of glory." These are the "old lies" of which Ezra Pound wrote in his 1920 poem "Hugh Selwyn Mauberley." They are lies that were supposed to have died on the Somme in 1916, but which it has been in the interests of later generations of veterans to nurture. This Morgan's father sentimentally recalls of his own war (the Second World War): "You never got closer to anyone than the men you fought a war with." In *Beyond the Flag* (1981) by American Christopher Buonanno, the historical perspective that enables ideas of the heroic in war is relentlessly subjected to irony.[22] The headings of the chapters about this war in Vietnam carry incongruous rallying calls and remembrances of past conflicts: "The Glorious First of June," "Death to the French," "The Bonnie Blue Flag." Their grisly, comic inappropriateness is one of the author's ways of insisting that Vietnam cannot be assimilated into traditions of military glory.

For Australian novelists, such comparisons with earlier wars can be wistful rather than mocking. In Pollard's *The Cream Machine,* the narrator almost suppresses the possibility of irony in this reflection: "Looking along the row of slouch hats and rifles I grope for the supposed similarity between us and the traditional national image: where are all the tall bronzed Anzacs? the once-famed Diggers who stormed the ragged impossibility of Anzac Cove or died jeeringly in the mud beneath Mont St Quentin? Where is the morale and endurance of Tobruk or the Kokoda trail, the dash and inexorability of Kapyong? Perhaps it lies in the unconscripted element?"[23] It is a confused passage that repays attention. The suggestive force of the proper names—Anzacs, Diggers, Tobruk, Kokoda—is not reduced by the clichéd qualifications that accompany them: "tall bronzed," "died jeeringly" (at whom? looking in what direction?), "dash and inexorability." The diction belongs to an earlier era in which heroism and glory in battle were less dubious concepts. They are samples of the '"raised," essentially "feudal language," "the old rhetoric" of pre-Somme accounts of "strife" that Fussell analyzed. Notwithstanding, the Australian conscript pays them uneasy deference on the eve of his battle. The bolster of military and national legend is less easily discarded by Australians who write of the Vietnam War than by their American counterparts.

According to Jeffrey Walsh: "The myth of a lost generation of soldiers is one of the most potent imaginative impulses and orientations in the traditions of American war writing; it communicates an aura of betrayal, of inter-generational conflict, of a youthful and distinctively alternative value system contending with one expressive of a paternalistic dominant culture: the older culture is rejected as it is deemed responsible for the moral conduct of the war."[24]

Such a sense of their abandonment by and their antipathy toward the authority of the parent culture is stronger than ever before in the American literature of Vietnam. It is marked in the Australian literature also ("It's a politicians' war, not a soldiers' war"), where the commitment of so small a force to the conflict made its losses appear to be needless sacrifices on behalf of a society unwilling to give wholesale support to the war.

The discernment of the enemy on one's own side—whether incompetent generals, profiteers on the home front, or self-serving politicians of the older generation—begins long before the war in Vietnam. Less tangibly, the rhetoric of these groups that attempts to justify war aims becomes an intractable and tormenting enemy of the serving men, at least from the time of the First World War. Such rhetoric was famously assailed by Frederic Henry in Ernest Hemingway's 1929 classic, *A Farewell to Arms:* "There were many words that you could not stand to hear and finally only the names of places had dignity. Certain numbers were the same way and certain dates and these with the names of the places were all you could say and have them mean anything. Abstract words such as glory, honor, courage or hallow were obscene beside the concrete names of villages, the numbers of regiments and their dates."[25]

Speaking for his "lost generation" of soldiers, Henry shifts into the second person. As for Pollard's narrator in *The Cream Machine,* "the names of the places were all you could say and have them mean anything."

For one American Vietnam veteran, the litany of proper names of war had lost its consolation. William Jayne said of Hemingway's lines: "We had such concrete names embedded in our psyches too. Names like Con Thieu and the Arizona Territory; the Rock-pile and Hill 881; the 9th Marines and the 5th Marines . . . the concrete names of World War Two, the Marines' heroic quest across the Pacific, are part of our national mythology. No one knows that over 6,000 Marines died in Quang Nam province in the course of the Vietnam War." On behalf, then, of a forgotten as well as a lost generation, one whose experience of "the culture of combat . . . made us aliens when we returned," and with pain sharpened by his self-conscious, high literariness, Jayne added: "Our memories were dominated by the feeling that these concrete names—and all they represented—were useless. Our combat experience, the seminal event in our lives, was not viewed in the context of being right, wrong, glorious or respectful. It was simply useless."[26] This is one of the most forlorn voices of all these "lost generations." This is the note that is sounded so often in both Australian and American Vietnam War fiction. It expresses one belief about their condition that helps to determine the "predictable" structures of Vietnam narratives.

The rhetoric of American imperialism, the clichés to which the eponymous hero Alden Pyle adheres, were depicted as additional dangers in Greene's *The Quiet American.* Recollecting his first meeting with Pyle, the narrator reflects of this self-confident ingénue: "Perhaps only ten days ago he had been walking back across the Common in Boston, his arms full of books he had been reading in advance on the Far East and the problems of China. He didn't even hear what I said; he was absorbed already in the dilemmas of Democracy and the responsibilities of the West; he was determined—I learned very soon—to do good; not to any individual person, but to a country, a continent, a world." Appropriately, Pyle's epitaph is a cliché. The U.S. economic attaché sends this telegram to Pyle's parents: "Grieved to report your son died a soldier's death in the cause of Democracy."[27] Greene's perception of the destructive consequences of the rhetoric of idealistic imperialism would be analyzed and confirmed by other writers, American and Australian, in the later stages of the Indochinese wars.

The language of war makers as it is represented in American literature was dissected by James F. Mersmann, who argued that "the historical relationship between war and the decay of language is documented as far back as the Peloponnesian War." He sought to define the peculiarities of the language of the men who directed the American war effort in Vietnam: "Tautological and circular in structure, the language of the political-military establishment is also Latinate and abstract, verb-poor and noun-heavy. 'Escalation,' 'pacification,' 'Vietnamization,' 'liberation,' 'saturation,' and 'defoliation' intersperse 'kill-ratios' and 'free-fire zones'."[28] A similar point is made in Del Vecchio's *The 13th Valley,* when Lt. Rufus Brooks muses on "Politicians and Political Rhetoric," on "some of the word games we play at war. Pacification. Vietnamization."[29] What a barbarous obfuscation of political and moral intentions that last word denotes.

Not just the language of the military establishment, but also the clichés of war reporting became objects of particular antagonism during the war in Vietnam. Already in Hemingway's sights in *A Farewell to Arms,* such clichés were another of the targets of the prescient Graham Greene. In *The Short-timers* (1979), by American Gustav Hasford (the novel upon which Stanley Kubrick's film *Full Metal Jacket* was loosely based), a war correspondent mocks the currency of his vocation: "My stories are paper bullets fired into the black heart of communism. I've fought to make the world safe for hypocrisy."[30] At the point of crisis in Frazer's *Nasho,* Turner of the Australian Service Newspaper Unit is interviewed by an army psychologist whom he informs: "We all use a set of clichés which are up on the wall of the office. Saigon is depicted as quote this war-torn Asian capital unquote. 'War-torn? War-torn?' he ranted. 'Saigon is peace-torn—that's what it should say."[31] Turner eventually goes back to a mental hospital in Australia. Hasford's protagonist, "the Joker," tries to quell his revulsion at what he sees and how he can write of it by a stylized, macabre humor. Incinerated bodies are "crispy critters;" "the aroma of roasted flesh is, admittedly, an acquired taste." Thoughts of leaving Vietnam can only be entertained in parody, as in "erect-nipple wet dreams about Mary Jane Rottencrutch and the Great Homecoming Fuck Fantasy." Official pronouncements and private consolations alike are thus sardonically demolished.[32]

In Buonanno's *Beyond the Flag,* the ruination of such slogans as "fighting for your freedom" proceeds energetically. They are as surely "wasted" as the flora and fauna of what another ironist in the book calls "this idyllic land." Buonanno is sensible of the cost of such corrosion of language. His protagonist Vanderpool, who is—incidentally—one of the few not to make it home, in whatever condition, in these fictions, puzzles out the indecorous mixing of levels of language in the speech of Von Marshall, a fellow soldier: "Anyone who could glide through a line of Shakespeare or a verse from Browning, then instantly regress to the vilest obscenities, is just as dangerous to himself as he is to others."[33] In this unusually moralizing view, the opportunistic use of still-hallowed authors, its juxtaposition with the vile, devalues the bases of any language.

The ironic tone of Wright's *Meditations in Green* is the more unsettling because it is always on the verge of collapsing into a recognition that the bizarre events being catalogued are the norm; that there exists no other frame of reference by which they could be judged insane—that is, no place from which irony could be generated. The process in which ironies become unironic is registered in various ways: "Sensory evidence provided no clues to contradict [Tripp's] theory that they had not in fact left the United States at all but were prisoners in a bizarre behavioral study in Utah." Grumbacher is made "awards and decorations clerk" because he has "completed a couple of courses of college creative writing." The army intends no irony here. Grumbacher's task is to write the war, however "few of his compositions, he later admitted without false modesty, could equal the naive narrative flow, the melodramatic suspense, the unconscious art of those fabulous mission reports the officers themselves had written as testimony to their deeds of heroism meriting special recognition."[34] The officers, that is, were prepared to write, if not to fight, a good war.

Another "writer" who contributes to the sour texture of Wright's novel is Lew Simon, whose letters to Ma and Pa back home are his sardonic reprisals for their comfortable incomprehension of his lot. Not just his own American background is being ironically regarded here, but another tradition of war literature, in which recollections of an idyllic past provide consolation for the distresses of the present. This mode of digressive reverie, instanced by Robert Jordan in Hemingway's *For Whom the Bell Tolls* (1940) and by Paul Berlin in O'Brien's *Going After Cacciato*, is a form of escape from battle that knows itself to be temporary. It is a more extensive counterpart of the escape that simile affords in the figurative language of so many accounts of Vietnam.

Lew Simon's response to such revisitings of the past and home is in the mode of parody. Using cliché, he mocks those who are not in Vietnam and does so (distantly, jestingly recalling the "band of brothers" speech in Shakespeare's *Henry V*) in the idiom of stoic, good-humored, folksy companionship: "Last night a few of the guys gathered in my room to share some conversation and that tin of chocolate chip cookies (Thanks Mom) when Sam, you remember Sam? He's the boy from Arkansas who stands guard duty in his bare feet despite the danger of snake bite. Anyway, he pulled out his mouth harp (another word for harmonica) and started playing a rendition of 'Shortenin' Bread' that was absolutely amazing." Lew opines that "it's moments like last night that redeem the other times of this awful war." But there is a characteristic final flourish, in the PS to the letter: "The other night one of our sergeants went crazy with tension and started running around screaming and shouting at people until the OD hit him over the head with an entrenching tool. Lucky there was no one seriously hurt."[35] Some time later, when the first sergeant receives an emergency call initiated by Simon's parents, the soldier's writing career is terminated. Whether he is being punished for writing fact or fiction is not disclosed.

These examples make it possible to speak more precisely of how and why "language"—the rhetoric of war makers, the confections of some war correspondents, the clichés by which folks at home console themselves, the "visions of glory" that war literature may once have enshrined—becomes an enemy in American, and less elaborately so, in Australian literature of the Vietnam War. In *Dispatches*, Herr's essential subject was such language, together with the kinds of vernacular, figurative resistance that developed toward it. After a black paratrooper tells him, "I been scaled man, I'm smooth now," Herr reflects that this left him to wonder "not what he meant (that was easy) but where he'd been to get his language." Herr's book traces the unended conflict between military jargon and soldiers' deflating translations of it. He writes of how language collapses in situations of terror that official placebos never help. There are, he suggests, two versions of the Soldiers' Prayer: "Standard, printed on a plastic-coated card by the Defense Department, and Standard Revised, impossible to convey because it got translated outside of language, into chaos—screams, begging, promises, threats, sobs, repetition of holy names until their throats were cracked and dry, until some men had bitten through their collar points and rifle straps and even their dog-tag chains."[36]

The most famous American slogan of the Vietnam War was the enervated conclusion that "It don't mean nothin'." The rhetoric and ideology of the military establishment may have been mocked, derided, resisted, or translated into parodies of itself, but "it" had not been defeated. Finally, such language was as elusive a target as the notional enemies, the Vietcong and the NVA (as American and Australian authors have preferred to call them, rather than using the acronyms NLF and PAVN that those enemies employed).

Australian poets of the war sought to simplify this matter of enemies. Typically for them, the enemy was not Vietnamese. When Vietnamese people appeared, it was often as the victims of Australian or American atrocities. Poets sought empathy with them. David Campbell, for instance, made a stagy entrance into the heart and mind of a defenseless peasant: "I was milking that old cow when a row of tall bamboo/Was mowed by rifle fire." Other voices are heard in the poem—guttural, childish, American: "Put a rocket in that old cow,/Then it's time to line for chow." Nevertheless, the war may have contributed to a shift of Campbell's poetic concerns in the latter part of his career. James Tulip suggested that Campbell's dilemma "as a World War II hero, over how to deal with the Vietnam War surfaced in his writing. It flowed across into a reassessment of Australian society; and his several volumes of verse in the 1970s mark a most penetrating exploration of cultural change in Australian society."[37] To the extent that this was true, Campbell's case is uncommon in postwar Australian poetry, where few careers were so affected in their directions as those of several American poets, Denise Levertov and Robert Bly among them. In 1966, the latter founded, with David Ray, American Writers Against the Vietnam War.

Campbell's fellow poet Bruce Beaver focused on the language of the military establishment in a poem he wrote concerning "this century of total war." The speaking voice in the poem is bland, technocratic, morally indifferent. Both Beaver and Campbell resented those American voices because, in large part, the United States was perceived to be dictating Australia's participation in the war. Such reliance was Andrew Taylor's subject in "Demonstration Poem." While "things usually hang straight":

> Australia though has come to hang crooked
> dependent in a southwesterly direction
> from the United States
> like a piece of something stuck to a top.

The dependent relationship, for Taylor, is demeaning, ludicrous, and infantile.

Australian prose writers on Vietnam did not altogether banish their official Asian enemy, although he was perceived with less hostility than were the Japanese in Second World War fiction. In Norman Bartlett's *Island Victory* (1955) they were "apes with pants on," "little, grinning, mustard-coloured Japanese," while for Ron Fisher, in *The Last Blue Sea*

(1959) by "David Forrest," "From the dark ages they came."[38] In the crop of Australian novels published since the mid-1970s, which are set in Asia but do not deal directly with Vietnam, Asian figures are often the valued mentors of naive and sometimes guilt-ridden Australian sojourners. This is the moral core of Nigel Krauth's *Freedom Highway* (1999), another novel heavily influenced by *The Quiet American,* which begins in Thailand on the day of a bloodless coup in 1957. Seeking uncritically for Asian mentors, in part out of a kind of cultural death wish, Australians enter into yet another relationship of dependence.

In Cook's portentously titled novel *The Wine of God's Anger,* the narrator—who has volunteered to save the world from communism—believes that his enemy is alien ideology. In the climactic battle against the Vietcong, he kills "the gentle little chance acquaintance who'd looked after me when I was drunk. . . . I had killed a man I knew."[39] The enemy in theory is the veritable friend. Even for this confused young man, who goes AWOL after the battle, another (American) ideology is on the way to being perceived as his real enemy.

During the 1950s, officer-trainee Brian Fitzgerald, in Thomas Keneally's novel *Passenger* (1979), is exposed to the dark side of Alden Pyle's American rhetoric when—in the course of his military induction at Portsea, Victoria—he hears of the threat of "atheistical communist Russia."[40] After service in the Malayan Emergency on behalf of British imperial interests, or Australia's northern defense, Fitzgerald begins to perceive bellicose, anticommunist rhetoric as alien and inimical to him. Left without moral or ideological bearings, Fitzgerald's state is at least one of worthy confusion. Much of the Australian protest poetry of the Vietnam War, such as that collected in *We Took Their Orders and Are Dead* (1971), did not distinguish between the rejection of imperialist rhetoric and the disparagement of the American ally.[41] As Mersmann said, much of this verse was "poemic": "poems that are more polemic than poetry."[42]

On those occasions when Australians appear in American Vietnam novels and vice versa, there is generally a degree of benign ignorance in their apprehensions of one another, as if the characters are less ideologically agitated than their authors. In some respects, these characters recognize an ultimate enemy in different ways. American ideology and dependence on the United States rankles deeply with Australians, whereas Americans apprehend a ubiquitous, indefatigable morass of enemy toward them: from allies and foes, in Asia and back home. Rowe made iconoclastic use of American opinions of Australia in *Count Your Dead.* Robert Allen's novel, *Saigon, South of Beyond* (1990), by treating the uncertain years between 1960 and 1963 in Vietnam, shows with hindsight the moral and political confusion into which Australians would be drawn.[43] "Alexander's" plaint for the wasted skills of Australian warriors in a war managed by Americans was made in reductive despair. Moorhouse portrayed Australian perceptions of "the blandishments" of their accents, their "gregariousness," and their "enervating enthusiasms." Yet, as his characters remark, these folk lynch the "Negro" and drop napalm. This ambivalence is static and impotent. The American phenomenon is to be wondered at, but it cannot be resisted. In Frazer's *Nasho* there is a cheeky scene concerning the mutual incomprehensibility of the allies' languages. The black man Horace asks, "What language you talk in haustralia?" "Hey Bluey," comes the reply, "Wombat, Geelong, Woolloomooloo, knapsack, SP bookie how's yer father?"[43] The teasing goes undetected, but the Australian jokers are at risk, having to retreat into comic mystification of their origins rather than own to whose language it is that they speak.

The sense of frustration that novels by both Americans and Australians express so vehemently arises in part from different circumstances. Peter Bourne wrote in 1970 that the Australians are "a token force and they know it"; they may be dying merely as "an act of political symbolism with little or no practical military value"; they feel that theirs is an army of quality "rendered virtually impotent by its diminutive size."[44] Several novels corroborate Bourne's comments, either through such title metaphors as Carroll's *Token Soldiers* or in the disgruntled discussion among troops in Nagle's *The Odd Angry Shot.* Bourne attempted to explain why a reporter declared: "The Vietnamese hate the Americans. The Americans hate the Vietnamese. Americans hate other Americans. The local Chinese are hated by both the Vietnamese and the Americans. The Australians hate everybody."[45] Here was the profusion of enemies that Australians do and do not want: the need to ensure their enlistment in history and fear as threats to their survival. Here also were explanations of American frustrations with the war, contempt for the indigenous ally among them. Abetting this was a belief that they had been abandoned by "the World"—the U.S. government, their families, and by values once unambiguously held (at least as legend had it). The deeply entrenched cynicism toward warlike and imperialist language and those who used it was a prominent consequence. Thence the impasse: This was the language and prevailing ideology of their own country.

Some Australian authors, prompted by the war in Vietnam, redefined the national enemy as American culture, language, and ideology—terms of hegemony less concrete than the military alliance that might be resented, but not repudiated. An enemy was constructed, moreover, with which it was not necessary to go to war. Such a move was hardly available to American authors, who sought more energetically than their Australian counterparts to escape from the war and from the habit of telling the same old war story. They looked not for a redefinition of the enemy, as the Australians had, but for an escape from enmity, from a condition whose terminal stage was reached when veterans came to be regarded as inimical to their own society. This anxiety deepened, as John Hellmann has argued, because if their war story was always the same, their mythical, inherited story of the meaning of America had changed: "On the deepest level, the legacy of Vietnam is the disruption of our story, of our explanation of the past and vision of the future."[46]

The expectation that their lot in war will be demoralizing in its defeat of preconceptions accompanies many literary characters to Vietnam, or is one of the first lessons that they learn there. The consequences of this expectation—a sense of impotent abandonment, of severance from the world left behind—are major constituents of the war fiction. Here is a source of the apparent predictability of the unfolding of many narratives and the cause of Bryan's and Kakutani's descriptions of them. Neither critic examines the attempts of writers, Australian or American, to reconstitute their worlds by rejuvenating the possibility of metaphor, by finding—with deference to General Sherman—what else war is besides "all hell." Of that often misquoted aphorism, Tim O'Brien wrote: "As a moral declaration the old truism seems perfectly true and yet because it abstracts, because it generalizes, I can't believe it with my stomach. Nothing turns inside."[47]

Joseph Heller's novel *Catch-22* (1961) provided, in its title, one of the most potent metaphors ever made in war literature. Its expression of the absurdity of the conduct of war has been generalized to refer promiscuously to many other forms of human activity. Instances of irony abound in the novel: "Men went mad and were rewarded with medals"; "a crazy bastard may be the only sane one"; the German enemies with whom Milo Minderbinder trades "are also members in good standing of the syndicate."[48] Here, irony has become routine. As in Wright's *Meditations in Green*, the ironic circumstances of war are so pervasive that there is no alternative frame of reference against which to regard them. Irony thus is disfranchised. Heller moves slickly into that postironic mode in which metaphor may be renewed, and establishes his notorious, catchall, "Catch-22" metaphor.

For novelists of Vietnam, that path was not so easily followed. In the hands of some writers and commentators, "Vietnam" has been a conveniently vague metaphorical device for the exculpation of all kinds of failures, national and personal. More often, the literature of the war suggests that it was a remarkable stimulus to the provisional illuminations of simile, and nearly intractable for metaphorical understanding. The metaphorical renewal that Heller so deftly achieved could now scarcely be won at all. Moreover, Kakutani wrote that "a large novel that embraces the entire scene" has yet to be written, although James Webb made such an attempt with *A Country Such as This* (1983).[49] The Australians' restricted sphere of military operations militates against such an undertaking. The nearest to it has been Christopher Koch's *Highways to a War* (1995), based in part on the life of Australian war cameraman Neil Davis, who was killed in a botched Bangkok coup in 1985.

Nostalgia for a perspective on war that is serenely omniscient rather than bewildered or personal is unlikely to be satisfied. The kind of realistic prose narrative that Kakutani wanted is not readily enabled by the sameness of soldiers' experience of Vietnam: the intensely occupied 365-day tour of duty (for Americans at least), and the horribly predictable sequence of shocks and disillusionments (for all who served and wrote of it). A novel written from the generals' point of view is hardly conceivable. The alienation from home of ordinary soldiers meant that digression into past lives has seldom been undertaken for long in these fictions, so difficult was it to believe in the reality of that time, or to hope to return there. This is not to say that ways of escape from war and from the scarcely varying war story lived in Vietnam have not desperately been sought. The characteristic means of seeking such an escape in this war literature, its emblematic literary figure, is the simile.

Similes offer the opportunity to vary the stock narrative in which the characters in Vietnam War fictions find themselves. They represent the potential chance, although it is never fully realized, of brief participation in other narratives besides the fixed plot, the inexorable sequence of events, in which the characters in stories of this war feel themselves to be imprisoned. Epic simile is a resort in descriptions of war that is as old as Homer's *Iliad*. In such a context it works to personalize a combatant, to allow us the ease of digressive and nostalgic reference to him. Such functions are radically undermined, even as they seem to be present, in the literature of the Vietnam War.

Mark Baker introduced *'Nam* (1981), his collection of veterans' reminiscences, with a group of similes: "The Technicolor blotch of napalm flickering on the screen while Walter recited the day's body count like a grim blessing over our suppers had little to do with gagging on the stench of a burning man. . . . Because Vietnam veterans lived through it, the account they give is as raw and shocking as an open wound. Death and brutality pervade this book, like the heavy ticking of a clock echoing through the entire house on a sleepless night."[50] Several of the many purposes that simile served in Vietnam War literature are illustrated here. The last of Baker's similes, awkward as it is, does not domesticate "death and brutality" so much as introduce them into the house, bringing them home, where they are neither wanted nor expected. The same point is more bluntly made through the first simile, where newsreader Walter Cronkite's assumption of a priestly function is mocked for its pretensions and for its irrelevance to an understanding of the war. Neither does the smell of home cooking prepare one for the aroma of "burning man." Perhaps Baker's similes represent not so much the yearning for escape as the impossibility of veterans truly returning home. His second simile, of the open wound, is well on the way to becoming a cliché—the kind of blurb that books such as his should shrink from. This is a figure of speech dissected by Keith Beattie in *The Scar That Binds.* In other narratives of the war the capacity of simile to turn into the familiar, and the comfortable into cliché is strenuously opposed.

In *Vietnam: A Reporter's War* (1985), Australian journalist Hugh Lunn introduced the chapter and the notion "Under Fire" through simile: "Then we were hit. The copter lurched. It was the ground. Suddenly everything was much more real—like the moment when they finally wheel you into the operating theatre after all the waiting and preparation." Among his registered first things is the sight of napalm being dropped: "I could see the tin cans rolling and tumbling down out of the sky. They were like the unpainted, ribbed tin cans of apple my father used to use in his cake shop. . . . Tiredness was now overtaking me like an anaesthetic. Watching all this from the ground was like being at a big movie."[51] Similes cluster, as with Baker. The events that stimulate their coining make more urgent the desire for escape from war. They arouse memories of the domestic, the nonmartial, that which is comfortably in the past, elsewhere.

In several American novels about the war, similes occur from the first page as vital points of inception for the narrative. The recruit depot, in Hasford's *The Short-Timers,* is "like a death camp." Vietnam, in Fuller's *Fragments,* smells "like spice on bad meat"; its air is "like poison." Hasford's simile occurs in other war novels, Australian as well as American. In Cook's *The Wine of God's Anger,* dead bodies "were lying like those tangles of corpses during World War Two." Buonanno's character Vanderpool "was as content as any Jew in the death camp." This comparison is both a wishing away from the present of Vietnam and an attempt to judge it with reference to the worst human precedent for suffering.

Other similes are enlisted to render animate, at least for a moment, the inanimate, inhuman objects of the war. Herr writes of a helicopter "looking like a great, gross beast getting a body purchase on some mud."

To Australian author Hugh Atkinson, a helicopter in flight is more graceful, "like a dragonfly."[52] For one of Hasford's characters they are "like monster grasshoppers." The Kilgore-style colonel in Rowe's *Count Your Dead* loves air strikes—if not, as in the movie *Apocalypse Now,* for "the smell of napalm in the morning"—then because they are "silver birds flashing and striking like marlins." The "linked belt" of a machine gun "snaps down the ditch like a length of golden intestine following him into the slime"; napalm was "like a wave rolling up a steep surf beach." The similes also function in another way: they try to turn the human into something less than that. To Robert Riggan, a scared American soldier thrashes "like a trash fish." Unzipping a body bag is "like turning over a rock."[53]

In conventionally ordered war narratives, such as Smith's *American Boys* and Del Vecchio's *The 13th Valley,* the incidence of similes is much lower. War is the place the books want to be: Why dream of other places? In *The 13th Valley,* one simile works against first-person accounts of the dishevelment of battle to suggest the cohesion of a unit in action: "Alpha slithered away from Campobasso, slithered into the still night like one segmented snake seeking prey." A first glimpse of battlefield horrors initiates similes in Smith's book, but when they occur they are inert and uninventive: soldiers "howling like crazed savages," mountains "like a giant dead man," lunacy spread "like fertilizer."

Vietnam is no longer the magical, mysterious East of imperial celebration and possession: "the dawn doesn't come up like thunder" in Cook's novel. It does for Buonanno, but the advent is recorded in jest. Similes become clichés when they begin to give bogus consolation or information about the war; when they are used by its promoters as instruments of that bellicosity whose attendant language writers came to see as their ultimate enemy. In *Fragments,* Jack Fuller mordantly criticized such similes and their capacity for being put to corrupt use. When a soldier "back in the World" cons two girls with an atrocity tale, Fuller's Morgan says with asperity, "He's as phony as a body count." In his parents' home, Morgan is disquieted by the fuss over his medals. His father is moved sentimentally to recollect his own war and then to this injunction concerning comradeship in arms: "You've got to be as honest as steel." There is no "fragment" here to shore against the ruins of Morgan's world after his return from Vietnam.

Rarely is a war said explicitly to be, as Riggan says once, "like a dream." Instead, the profusion of similes and their use in these Australian and American works is intended as a means of escape from waking, present horrors. The similes might express the wish that this present time is a dream, but that their authors know it is not. Thus Vanderpool, in *Beyond the Flag*, "watches the roadside hooches and the green checkerboard squares of rice paddies monotonously glide past, as if they were only printed canvas on an old Hollywood revolving prop from the silent film era." The navy corpsman Donaldson is "a tall lanky fellow, like the tin man in The Wizard of Oz."[54] Wright provides a correction to any view of the war as a dream. This simile from *Meditations in Green* insists on Vietnam's power to obliterate most remembrance of the past times before the war: "The war was real; he was not. It was like memory, and therefore his most profound sense of self was a tub of tepid water into which chunks of rock (the war) fell almost daily now in wide splashes, spilling his life onto a cold black-and-white linoleum floor."[55]

Jeffrey Walsh thought that the use of similes in Vietnam War literature might typify "an intellectual bewilderment"; indicate a wry apartness or "gentle bewilderment." Instead they represent a much more energetic, unavailing attempt by authors to move beyond the constraints of their situation. Severed from the contiguities of personal past and social life, the participants in these fictions have their war reported in fragments, as the responses of individuals to terrors and routines that are altogether unindividual. Metonymic narrative at any level beyond simile is defeated, yet in the uses of simile the most daring and characteristic figurative language of the literature of the Vietnam War can be found.

Unexpected but perhaps explicable affinities are evident between Australian literature of Vietnam and Australian poetry of the 1970s and 1980s, which does not explicitly treat the war. In many of Robert Gray's poems, simile is the dominant figure of speech. It enables the tentative movement from one uncertain vantage point to another. The declarative confidence of metaphor is usually eschewed.[56] The legacy of the Vietnam War and its literature is there in the shadows.

Often what looks like a metaphor for the Vietnam War is in fact simile. A good example is when Herr recalls that "the Elephant would be there kneeling on my chest." Several of the titles of Vietnam novels look metaphorical—*The Most Savage Animal, The Short-Timers, Token Soldiers*—but are in practice bitterly literal descriptions of the present realities of Vietnam rather than transformations of it. The title of *Going After Cacciato* reveals the governing metaphor of the novel. Its epigraph, "soldiers are dreamers," comes from a First World War poem by Siegfried Sassoon. Ways to escape from battle—through reverie, reminiscence, and actual or imagined flight—are the concerns of this story. Its postironic temper makes it the most distinctive novel of the war yet to appear. Yet O'Brien's work persistently reaches toward other kinds of war literature (whose examples ultimately it will not accept): memoir in the manner of Remarque, the themes of separate peace and farewell to arms from Hemingway, that of the lost patrol from Mailer (and countless films). Relating the journey of a platoon from Vietnam to Paris in search of the deserter Cacciato (whose name, signifying "hunter," reverses the participants' roles), the novel parodies American myths of the frontier, of the regenerative westward movement in search of unsullied places in which to settle. Paul Berlin's memories of childhood are in the mainstream of American Romanticism from Thoreau through Twain to Hemingway, yet his nostalgia is delicately criticized. Only in the dream narrative of pursuit can he travel that westerly way that would eventually lead him home. The spiritual autobiography central to this Romantic literature can no longer be retrieved by memories of Walden Pond, or rafting down the Mississippi, or of time spent "up in Michigan." For a soldier in this "bad time," the self's center is irrevocably in Vietnam.

"By a stretch of the imagination," Berlin can for a while wish himself away from the war. But the interlude is temporary. Some of the power of O'Brien's metaphor lies in its fragile self-knowledge. The world it reconstitutes is magical—and illusory. The desire for homecoming that it expresses is impossible for many in life and occasions shocking dislocations for others. Somber complements to O'Brien's novel are two poems by Australian Bruce Dawe.[57] In "The Fate of Armies," Dawe imagined men's escape as in dream from battle:

> Now I know to what cool earth the armies
> return, return, in absolute silence,
> under the hurt gaze of the moon.
>
> Slim, nude, beautiful, each combatant
> rises into that injured light, shrugging off
> the last fox-hole sand . . .
>
> Alive with enquiry then, and anxious for
> a solace dreamed of while the brute weather
> exploded above them, they roil, roil, writhe
>
> As if bewitched on the pure blebs besprinkling
> the vast yard. If the could sing, they would;
> if they could travel speedily enough
>
> Over the surface of their world to inhabit
> perpetual night, that would be something,
> and better than retreating, as they must.

Dawe's poem "Homecoming" is a literal counterpart of such dreams. It is also one of the finest threnodies in the war literature of Vietnam, telling with grave tenderness of the return of the bodies of slain men, belatedly, to their proper places of rest:

> to cities in whose wide web of suburbs
> telegrams like leaves from a wintering tree
> and the spider grief swings in his bitter geometry
> —they're bringing them home, now, too late, too early.

In "Homecoming." Dawe speaks without evasiveness, but obliquely, of the Vietnam War. It was a pronounced habit of Australian literature written during and after the war to treat this morally and aesthetically troubling conflict by indirection. That is, on those occasions when it was allowed to come to mind and memory at all. Poetry, fiction, and much historical writing revived the First World War, seeking to represent it—rather than Vietnam—as a moral and historical watershed in Australian life. The fiction of Roger McDonald, David Malouf, and Geoff Page, and poetry of Les Murray and Chris Wallace-Crabbe insisted on a divide between an innocent, rurally oriented, antebellum Australia and the postwar society whose idealism had been misplaced, although its role in history had properly begun. The First World War was a domestically divisive conflict, as was Vietnam. It was a foreign war to which Australians at first rushed willingly and supported stridently, as most did the war in Vietnam. The nostalgic return to 1914–18 in this writing may have suggested implicitly that the innocence supposedly lost then, the dependence willingly embraced, had prepared at long range for Vietnam.

By indirection, also, "Vietnam" was examined in a range of Australian novels written since the mid-1960s (Koch's *Across the Sea Wall* was published in 1965). They were set in other Asian countries and were guardedly silent concerning national participation in the Vietnam War. This was a conflict that unobligingly provided no heroes, whether as individuals—such as Capt. Albert Jacka, VC, in the First World War—or corporate, such as the First and Second AIF. The Anzac legend was tarnished treacherously (so some of the literature asserted) by domestic protesters and incompetent allies. To compensate, assiduous legend-making work went on in Australia in the 1970s. Michael Boddy and Bob Ellis revived the fortunes of eccentrics and outcasts—the American-born politician King O'Malley and the bushranger Martin Cash—in polemical musicals. Paul Sherman (in 1974) and Jack Hibberd (in 1976)—the former respectfully, the latter with a semblance of iconoclasm—put opera singer Dame Nellie Melba back on the stage. Kenneth Ross wrote *Breaker Morant* (1978), a play about the sometime *Bulletin* poet and outback adventurer who was executed by the British in 1902 for shooting prisoners during the Boer War. This became a film by Bruce

Beresford, in which Morant was portrayed as a victim, not so much of the notional Boer foe, but of the notional British ally. Historian Manning Clark went *In Search of Henry Lawson* (1978), while Jean Bedford related the adventures of bushranger Ned Kelly's *Sister Kate* (1982). These legendary figures, resuscitated or manufactured since the early 1970s, were rebels and renegades, folk both morally tarnished yet "typically" Australian. The coincident experience of the Australian withdrawal from Vietnam in 1972, then the fall of Saigon in 1975, may have contributed to the tone of these works: defensive, hectoring, sour, and suspicious of heroism and celebrity, for all their often raucous injections of humor.

In the 1990s, Australian novelists have ventured a more direct encounter with the events and the legacies of the war in Vietnam. Koch's *Highways to a War* gained its wide angle of view by basing itself on the adventures of Mike Langford, a war photographer who ranged across the sites of conflict in Southeast Asia before disappearing in Cambodia in 1976. Georgia Savage's *Ceremony at Long Nho* (1995) concerns a middle-aged woman's journey of self-healing to Vietnam where her former husband, another photographer, was crippled in action. Many deep ambivalences about Australians at war, in Vietnam in particular, are treated in Savage's novel. Despite the large number of Vietnamese who have settled in Australia during the last quarter of a century, there is as yet no imaginative literature to compare with the fiction of Robert Olen Butler (a Vietnamese linguist who served in that country in 1971 with the U.S. Army), notably in his collection of short stories focusing on a Vietnamese-American community in Louisiana.[58]

It is still fair to say that Australian Vietnam War literature—for complex and anxious reasons—faces the war less directly than does the American. Nevertheless, the various tangential treatments it has received suggest the powerful, if imprecise importance of the war for writers of the past two decades. In Australia there is no pulp literature of the war equivalent to Don Pendleton's "Mack Bolan" and Eric Helm's "Vietnam: Ground Zero" series, or such Vietnam adventure stories as Dennis K. Philburn's *Freedom Bird* (1987), presented by *Soldier of Fortune* magazine.[59] Nearest to it perhaps was Peter Corris's opportunistic use of the trope of a veteran's return to the country in the *Vietnam Volunteer* (2000). More importantly, there is in Australia no extensive literature portraying returned servicemen from Vietnam as outlaw-victims. The works by Williamson, Cairncross, and Lord, mentioned already, are exceptions. The Gallipoli veteran who returns to an unwelcoming Australia in the 1976 film *Break of Day* features another transposed treatment of Vietnam.

Most Americans reckoned with a war lost, perhaps needlessly, in which a tradition of national idealism, a concept of special destiny, was forever compromised. Many Australian authors either ignored the war or treated it indirectly, thus abetting public amnesia regarding its causes and consequences. A few in desperation supported the valiant reputation of Australian troops who supposedly had been drawn into a mire and betrayed by their putative allies. Some then saw Vietnam as a war in which the United States, as the true enemy of Australian culture and nationhood, was exposed. Doing the state this presumed service, writers played another variation on that plaintive theme of Australian dependence, which even now too few have heard or sought to vary.

JEFF DOYLE

8 Reading and Building the Australian Vietnam Forces National Memorial

From the beginning of 1988 until Friday, 6 September 1991, one of the niches set aside for monuments to honor the nation's warriors along Anzac Parade in Canberra contained a small cross and, next to it, a notice board. The cross was made of plain wood, painted white; the wording on the notice board read: "On this site will be erected a memorial for those who died & served in the Vietnam War."

Until September, 1991, this spare duo of signs was all that marked the Australian national capital's and, at least symbolically, parliament's and the nation's official intention to memorialize Australia's Vietnam veterans. Those signs announced the intention of establishing another sacred "site"—this one for the sometimes tenuous consolidation of Australia's European heritage.

The day the memorial was dedicated, 3 October 1992, marked the fifth anniversary of the 1987 Sydney Welcome Home March. That occasion has been claimed, at the time and since, as marking for the veterans their first national acknowledgment, the first move on a national scale of acceptance of Vietnam veterans back within the folds of the nation's mythical self-images and identities, specifically those clustering around the Anzac legend. This chapter is not the place to recount the precise details of the many histories surrounding that march—nor the more or less documentary histories, which "prove" that many veterans indeed had their welcome home marches at the end of their tours of duty, nor equally those personal narratives, those mythical or "errant" (rather than completely erroneous) histories, in which anecdote assures that seemingly every Vietnam veteran was demobilized unceremoniously, and after midnight, in some airport farther west than the boondocks.[1] Nor is that Americanism an accidental replacement for what an earlier generation might have termed "beyond the black stump"; it instead signifies the substantial replacement of certain elements of the wider Australian experience of Vietnam with the remembrances of only a few. Even more, it signifies a kind of reversed or inverted appropriation of American myths of the revenant warrior despised, which characterized the United States in the decade following the fall of Saigon, into an Australian context at once supportive and nurturing of it, and one that might have been more generally understood as politically and historically at odds. "Might have been" understood, if the Australian people had an ability to remember its more recent history as more than a series of sporting encounters and political exposés of faceless men and "reds under beds," and had thereby comprehended it more analytically than the political and journalistic catchphrases of the late 1970s encouraged us to remember the Menzies years.

If the march was one move, one sign on the historical pathway to "recovery," in the following few years some elements of the veteran community began the process of making those signs more definite, much more substantial and lasting. And again the pathway chosen by the veteran community had an integrity all its own. It wanted a memorial, a sacred site on Anzac Parade. The fact that, like the march, that impetus had a parallel in the American veteran community should not go unnoticed, for it suggests that while much of the drive within the veteran community seeks solutions appropriate to Australian experiences, many of the underlying structures have been borrowed willfully or unintentionally from the actions and reactions of their American counterparts. The acculturation of the Vietnam experience within Australia has all too often had an underlying American substratum (though this is not surprising in many cases), which has led to unhappy consequences. However, this pathway of analysis follows the competition for and design of a national monument to the veterans, a monument situated not merely within the national capital but significantly within the precincts of one of the key axes of the city, designed by Walter Burley Griffin, and hence symbolically a key avenue of the nation.

Although the sod turning occurred on 6 September 1991, the process of selecting the design, estimating its cost, modifying it, and getting the tender for its construction had been under way for more than three years. Before charting the several brief histories of the Australian Vietnam Forces National Memorial, however, I want to turn to the major American memorial, "the Wall," in Washington, D.C. It is neither the first nor the last of the American monuments to the war, but it is the best known, the most controversial, the most visited (and despite or because of the intentions of the Australian groups to separate ours from theirs, so to speak) it looms large in any discussion of monuments devoted to Vietnam. It is also instructive to look at the processes and responses to that memorial before looking at our own, if for no other reason than that the several Australian groups involved since 1988–89 had looked very hard at the Wall.

The Washington Vietnam Memorial

The Wall seems simple in design, a chevron-shaped sunken wall consisting of two half walls of polished black granite panels (140 altogether), meeting at a 125-degree, twelve-minutes angle, twelve feet high at the middle and tapering off toward the tips of the chevrons. These tips point like arrowheads to the Washington and Lincoln Monuments, respectively. The angle of the chevron is therefore deliberate. The idea of the monument is quite straightforward. The names of the dead (some fifty-eight thousand) have been photochemically sand-blasted in chronological order of their deaths on the 140 panels. The only deviation from what might be seen as a very simple though elegant handling of the material is the design decision to begin the chronological listing of the names in the middle of the chevron. Thus, while the monument is totally symmetrical, the two halves being identical except for the names and other inscriptions (two only, on the wings) it is not a simple matter of walking from one end to the other to "encapsulate" or "incorporate" the temporal (and human) sweep of the war. Such a process has to have two elements, and walking through the monument requires two distinct phases: if one starts from the middle and faces east, one finds on the first panel, panel Number One East, the name of Dale Buis, an adviser killed on 8 July 1959. (Since the dedication another name, that of Harry G. Cramer, an army captain killed two years earlier, has been added.) At the end of the east wing, Number Seventy East, one must walk the full length of the Wall in a westerly direction to the far end, panel Number Seventy West, and then walk again to the middle to finish in the angle of the two wings with the last panel, Number One West, dated 1975, where the last name, Richard Vande Geer, refers to one of the men killed on the USS *Mayaguez* on 15 May 1975. Each name is preceded on the west wing or followed on the east wing by a diamond or a cross: a diamond symbolizes that the death was confirmed, whereas a cross marks each of the approximately thirteen hundred who are still missing. Here the cross signifies hope. If remains subsequently are returned, crosses are filled in to form diamonds. If any are returned alive, a circle symbolizing life will be engraved around the cross.[2]

The idea for the memorial came from Jan Scruggs, a decorated and combat-wounded veteran of the U.S. Army's 199th Light Infantry Brigade.[3] He founded the Vietnam Veterans' Memorial Fund on 27 April 1979, and together with other veterans set about organizing a national competition to select a design. By 31 March 1981 the competition had attracted 1,421 entrants. On 1 May the committee unanimously chose Maya Ying Lin's design.

The design criteria as set out by the committee required that the monument:

1. be reflective and contemplative in character;
2. be harmonious with its site and surroundings;
3. provide for the inscription of the names of the nearly fifty-eight thousand who gave their lives or remain missing;
4. make no political statement about the war; and
5. occupy no more than two acres of land.

Maya Lin has been quoted widely offering interpretations of the Wall, as in the May, 1985, *National Geographic,* in which she said: "I didn't want a static object that people would just look at, but something they could relate to as on a journey, or passage, that would bring each to his own conclusions. I had [an] impulse to cut open the earth . . . an initial violence that in time would heal. The grass would grow back, but the cut would remain, a pure, flat surface, like a geode when you cut into it and polish the edge. I didn't visualize heavy physical objects implanted in the earth; instead it was as if the black-brown earth were polished and made into an interface between the sunny world and the quiet, dark world beyond that we can't enter."[4]

Despite the unanimous choice of the committee, many veterans and media analysts thought the Lin memorial was less than satisfactory. On 13 October 1981, a veteran objected to the design at a public meeting of the Fine Arts Commission. Numerous journalistic attacks soon followed, and opposition grew steadily. Secretary of the Interior James Watt sided with those wanting to celebrate a war that had been so recently ennobled by Pres. Ronald Reagan. By January, 1982, a solution to the continuing dispute was reached with the addition of a flagpole and some figurative elements. A review of the 1,421 original designs containing statuary was conducted, and Frederick Hart was subsequently asked to submit another figurative design. His fifteen-inch maquette of three soldiers "looking" toward the wall was unveiled on 20 September 1982. It was approved but its location became another contentious issue that was finally resolved by placing the three eight-foot-tall figures forty yards from the Wall in October, 1984. On 20 October 1982, Hart told the Fine Arts Commission: "I have . . . three goals in mind: first to preserve and enhance the elegant simplicity and austerity of the existing design by Maya Lin; second to create a work which interacts with the Wall to form a unified totality; and finally, to create a sculpture which is in itself a moving evocation of the experience and service of the Vietnam veteran. . . . I see the Wall as a kind of ocean, a sea of sacrifice that is overwhelming and nearly incomprehensible in its sweep of names. I place these figures upon the shore of that sea gazing upon it, standing vigil before it, reflecting the human face of it, the human heart."[5]

Coming to the Wall seems more or less a chance affair. Either one enters it or misses it entirely, although with the addition of the statuary these aspects have altered. For the last ten years or more the first thing seen when entering from the northeast is the stand manned by veterans soliciting support for their comrades who are still missing in action (MIA). There is another stand at the southwestern approach. Many commentators consider these to be part of the monument. It is currently impossible to visit the Wall without encountering veterans. For many, the statues solve the need for a celebration of the soldiery. The soldiers seem to have emerged from the trees and to be contemplating the names inscribed on the memorial. Their look is unheroic; they are tired men, exhausted and stressed. The flagpole is another eighteen yards closer to the Lincoln memorial. Seals of the five armed services (the Coast Guard, Army, Navy, Air Force, and Marine Corps) adorn the base. The additions add a representational dimension but at such distance that they do not totally compromise the memorial. Some have suggested that the threefold aspect of the finished memorial conveys faint echoes of the old and bitter debates about the war.

With or without these echoes, the thrust of the Wall is interrogative. Are the deaths remembered here in keeping with the best traditions of the nation as exemplified by the other monuments? For what and for whom should Americans die in war? Looking at the Vietnam Veterans' Memorial implicates the visitor in these questions, as the reflective granite surface acts as a mirror, mitigating any sense that it is just a tomb. When visitors look at a name, they see themselves reflected back through it. This reflexivity is evident in the many striking photographic images of the memorial, most of which make the point of this specular identification between the living and the dead. This attempts to maintain the Wall's contemporary relevance; but while it may heal, a scar will remain.[6] While Lin's stated design intentions opted for a therapeutic effect in the form of a nonglorifying, unheroic mnemonic, this reflective aspect throws the memorial open to wide political interpretation. That impact has been reduced by the additions and the subsequent contradiction that exists between forms. By effectively introducing the Wall, the entrance plaza and the statues circumscribe Lin's radical execution of a not-so-radical intention with a conservative balm, as if conservative celebration of soldierly heroism (albeit a naturalistic, exhausted heroism) allows the radical gesture. In contrast, the selection and construction of the Australian Vietnam Forces National Memorial (AVFNM) presents a picture of consensual process vindicated.

The Australian Vietnam Forces National Memorial Project

The Australian Vietnam Forces National Memorial Project began in the aftermath of the 1987 Welcome Home March. Interested veterans moved to set up a steering committee that developed into the Australian Vietnam Forces National Memorial Committee, and then looked for participation from various government bodies such as the Departments of Veterans Affairs, Arts, Sports, and Territories, the National Capital Memorial Committee and, notably, the National Capital Planning Authority (NCPA). In the long term, this latter agency acted in a largely administrative and supervisory role, prescribing as essential that the memorial fit within the overall plan not only of Anzac Parade but more widely within the national capital plan itself.

The early steering committee decided on the appropriate location on the western side of Anzac Parade, opposite the Tobruk monument, although the final site provided is opposite the Royal Australian Air Force memorial. At the same time, a committee composed of members from the veterans' groups and the various government agencies and departments developed a set of criteria for the type of design. One major feature of the design was decided early. Unlike the American memorial, which marks the dead and missing, and unlike the other monuments along Anzac Parade that mark specific services or specific localized events such as Tobruk, the AVFNM would be for all those who served and died.

The Australian monument memorializes all those who served in Vietnam, including nonmilitary personnel, with a special aspect devoted only to those who died. Somewhere within the winning design there was to be recognition of the names of the dead, although in what form this recognition was to be made was at that stage still to be determined. What is of importance was that the committee reflected the diverse views of the Vietnam veteran community and those of the other, more "general" committee members. Intentional or not, this breadth ensured that the design finally chosen would not represent the ideological concerns of any narrow faction. The working group of the Memorial Committee that met on 16 August 1989 consisted of five members of the Australian Vietnam Forces National Memorial Committee, two members of the NCPA, two representatives from the Department of Veterans Affairs, and one each from the Australian Capital Territory Administration and the Arts, Sports, Environment, Tourism, and Territories Departments.

This committee chose an assessor panel consisting of five of their own number to which they added two "artistic advisers." Having devised a set of criteria to satisfy their general requirements, an international campaign requesting "expressions of interest" was begun in the press in July, 1989: "The National Capital Planning Authority, acting on behalf of the Commonwealth Government of Australia and the Australian Vietnam Forces National Memorial Committee, invites submissions from suitably qualified persons (Sculptors, Architects, etc.) acting singly or jointly who are interested in the design and execution of a national memorial to the Australian Vietnam Forces."

The competition was to be a limited, two-stage design competition. Submissions would be judged by "a panel of assessors" that included two well-known sculptors, although the panel's composition was not announced publicly for good and sensible reasons. Up to fifteen entrants selected from the initial open-entry field would be invited to submit "stage one" design proposals, for which they would be paid AUS$2,000. Five of the entrants submitting stage-one proposals would then be invited to submit "stage two" entries—in which more detail of the design, including a maquette, would be required—for which they would receive an additional AUS$2,500. The assessors would then submit their choice to the full committee for approval.

Those expressing interest were provided with a full set of design criteria and other relevant information in an eighty-six-page booklet, *National Memorial to the Australian Vietnam Forces: Conditions for a Two Stage Design Competition,* issued by the NCPA in October, 1989. Entrants were asked to provide a written description, together with relevant illustrative material, and in particular to describe the materials to be used, details of the method of construction, and an estimate of the cost, which at 1989 prices was not to exceed AUS$800,000 (roughly U.S.$500,000 at the time). The money would come from public donations, with the balance provided by the government.

With this booklet, the committee stated publicly that it had no preconceptions about the formal aspects of the memorial. It considered only that it "should be a sculpture, being representational rather than abstract in its symbolism," and that the following wording was to be inscribed on the memorial: "For all those who served, suffered, and died. Vietnam 1962–1973."[7] Elaborating on the rationale for and atmosphere desired in the memorial, the committee continued: "The Memorial should reflect on those who died and those who served in the Vietnam conflict, it should depict the environment and conditions in which Australian service personnel served, including the feeling of night, and capture the mood and feeling of that era. Symbolism of the link between the Australian

Vietnam Forces and the original ANZAC Force is also to be expressed in the memorial. Consideration is to be given also to the controversy at home that surrounded Australia's involvement in Vietnam."[8]

It may appear that the committee was setting a fairly tall order. To get all that information, and to be representational too, seemed to demand a great deal, suggesting (as it did to a number of the entrants) not only some kind of paneling on which scenes might be inscribed, but also very strongly the desirability of other figurative elements. However, the committee had more suggestions: "Allowance was to be made within the design for a scroll bearing the names of those who died. . . . Once sealed within the memorial no more names will be added to the scroll. . . . The sculpture should be monumental in scale and compatible with the character of Anzac Parade. Provision should also be made . . . for areas allowing visitors to spend some time in reflection. . . . [The] design, which must have visual legibility, should take full cognisance of future ceremonial activities. . . . For this end it should contain a small forecourt apron area to allow for small gatherings."[9]

The criteria suggested that, consistent with other monuments along Anzac Parade, height might be achieved through small flights of steps, giving the monument prominence. Where the American memorial had, if anything, been underpinned by Spartan design criteria, the NCPA booklet erred on the side of fullness. Although in the long run the plethora of suggestions made may have been as liberating as the few provided to the 1,421 entrants in the United States, the committee's booklet seems determined to leave nothing to chance. The committee added:

> "It is expected that the proposed design may combine figurative and architectural elements, stairs, raised areas, carved inscriptions, appropriate commemorative plaques, relief or three-dimensional sculpture, and flagpoles."[10]

The committee attached to this a substantial package of reference material that included maps, photographs of the other monuments, and a bibliography—these to assist in getting a "fuller [*sic*] understanding of the purpose and significance" of the memorial.[11] The first and one of the key elements in aiding the understanding of prospective entrants was the text of a Dawn Service address given by Brigadier Colin Kahn, DSO, at the Martin Plaza Cenotaph in Sydney on 3 October 1987. In his address, Kahn, a former commanding officer of the 5th Battalion, Royal Australian Regiment, on its second tour and a member of both the full committee and the assessor panel of seven, described a series of mental images that summed up Vietnam for him. The first was of HMAS *Hobart* serving with the U.S. Seventh Fleet off Quang Tri. The second was the "thud thud thud" of the helicopter, which he described as "our sound," and which conjured up visions of No. 9 Squadron RAAF coming out at dawn to pick up infantry at Nui Dat, or to effect "dust-off" (medical evacuation) missions. He described "lumbering" Caribous of No. 35 Squadron at outposts such as Duc Co, Canberra bombers of No, 2 Squadron, and so on. Notably, he concludes his series of images with two of the most telling: "But then I saw *"the man who walked out front,"* the infantryman so many of whom are the men we honour today. I saw a rain and sweat drenched man in green, laden like a pack mule, aged 21 going on 50, cutting his way through jungle by day to find and attack the enemy, then laying all night in paddy fields or on trails in ambush [emphasis in original]."[12] Kahn's final image epitomizes Australia's experience of Vietnam: "Finally, I saw an image . . . I saw TRA BONG VALLEY in 1965 and two isolated Australian Infantry Warrant Officers from our *famous Training Team*. They are under attack—one is dying from his wounds but the other will not leave his mate to the enemy. They are later found dead together [emphasis in original]."[13]

However true these images are of the Australian experience of Vietnam, and who could doubt their veracity, they also suggest a strong undercurrent of accommodation to Anzac symbolism. The "man out front" attempts to localize the specifics of the Anzac icon to the jungles of Vietnam, but it could easily stand in the jungles of New Guinea or Malaya. Kahn's last image is, moreover, redolently Anzac: an image of mateship that entails one's willingness to lay down one's life despite the futility of the action. Behind Kahn's speech lies the image of the First World War "hero" Simpson at Gallipoli, the Rats of Tobruk and "fuzzy wuzzy angels" in Papua.[14] These all owe allegiance to the blend of the soldier and pieta-like images in which Mary, cradling the dead Christ, is symbolically transposed into a dead or dying soldier clasped in his best mate's arms. The obvious religious statues behind these images also have a dramatic paralleling back to Shakespearian images from the earliest historical plays such as *Henry VI* act 3 to Horatio holding a dying Hamlet. In the film *Breaker Morant* (1979), Morant clasps his dead friend in such a pieta. Chauvel's *40,000 Horsemen* (1946) and Peter Weir's film *Gallipoli* (1981) have similar scenes, and many early Anzac memorials are emphatically pietistic. Kahn's image validates the Vietnam experience into the larger Anzac legend largely through this strong image of quiet rather than combative courage.

The rest of the NCPA booklet gives a more detailed description of the processes of the two-stage competition that had evolved from the experience of the NCPA and others in handling earlier competitions for memorials in and around Canberra. For the specific designs to meet such a long-standing and national need, the multiple-stage process allowed the committee wide-ranging input and advisory capacity. Indeed, it was possible for the committee to suggest through the multiple stages how some groups might well adjust their designs for the better by adoption of elements from other designs, without any specific direct reference to those other designs. Of course the committee could not do this directly, but by a process of consistently referring to the guidelines, emphasizing this criterion over that one, it achieved subtle and desired changes within the more favored designs without compromising the integrity of any participant. Contrary to popular belief in the ills of the bureaucratic process, particularly in Canberra, this competition seems a masterful use of compromise and negotiation. It also moved very quickly. Having advertised the competition in July, 1989, preliminary selections had been made by October, when a press release identified the fifteen entrants selected to submit stage-one design proposals.

A total of eighty-eight entries were accepted, and they reflected a wide range of interests and abilities. The committee noted that the spread of entrants covered all the states, included a generous sprinkle of professional sculptors (nine) and architects (six), together with a significant number of entries from veterans (three). The winning fifteen were asked to submit more detail by 8 December, and to make an oral presentation to the committee on 12–13 December. This, it was felt, offered wider explanations than the anonymous and once-off process employed in the United States. Designs that might be intriguing and acceptable on paper at first glance were subject to further explanation and scrutiny through this process of further assessment.

The effects of the committee's long and detailed comments, especially those images pictured in Kahn's address, were reflected in the monumental "vocabulary" of many of the fifteen selections. One entry depicted a "Mound of Silence," a raised space in red polished granite with green surroundings, with side lighting and a feeling of night. In another, helicopters and defoliated trees were used to convey compassion rather than conflict, presumably representing Kahn's dust-off image. The figures in another invited the onlooker to walk among them as if one were talking to the veterans. Indeed, many of the designs were at pains to stress that their emphasis was on contemplation, that despite elements such as helicopters and weapons, their designs were not "aggressive." A number of themes typical of the more general vocabulary of memorials to the dead were evident: eternal flames and columns were typical; crosses were not evident, although one design used the specific effects of sunlight to cast cross-shaped shadows onto its back walls for one hour only per day.

Not surprisingly, both Kahn's "man out front" and the image of mateship in adversity featured in a number of designs. One very impressive design captured most, if not all, of the committee's recommended suggestions and hinted at the trenchlike character of the Washington Vietnam memorial to boot. This design featured a large statue of the "man out front," behind which was a large wall-like structure on which a sculpture of a dust-off crewman was seen lowering a rope. Behind the wall was a trench into which the visitor would walk, symbolically encountering the experience of some aspects of Vietnam. This echoes, without copying it, the sense of wounding in Maya Lin's Washington memorial. On one of the trench walls, but placed so that they could not be touched (a distinction from Lin's Wall), would be twelve bronze panels (one for each year of the war) depicting typical scenes in low relief, with titles such as "Contact Front," "Tunnel Rat," "Reposition 180 degrees," "Short Final," "Main Guns Fire," "You need me here, Doc?" and "The Pain of Separation" covering Kahn's list.

Having selected their list for stage-one proposals, the committee wrote to each entrant and suggested areas in need of clarification and/or modification. Letters containing both general competition and specific information were sent to each of the design teams on 22 December 1989. These recommendations suggest the ways in which the committee cross-pollinated the best elements of selected designs, and the ways in which the committee itself had come to understand the potential of the monumental languages offered to them. To the team of sculptor Ken Unsworth and the architectural firm Tonkin Zulaikha Harford (Unsworth/TZH), which had "submitted a design incorporating three huge stelae rising from a pool and supporting a ring of 500 'floating stones'," the committee recommended that the word *Vietnam* be included, perhaps as a set of large bronze letters at the front, and that the design remove the jets of flame and allow the oft-cited light dappled from both the background canopy and the effects of the ring of suspended stones to simulate the flame. The designers were asked to look again at their intentions to incise the treated inner surfaces of the stelae, and at methods and designs for incorporating unit badges and labels. Most significantly, the committee asked that Unsworth/TZH reduce the scale a little—10 percent was suggested. Last, they were asked to reconsider the external wall cladding, initially suggested as a grid of polished granite tiles.

Compromise is not what the public or a large proportion of the intellectual community considers to be the stuff of great art. Practice, at least in public buildings, works to the contrary. Great art, particularly civic art, is more than likely the stuff of negotiated and often constantly modified gestures between creative and commercial or civil desires. Of course, there can be recriminatory responses to such processes. The Washington Vietnam memorial is one such case in point where the constant bickering and modification of the monument has all but remodeled it into a collage, a truly postmodern monument. In contrast, the Australian National Memorial and the process of its choice was a model of consensus. In part, the focus of this chapter is to demonstrate not merely that the process was consensual, but also that the process as consensus means that the monument itself is the more rich, the more impressive, and just perhaps the more typically Australian for all that. In that emphasis upon the process, I want to suggest, too, that the technical aspects of the selection process as well as their end result—the single chosen design—are not appendages to the monument but become an inherent and coherent part of it. True, visitors to the finished memorial may not see the joins, as it were, but they are there nonetheless, and integral to the monument that will remain. This monument has many creators. It also speaks with many voices, in a fashion that enunciates the many stances about the war both then and now, and for the future when the specific, personal, human dimensions will have faded, if they have not completely disappeared from popular and even family memories.

The Chosen Design Unfolds

Prime Minister R. J. L. Hawke announced the winner of the competition on 3 October 1990. The chosen design was created by the combined team of Ken Unsworth, AM, a well-known and highly regarded sculptor and spatial performance artist, and the relatively youthful architectural firm of Tonkin, Zulaikha, and Harford, with the main work for this brief coming from Peter Tonkin. To this point, this chapter has tracked the documentary pathway of the official competition. It is appropriate now to backtrack, to start another time line charting the Unsworth/TZH pathway to the winning design.

Ken Unsworth reports that although he noticed the advertisement for the monument, it was only in passing, and that initially the project was not of much interest to him. His own style of sculpture, installation work and performance art, owed more to the liberating effects of the tradition of Joseph Beuys. He personally favors sometimes-large collections of suspended objects—mostly stones, but occasionally pianos and other cultural artifacts. He has produced major public works on commission for public space, such as his Nike for the Wollongong City Art Gallery, a ten-ton bronze for Sydney's Darling Harbour Authority, and a large stonework for the Reide Park Art Gallery in Melbourne. Even so, he thought little of the brief until he received two telephone calls from architects suggesting partnerships. The second call, from Peter Tonkin, sparked the partnership.[15]

Driving most of the ideas was Unsworth's desire to create a contemplative place. His interest in the material qualities of stone linked to calming though elevating thought is consistent with his strong love of Romanesque church architecture and its serenely solid spaces. Most of his preliminary sketches demonstrate how much he wanted that space to be inviting, leading the visitor into its monumental interior, a site of comfort and calming. Many of his designs were huge and soaring blocks, pillars or columns in squares and circles, topped by semitransparent "ceilings" of glass or metal or stone, through which the light would filter, dappling the space beneath. Working through dozens of sketches, Unsworth returned to a favored model—the "four-square" model, in which four huge orthogonal stelae rise up from a pool of shallow water and shoot jets of flame. A ring of five hundred stones is suspended from the upper inner sides of these stelae. Inscriptions, ramps, and steps were added to the margins to complete the design. The initial sketches suggest a truly monumental scale, with the stelae rising what seems to be about fifty feet. Unsworth passed these sketches to Tonkin, who worked on the more promising ones. Tonkin was looking for an open, inviting, and involving monument without a strong figurative feel, although that could be a part of it if Unsworth and the committee so desired. Tonkin had more of a building in mind, as did Unsworth.

Tonkin also decided that the stelae model was the most promising. As a preliminary move, Unsworth had made a 1:15-scale chipboard model, but it did not offer enough access. Tonkin made a more modest model, about 1:25 scale, and photographed it from various angles to see how it would look. It was clear that power and strength were the key elements of this design, but it was also seen as rather static, overpowering even, in a word "daunting"—a monument that might overawe rather than calm.

Tonkin decided that the static rhythm of the "four-square" model had to be modified, and this is where the mutually creative effect is at its most powerful. Applied to Unsworth's extraordinary concept, Tonkin's modification is apparently a fundamental one: three stelae instead of four, at once imparting a dynamic, inviting rhythm. Tonkin added more to this, in a brilliant and incisive stroke. Once taken, its elegance speaks clearly. He modified the orthogonality of each of the stela. Where Unsworth's plan called for each stela to lean inward, with a slight tapering at the top margins, Tonkin suggested that each stela be twisted around the vertical plane, wrenching the overall design (best seen from above) into a tight helix, a spiral that sets the whole design in motion. The effect is staggeringly original and brilliant, since not only is the monumental height, the awe, and the calm preserved, but the monument becomes like a building, much as one might wish a church to be (and as Unsworth feels Romanesque space to be), inviting, drawing the eye, and subsequently the feet, ineluctably into the space.

The three-stelae form preserved the suspended five hundred stones so that they formed a constellation some twenty-five feet above the visitor's head. Five hundred stones; five hundred dead. In part an Unsworth signature, the beauty of the suspended stones could not be conveyed by the sketches, or subsequently by the 1:25-scale maquette. They were conceived to add to the play of light through the canopy of trees, adding to the filtered, dappled, forestlike gold and greens.

There was, of course, more to that internal space as well. The three inner walls would be covered with a polished veneer of granite fixed to the stressed concrete slabs at the core of the stelae. On one wall it was envisaged that there would be a photoengraving of a suitable Vietnam scene. Even at the earliest stage, the image chosen by Unsworth/TZH followed Kahn's observations and included a helicopter. On another wall there would be a series of inscriptions capturing the idiom of Vietnam at home and abroad, while the third was to be blank. There was the suggestion of some kind of altar in the middle of the interior on which there would be names of battles, maps, units, a list of the dead. Taken to the committee and subjected to the processes of selection, the design was modified. Unlike the post hoc recriminations and additions to the Washington Vietnam memorial, and the often bitter acrimony with which its construction was greeted, the winning design for the Australian monument was modified over a period of time, both before and after the winning design was announced. Indeed, in the final year of its construction, even after the first sod turning, there were minor modifications.

From 3 October 1990 the basic structural form of the three stelae model was not changed. The most significant changes undertaken during the course of selection and after were the removal of the jets of flame, which would be an unnecessary economic burden; a general reduction in scale of about 10 percent; specifying exactly what would be in the interior, the matters to be engraved or affixed to the inner walls; the nature of the actual surfaces cladding the inner and outer walls; and perhaps most notably, the determination to replace the ring of suspended stones with a suspended polished granite annulus. The suspended stones were among the first desired modifications, and the reason seems to have been that the stones were read as too representational in character. For some veterans, being in a confined space, no matter how monumental, with what appeared to be the effects of a shell burst above them, would be anything but composing and contemplative. Something more symbolic to replace Unsworth's beautiful stones was found. The polished stone annulus is a handsome solution.

As it neared its final stages, the design's surroundings included a ramp up to the monument from Anzac Parade, a set of steps to the right, two exit or circulation ramps to the sides, a large lettered sign reading "VIETNAM" above a wall appropriate for wreath laying to the left, and beside this, flagpoles. The design met most of that list of suggested needs published by the NCPA in 1989.

Inside the monument, the rear stela features an engraved photo wall. The image is a well-known photograph of combat troops boarding helicopters for a patrol insertion. On the right-hand wall, thirty-five quotations and catchphrases "typical" of the war are affixed in steel letters. The selection process for these was a long and difficult one, attempting to choose the more concise and most typical examples from the period. Less happily for some future critics, the subject matter of the quotations will seem sanitized in comparison to what they know of the linguistic practices of the Vietnam era, typical but censored of anything remotely obscene. This is disappointing, if unanswerable in a public monument, since the intention seems to have been otherwise. A 23 July 1990 press release requested interested parties to submit suitable photographs and quotations, one-line sentences in fact. The one-line sentences had to possess a "ring of authenticity of having been written at the time and in colloquial rather than literary style." The release continued: "These quotations will represent to future generations the unique vocabulary developed during the war." As examples, the media release cites dust off, gun line, and gun ship. At the meeting that suggested the public request via the press, the chairman suggested that at least two quotations be included. These were Pres. Richard Nixon's "Peace with honor," and the *Melbourne Age*'s caustic parody, "Peace without honour."

Insistently Australian as the brief is, there is here also a censorship beyond that of the obscenities of men at war. Much that might be included was always unlikely to find enunciation on the inner stela wall, robbing an otherwise polyphonic memorial of further choruses. True, some of those choruses, such as "Free Zarb" (a well-known peace activist), or S[ave] O[ur] S[ons], or the Moratorium movement's "peace-flower" graph, may well be so obscure in a generation or two (as indeed they are now to most Australians under thirty-five), that the need for the memorial to be to some extent self-explanatory selects these quotations, and others like them, out.[16]

But there is a more insistent site of rupture in the elliptical nature of the inscriptions. That Australian emphasis marks the wall as possessing the curious absence of the kind of "big" quotation that might be appended to Australia's Vietnam. At one time in the decision-making process it seemed likely that the two "big" quotations on the wall were to be President Nixon's "Peace with honor," and Prime Minister Harold

Holt's appropriation of the well-established American campaign slogan, "All the way with LBJ." Ironically, the selection processes applied to localize the Australian experience of Vietnam threatened to impose a ventriloquial chorus onto the wall. Of course it would have been reasonable to do so, for it would have captured much of the impetus of the war and its aftermath: how often others have spoken of the experiences of Australians in Vietnam. In the long run, neither of those quotations appeared. Both would acknowledge too far the influence of the United States on an Australian experience. Nixon's appearance on the wall was the bland: "More than ever before TV showed the terrible human suffering and sacrifice of war."

The altar was placed initially in the center of the inner space, but was finally located on the side of the third blank wall. On its top is a map of Vietnam engraved on a bronze plate; the base contains unit badges. A laser-engraved metal scroll containing the names of the dead is sealed in one of the segments of the suspended annulus. Unlike the American monument, no further additions will be made to the Australian list. The scroll will be unreadable, suitable only for the "other" world. In fact, the names of the dead have long been inscribed on the cloister walls of the Australian War Memorial nearby, along with all of Australia's dead from previous wars.

With the announcement of the winner, the two processes met. The committee and the AVFNM group ensured that the design had wide exposure within the veterans' community and the community at large. By 14 September 1990, just before the announcement was made officially, an itinerary was in place for displaying the 1:25-scale model in all states, mostly at Westpac Bank branches, between 7 December 1990 and 25 January 1991. In fact, the model stayed on display until March 1991, and after that time the "selling" of the design was continued through the touring "Nambus" exhibits, updating letters and a pamphlet produced by the AVFNM committee. The pamphlet quotes partially from the description of the design, detailing its rationale and symbolism from the documents the Unsworth/TZH team attached to its submission. In the pamphlet, the design is described as consisting of "three precast concrete forms, tapered and inclined to the centre." These forms are inspired by ancient standing stones and by the classical Greek stelae. Such forms have always symbolized commemoration and contemplation, and remain amongst the most durable and potent of man's creations. It continues:

> the corners of the stelae are open, inviting and providing a passage into the interior. The Stela forms have acutely pointed edges, producing a contrast of shape and scale and

> formalising the emotional response to war. These great 'stones' stand in a shallow pool, forming a cordon against [the] bustle of the outside world which is bridged by the entry ramp and the side stairs . . . The open corners will give glimpses of the more intricate interior, a powerful inducement to stop, to . . . enter, to contemplate, appreciate and remember. . . . The interior fulfills the role of . . . the subtle dramatic centre of the work. It unites directly representational images with abstract symbols in the most powerful and comprehensible fashion.

The description continues, indicating the means of understanding: the photographic image prevents any artistic reinterpretation or distortion, while the "wall of words" educates and focuses visitors' thoughts on the unique language of the war. Most interesting is the way that the modified annulus has been incorporated into the symbolic design. The "roof" formed by a suspended ring of polished black granite segments "denies the physical past, its seemingly disembodied earthliness" recalls the sacrifices made by the individuals who fought and died.

On the morning of 3 October 1992, Governor-General Bill Hayden officially dedicated the Australian Vietnam Forces National Memorial. An estimated 30,000 marched in honor of the memorial, and something like 25,000–30,000 spectators cheered them on for more than three hours. The afternoon saw many unit functions and another concert. The whole day mirrored the 1987 Welcome Home March, and like that march for many it was another major move within the longed for reconciliation. Not for everyone, however. Some veterans chose not to attend, seeing the whole enterprise as conservative and normalizing of the Vietnam experience within ANZAC in ways opposed to their best interests. For many others there was healing and a sense of being home again. Again, curiously for many, it was announced as their first welcome home march. The myths linger.

Reading the Washington Vietnam Memorial as American History

The zone of the Washington Mall and its structures belong to a particular species of recollective architecture, a species in which symbolic and normative content is prominent.[17] War memorials recall struggles to the death over values. Moreover, the architecture by which people memorialize themselves is a species of pedagogy, seeking to instruct posterity about the past, and to do this it must seek to decide what it is that is worth recovering. One cannot then view such memorials on purely aesthetic grounds, nor in isolation from their immediate surroundings—both physically and within the competing political iconographies of those who shaped and are shaped by the monument.

Maya Lin's Wall is located centrally in the Washington Mall, a trapezoidal area defined by the White House (north), the Capitol (east), and the monuments to Lincoln (west) and Jefferson (south). The very center of the Mall is the soaring obelisk of the Washington Monument. The other four may be said to orbit this central spike. The Mall is the place, the sacred site, where the American nation conserves its past, recollects it, honors it, and practices the democratic government within its precincts that these sacrifices have made possible and defended. Indeed, the monuments set up a defensive cordon, as it were, that symbolically defends the nation in the present through the deeds of the past.

It has been argued that the Mall's existence is a tribute to the federalism—the *e pluribus unum*—of American democracy, of the slow and bitter evolution from Washington and the first revolution through the second revolution led by Lincoln during the Civil War. All subsequent events that the controllers of the Mall may choose to honor add to this unfolding narrative of federalism. Within this pattern, C. L. Griswold has argued that the Wall functions interrogatively. The two wings of the Wall point to the two key points of that narrative of revolution—one arc points to the Washington Monument, the other to the Lincoln Monument. The siting of the Wall asks whether Vietnam was fought within the traditions, within the boundaries, of the principles that articulate its arcs. While finding that the Wall is far from neutral, Griswold concludes:

> it neither separates war and politics completely nor proclaims a given political interpretation of the Vietnam War. This accomplishment of the memorial tends to be missed by critics. Differently put, the architecture of the Vietnam Veterans Memorial encourages us to question America's involvement in the Vietnam War on the basis of a firm sense of both the value of human life and the still higher value of the American principles so eloquently articulated by Washington and Lincoln, among others. This is the key to the memorial's therapeutic potential. Because they have failed to understand this, critics of the VVM have held that the Memorial would quickly become a rallying place for all sorts of "anti-American" groups.[18]

Griswold identifies the Wall as a significant example of a long tradition of American monumentalizing of warfare and patriotism. There is no simple glorification; rather the Wall interrogates its self and the virtues of its nation as it laments the dead and reflects on the value and meanings of their deaths. Philosophically so refracted such monuments do not in any sense wave their flags with less than careful attention to the moral details and indeed the morale of the wars they remember. As Griswold implies, such monuments are indeed admirable. The question is whether the Australian process and site allowed an Australian variation of the admirable or something else.

Anzac Parade: A Not So Celestial Axis of a Nation?

Anzac Parade in Canberra was envisaged as one of the key axes of architect Walter Burley Griffin's plans for the avenues and circuits of the nation's capital, and as such it can be read as a syllogism of the kind through which Griswold reads the Washington Mall. The longest and widest avenue in the city (indeed the largest open feature in any Australian city), Anzac Parade directly links Capital Hill and the Parliamentary Triangle with the War Memorial and Mount Ainslie beyond it, covering two miles including the lake. And pace Griswold, it offers this narrative: that Parliament's capacity to govern the federated states was founded in and proven in the blood sacrifice of the early nation's youth in the forges of Gallipoli and the subsequent engagements of the western front and throughout the Second World War.

The site of the Vietnam memorial is roughly in the middle of the avenue on the western side. The full sweep of the two miles of avenue and its trajectory across the lake, the width of the avenue (some 180 yards), and the height of the blue-gum canopy (fifty to seventy feet) means straightforwardly that the Vietnam memorial, like all its companions, will not dominate the Parade. Its size is commensurate with the character of the space and the masses of those enclosing buildings and trees. It fits snugly into its niche, not projecting too far out of the canopy as to be noticeable well before approaching it from the north or south, while from the front, approaching it walking west, it sits snugly back into the canopy. That is not to say that it is not a massive and inspirational building. It is. Also, by comparison with the other monuments, it is a more substantial building. Most of the others are either variations on the soaring obelisk or spire or figurative groups, large but not overwhelming. Despite this, the Vietnam memorial does not dominate the avenue. From a distance, only the thin edge of the leading two stelae are visible. In comparison with the relationships inhering between monuments in the Washington Mall, interconnection is less evident physically along Anzac Parade since each monument is snugly self-contained. They become a sequence of incidents along the boulevard rather than an ensemble perceived in its entirety at one glance.

It is difficult to read the sweep of Anzac Parade from the War Memorial to Parliament House as a consistent narrative without viewing the fragmentary effects of the detours required for each niche. Nor does the placement of the monuments form anything like a chronological sweep from the War Memorial to Parliament or back again. There is no sense in which Anzac Parade reads chronologically from at least the mythical national foundation at the War Memorial to contemporary practice at the new Parliament House site. Rather it is of a fragmented, almost unrelated, set of incidents, at best brought together by an actual physical tour of the avenue, such as occurs on Anzac Day when service personnel marching along the avenue toward the War Memorial forecourt concatenate the events of the past into the present, rolling up the human elements of each niche's history, and extrapolate that into the national future.

That conflationary effect is limited perhaps to the grand occasion, or to the individual who walks the avenue, linking his or her own biography to the particular elements of each niche. As a whole and for most of the time, the elements within each niche are fragments of a history, and symbolic or allegoric fragments at that, conveying only partial histories. In a peculiar fashion, the impetus for Maya Lin's metaphor of the Wall as a wounded earth, her hope that it might heal, comes to serve the fragmentary nature of Anzac Parade. The country whose war memorials do not add up to a totalizing inclusive narrative is perhaps the better for this, as they will not have a tradition of military behavior to fall back upon without at least some interrogation.

This last judgment is in part a pipedream, prompted by some of the readings of the Wall that have attempted to find a humane unity, but have left themselves in a deeply flawed conservative position that fosters the very wars the memorial and the readings eschew. A pipedream, since Australia does have a military tradition that, however fragmentary, is appealed to in a constant major key along the length of the eponymous Anzac Parade. But a pipedream perhaps the less useless if the comments of Unsworth/TZH, from the descriptive statement in their 20 September 1989 brief, come to any fruition in the acceptance of the monument. They perceived the monument as having both a symbolic and a civic role:

> The Memorial is conceived as an open structure, not a closed centralized object. Whilst presenting a monumental, archetypal exterior form, it has at its centre a resonant contemplative space. This enables the creation not only of a memorable emblematic object which will come to symbolize in an actual

> image the collective Australian memory of Vietnam, but also of an interior which in its tangible form will recall the physical experience of Vietnam . . . The final solution is a ring or halo of stainless steel, floating in constantly changing shafts of light and shadow . . . the halo denies the physical past, its seemingly disembodied earthliness recalls the sacrifices made by the individuals who fought and died. Endlessly becoming, the halo is air and light.

This seems to be crux of the design. Where the Wall acknowledges a past event—its names become the memorial Maya Lin offers—the other chronological movement it makes derives from its metaphoric status as a wound gradually healing, a gash for some, a grave for others. But whether of shame or not, written large is Lin's desire for it to be seen as part of, even the impetus for, a healing process. In that sense, the names will soon become merely static, their ceremonial, listing, incantatory effect will tend to remove the focus from the event to the men. The Unsworth/TZH memorial is more inclusive, certainly honoring the personnel but by a means of endlessly becoming, its emphasis is not upon the past but upon the present of the contemplative visitor. One aspect of monuments may well be the notion of glorification of the dead; exalting a nation to lament its loss, to be sure, but more centrally to celebrate its national bloodline, much as the monuments to earlier wars, especially those to the Great War, seem to do. In that sense, the location of Maya Lin's Wall within the historically refracted "text" of the Washington Mall is stylistically and symbolically no longer at odds with its context. As the kind of reading here proposed demonstrates, the Washington Wall closes Vietnam, despite Griswold's case that it is interrogative. For those who do not approve of the war, the names will fade. For those who do, the sentence of the Wall is a consistent pattern within the impetus of *e pluribus unum,* from Washington's monument itself to Lincoln's monument and all that this memorial "text" conveys.

Read against this impetus, the Unsworth/TZH monument is thankfully not speaking the language of typical war memorials. Its place in the narrative of Australian military history may yet speak with a discordant plurality.

These are not readings that many who visit the Canberra Vietnam memorial may well perceive or accept, and not simply on the grounds that they have not seen the Washington Vietnam memorial. Indeed, the selection committee seems to have been thoroughly consistent in its attempts to introduce a substantial element of the Anzac tradition, and equally, though not with any necessarily conscious object in mind, to keep the Australian design as far from emulating, imitating, or even remotely echoing the Washington memorial. In a curious fashion, that sub-/unconscious desire to suppress the Wall forced its intrusion into Anzac Parade. No student of Vietnam could read the Australian monument without comparing and contrasting it with the American model. In such circumstances, the winning design, whatever its provenance, is influenced by the other. That this is so cannot be proved directly except insofar as my readings and presentations of the "facts" of the selection process detect the suppressions. However, with the collateral effects of the very strong emphasis upon the Australian-ness of the finished monument, there is perhaps indirect proof of my assertion. Simply put, the image of the helicopters and the Australian troops engraved on the inner back wall speaks of that structure of alliance—of major power and client state. It is true, as Brigadier Kahn observed, that the helicopter was as much "our" sound of the war as it was the Americans'. Indeed, it seems to be almost everybody's sound of Vietnam. But it might also be remembered that many of the sounds of Vietnam were the sounds of America's technological behemoth at work; much of the imagery of the war, even that served to Australians in Australia, was American. Yet the monument tries to be almost emphatically Australian, and in the helicopter image above all. There is no visible insignia on the machine. The original photograph archived in the Australian War Memorial shows clearly that the machine is a U.S. Huey with definite and clear insignia. That is not surprising: the allies fought closely and shared such routine operations as this often.

The erasure of this evidence may be seen as a distortion much like those in American histories of the war in which there is no recognition of the participation of any allies (save stereotypically incompetent South Vietnamese forces), let alone the Australians. Some elements in Australia remember the Vietnam War as largely an American war in which Australian participation was as so much lickspittling to big brother. This is an error. It was in many ways Australia's war, and on a near equal footing of political necessity—not, to be sure, technologically or financially, but it was and needs to be recognized as Australia's war, too, both politically and ethically (even if this latter means that it opened inherent dissent and the threat of permanent rift within the community). That said, it was Australia's war under the purview of America's military power. Those structures remain to be considered in more detail in the wider community, more in need now, nearly thirty years after the war and in the wake of East Timor perhaps, than less. It thus is not surprising that it got little shrift in the memorial process, and that the final design made little reference to the larger ally, save perhaps for that watered down Nixon quotation. It is in the nature of the pendulums of alliance that we may come to despise that which we have perceived to need most for support. Australia's memorial response to Vietnam began in part with an impetus derived from the American models of the Welcome Home March and the Wall. Our veterans wanted their space and their acknowledgements, too. It is hard to blame them for that. Nor would it be sensible to point a caustic finger at the memorial design for having touched the upswing of the pendulum, in which the former great ally is all but erased from "our" war so that the stigma of his defeat will not tarnish our service.

APPENDIX

A Select Chronology of Australian Involvement in the Vietnam War

1950	14 January	Ho Chi Minh declares Democratic Republic of Vietnam.
	7 February	United States and United Kingdom recognize the French-sponsored government of the former emperor, Bao Dai.
	8 February	Australia recognizes Bao Dai Government.
	9 March	Percy Spender, minister of external affairs, speaks of the domino theory in the House of Representatives.
	8 May	United States provides $10 million in military and economic aid to the Bao Dai Government.
1951		ANZUS treaty signed.
1953		Jean Letourneau, French Minister in charge of Indochinese matters, invited to visit Australia to discuss aid.
1954		John Foster Dulles, U.S. secretary of state, encourages "united action" during the Indochina crisis.
	7 May	Battle of Dien Bien Phu lost by the French and Bao Dai forces.
	8 September	South East Asia Treaty Organisation (SEATO) formed with initial signatories: United States, United Kingdom, France, Australia, New Zealand, Pakistan, Thailand, and the Philippines.
	9 October	France leaves Hanoi.
1955		United States provides aid directly to Saigon; Australia sends troops to aid in Malayan Emergency.

1957	May	Ngo Dinh Diem, president of South Vietnam, visits United States.
	September	Ngo Dinh Diem visits Australia.
1960	20 December	National Liberation Front (NLF) is founded by Hanoi for the liberation of South Vietnam.
1961		Laotian crisis.
		Indonesia incorporates former Dutch West New Guinea colony as Irian Jaya.
	17 November	United States seeks diplomatic indications of Australia's stance on, and willingness to assist in, South Vietnam.
1962		Very Low Frequency "joint" U.S.-Australian naval communications station established at North West Cape, Western Australia.
	13 January	Operation Ranch Hand (defoliation) begins.
	24 May	Athol Townley, Minister of Defence, announces that thirty advisers are to be sent to South Vietnam.
	July-August	First AATTV personnel arrive in South Vietnam.
1963		Malaysia formed.
		Indonesia declares Confrontation with Malaysia.
	1 June	William Francis Hacking, an adviser, is the first Australian casualty, killed forty miles west of Hue.
		15,000 U.S. advisers in South Vietnam; U.S. gives $500 million in aid.
1964		83 Australian advisers committed to the Republic of Vietnam.
	June	Robert Menzies, Australian prime minister, visits Washington, D.C.
		AATTV members committed to active service.
	2 August	USS *Maddox* incident in the Gulf of Tonkin.
	4 August	USS *Turner Joy* incident.
	7 August	U.S. Congress passes Tonkin Gulf Resolution.
	10 November	National Service (Conscription) Act proclaimed.

1965	January	Agent Orange first used.
	March	U.S. Marines land at Da Nang.
	29 April	Menzies announces the commitment of Australian combat troops.
	May-June	1st Battalion, RAR (800 men), arrives in Bien Hoa to operate with the U.S. 173rd Airborne Brigade (Separate).
		U.S. troop commitment surpasses 50,000.
	13 May	Save Our Sons (SOS) founded.
	23–24 July	First Australian "teach-in" on Vietnam at the Australian National University, Canberra.
	September	Morgan Gallup Poll: 56 percent of Australians in favor of Australian participation, 28 percent in favor of withdrawal, 10 percent are undecided.
	22 October	First arrests (65 people) for antiwar demonstration in Sydney.
1966	26 January	Harold Holt succeeds Menzies as prime minister and leader of the Liberal Party.
	8 March	Government announces troop increase: two battalions and supporting units, and the Special Air Services, to be sent to Phuoc Tuy Province—a total of 4,500 men, including 500 conscripts.
	16 March	2,000 march in protest against the war organized by the SOS group.
	May	Seamen's Union refuses to load supplies for Vietnam on the *Boonaroo*.
	24 May	Errol Wayne Noack (first conscript) killed in action.
	14 June	5th and 6th Battalions, RAR, and supports in place at Nui Dat, with logistic support base at Vung Tau, 16 miles south.
	21 June	Attempted assassination of Arthur Calwell, leader of the Opposition, after an antiwar demonstration in Sydney.
	30 June	Holt visits Washington, D.C., and utters in a speech the famous "all the way" in support of Lyndon Johnson's Vietnam policy.
	18 August	Battle of Long Tan: Australia loses 18 killed, claims 245 Vietnamese killed.

	September	Arrest of schoolteacher William White, a conscientious objector.
	21–22 October	Lyndon Johnson visits Australia. A million Sydneysiders and 500,000 in Melbourne line the streets to welcome him on successive days.
	19 November	Morgan Gallup Poll: 68 percent in favor of conscription; 37 percent in favor of sending conscripts to Vietnam.
1967	8 February	E. G. "Gough" Whitlam succeeds Arthur Calwell as Opposition leader.
	May	Morgan Gallup Poll: 62 percent in favor of the war, 24 percent in favor of Australian withdrawal, and 14 percent are undecided.
	2 October	Teach-in titled "National Forum on Vietnam" held at Monash University, Melbourne.
	17 November	Holt missing presumed drowned. John McEwan (Country Party—the Liberals' coalition partner) temporarily becomes prime minister on 19 December.
	November-December	Australian troop commitment peaks at 8,300.
1968		Australian Draft Resister's Union established.
	10 January	John Grey Gorton, Liberal Party leader, becomes prime minister.
	31 January	Tet Offensive begins.
	12 February	Gorton announces semiofficially that there will be no increase in Australian commitment.
	16 March	My Lai massacre occurs but remains unknown until 16 November.
	May	National Services Act amended to impose two-year civil jail term for draft evaders.
	August	Paris student riots.
1969	June	President Richard Nixon announces withdrawal of 250,000 U.S. troops and the initiation of "Vietnamization."
	August	Morgan Gallup Poll: 55 percent in favor of with-

		drawal, 40 percent for continuing the war, and 6 percent are undecided.
	3 September	Ho Chi Minh dies at age 79.
	4 October	U.S. Morgan Poll: 58 percent believe the war is a mistake.
	15 October	Massive antiwar demonstration occurs in Washington, D.C.
1970	22 April	Government announces one battalion to be withdrawn.
	4 May	Kent State shootings in Ohio.
	8 May	Approximately 120,000 march in the first Moratorium March in Sydney; approximately 70,000 march in Melbourne.
	18 September	Second Moratorium Marches in Sydney (100,000) and Melbourne (50,000). More than 300 arrested.
1971	10 March	William McMahon succeeds as Liberal Prime Minister.
	30 March	1,000 men withdrawn.
	30 June	110,000 participate in third and final large antiwar march.
	18 August	McMahon announces that most troops will be home by Christmas.
	17 December	Last major troop withdrawal.
1972	2 December	Australian Labor Party wins. Whitlam becomes prime minister–elect.
	5 December	National service ended; imprisoned draft resisters released.
	8 December	Last Australian troops leave Vietnam.
	18 December	Last Advisers leave. Nixon renews bombing of Hanoi and Haiphong.
1973	23 January	Nixon announces "peace with honor."
	27 January	Cease fire initiated.
	26 February	Whitlam announces establishment of diplomatic relations with Hanoi, but continues diplomatic recognition of South Vietnam.

	29 March	Last American troops leave Vietnam.
1974	4 January	South Vietnam's Pres. Nguyen Van Thieu announces that war has been declared again.
1975	17 April	Phnom Penh falls to Khmer Rouge.
	25 April	Australian embassy in Saigon is closed.
	30 April	Fall of Saigon.
	December	Malcolm Fraser, Liberal leader, wins election.
		1,000 Indochinese refugees resettled in Australia.
1976	April	First Vietnamese "boat people" arrive in Australia.
1978		Fraser government introduces refugee component into immigration program.
1982		Arrival of the first Vietnamese migrants under the Orderly Departure Programme.
		Vietnam Veterans Counselling Service established.
1983	June	4,000 U.S. veterans begin class-action suit in New York State against the manufacturer of Agent Orange.
		Justice Philip Evatt charged with the Royal Commission to investigate the mortality of veterans.
1984		AVHS mortality report published.
1985	July	Evatt Royal Commission declares Agent Orange "Not Guilty"; Vietnam Veterans Association rejects findings.
1987	4 October	25,000 March in Sydney Welcome Home March.
1989	July	At the Geneva Conference on refugees, Australia votes with ASEAN nations for the mandatory repatriation of Vietnamese refugees. Australia is committed to resettle 11,000 people during 1989–1992.
	June-July	First Cambodian boat people arrive in Australia.

1990		Two more Cambodian boats arrive.
1992	3 October	Dedication of the Australian Vietnam Forces National Memorial, Anzac Parade, Canberra; 30,000 veterans march, watched by a crowd of about 30,000

NOTES

Introduction

1. For examples of these government reflections, see Desmond Ball, "The Official History of Vietnam and its Critics," *Quadrant* 37, no. 11 (Nov., 1993): 40–44; and Gregory Pemberton, "The Vietnam War and its Supporters," *Quadrant* 8, no. 4 (Apr., 1994): 51–52.
2. A corrective and more thoroughly documented version of the actual qualities of Australian horsemen in the Boer War can be found in the various essays in Peter Dennis and Jeffrey Grey, eds., *The Boer War: Army, Nation and Empire, 1999, Chief of Army/Australian War Memorial Military History Conference* (Canberra: Army History Unit, 2000). Notwithstanding the "history," the popular view of Australians in the Boer War through such "personalities" as poet/soldier Breaker Morant contributed to the developing legends of Australian fighting prowess and indiscipline.
3. This should be pronounced with a hard ess, as in "Ozzie," rather than as it so often is in the United States with a soft ess, as in "Ossie." Contraction is a favorite word creation device with Australians and has worked to minimize even Aussie, so that the hard ess gives rise to the identification of Australia as "Oz."
4. Until very recently, Korea has been *the* "forgotten war" despite what Vietnam veterans argue. For some analysis of the lapse of memory, nostalgia, and the history of the forgotten war see Peter Dennis and Jeffrey Grey, eds., *The Korean War 1950–53: A 50 Year Retrospective. The Chief of Army's History Conference 2000* (Canberra: Army History Unit, 2000), particularly Jeff Doyle, "Another Forgotten War Remembered," 179–99. In the volumes *Vietnam Days* (1991) and *Vietnam: War, Myth, and Memory* (1992), Peter Pierce, Jeffrey Grey, and Jeff Doyle address the issues of Vietnam and memory.

Chapter 1

1. This chapter summarizes some of the principal themes of Peter Edwards, *Crises and Commitments: The Politics and Diplomacy of Australia's Involvement in Southeast Asian Conflicts, 1948–1965,* the first volume of the official history of Australia's involvement in the Malayan Emergency, the Malaysian-Indonesian Confrontation, and the Vietnam War. In this chapter sources will be given only for direct quotations. The full references for the other material cited can be found in that volume.
2. Minute, Sir John Bunting to Sir Robert Menzies (quoting advice from Plimsoll), 13 Apr. 1965, CRS A1209, 65/6365.
3. Francis Stuart, *Towards Coming of Age: A Foreign Service Odyssey* (Nathan, Queensland: Centre for the Study of Australian-Asian Relations, Griffith University, 1989), 143.
4. The different spelling of *Labor* and *Labour* noted here between political parties of apparently similar persuasions rests with the Australian party's decision to use the spelling to differentiate, perhaps even distance itself, from other such parties.
5. See the coverage of this visit in the *Sydney Morning Herald,* 17–26 Apr. 1950.
6. Cabinet decision 241, 15 May 1962, CRS A494011, C4643, pt. 1.
7. *Commonwealth Parliamentary Debates,* H of R vol. 43, 13 Aug. 1964, 194.
8. Melbourne *Herald,* 12 May 1962.
9. Cabinet decision 204, 1 May 1962, CRS 4940/1, C3568.

10. C.V. Wedgwood, *William the Silent* (London: Jonathan Cape, 1967), 35.
11. Message, McEwen to Harold Wilson (with cover letter from Lawler to Oliver), 19 Jan. 1965, CRS A4940/1, C1473, pt. 2.

Chapter 2

The author wishes to thank Ashley Ekins and Col. David Chinn (Ret.) for their research assistance.

1. Robert J. O'Neill, *Australia in the Korean War, 1950–1953,* vol. 1, *Strategy and Diplomacy* (Canberra: Australian War Memorial and Australian Government Publishing Service, 1981), 404.
2. Ibid., 21.
3. "Defence Policy, The Vote and The Programme," D.P.C. Agendum no. 31, 28 Jan. 1954, AHQ file 23/441/55.
4. Other member nations were Great Britain, France, New Zealand, Pakistan, Thailand, and the Philippines.
5. Carlyle A. Thayer, *War By Other Means: National Liberation and Revolution in Viet Nam 1954–1960,* 192.
6. Estimates of the number killed have varied between 10,000 and 15,000, with a further 100,000 deported or imprisoned (many of whom were later released). See Joseph Buttinger, *Vietnam: A Dragon Embattled* (New York: Praeger, 1967), 912, 914, 974. A more recent source puts the number executed at closer to 5,000 (Thayer, *War By Other Means,* 93).
7. Le Duan, *Letters to the South* (Hanoi: Foreign Language Publishing House, 1986), 27.
8. Buttinger, *Vietnam,* 975. Buttinger is unable to estimate the number killed, but believes the official figures of 20,000 to 30,000 put into concentration camps were too low (ibid., 977).
9. Thayer, *War By Other Means,* 161.
10. Binh Gia Hinh Nam Bo, Communist Party paper, c. 1960, 32, as quoted in Thayer, *War By Other Means,* 192.
11. Jeffrey Race, *War Comes to Long An: Revolutionary Conflict in a Vietnamese Province* (Berkeley: University of California Press, 1972), 122.
12. Cabinet Decision no. 654, Feb., 1957.
13. For a full account see J. C. Blaxland, *Organising an Army: The Australian Experience, 1957–1965.*
14. Cabinet Decision no. 451 (FAD), 3 Sept. 1964.
15. Cabinet Decision no. 596, 5 Nov. 1964.
16. "AHQ Training Directive for 1963/64 and 1964/65," ARO 25/62, 21 Dec. 1962, Army Office Secretariat, Army Office.
17. AHQ letter 846-R1–1, 16 May 1963, Army file 846-R1–1, Army Office.
18. AHQ file A810-R1–13(1), Army Office.
19. The history of this force is contained in Ian McNeill, *The Team: Australian Army Advisers in Vietnam, 1962–1972.*
20. J. K. Waller, Australian ambassador, Washington, to Acting Minister for External Affairs, cable 3365, 4 Dec. 1964, AWM 121, DMO&P file 161/A/2.
21. The referenced cable actually stated "one division OR two battalions of American marines." In JPC Report no. 110/64, 11 Dec. 1964, AWM 121, DMO&P file 161/A/2 the assumption is stated that "or" should read 'and'. Later correspondence indicates that "and" was correct.
22. Waller to Acting Minister for External Affairs.

23. Comments by Wilton and senior staff on minute from Secretary for Defence to the Chairman, Chiefs of Staff Committee, and the Service Chiefs, 7 Dec. 1964, enclosing cables from Waller and Long, AWM 121, DMO&P file 161/A/2.

24. National Intelligence Board Report, Oct., 1964, summarized in *The Pentagon Papers: The Defense Department History of United States Decisionmaking on Vietnam,* Senator Gravel ed., vol. 3 (Boston: Beacon Press, 1971), 425.

25. Joint Intelligence Committee Report 3/1964, 21 Oct. 1964, 2; and Joint Planning Committee Report 110/1964, 11 Dec. 1964, 3, both in AWM 121, DMO&P file 161/A/2.

26. NSC Working Group on Vietnam, "Section 1: Intelligence Assessment: The Situation in Vietnam," 24 Nov. 1964. The assessment observed that "the tactical direction of VC efforts is in effect provided by North Vietnamese officers on detachment to the South—consequently any orders from Hanoi would in large measure be obeyed by the forces in South Vietnam" (Document 240, *Pentagon Papers,* 653).

27. NSC Working Group on Vietnam, "Section 1."

28. CIA-DIA Memo, "An Assessment of Present VC Military Capabilities," 21 Apr. 1965, *Pentagon Papers,* 438; Adm. U.S. G. Sharp and Gen. W. C. Westmoreland, *Report on the War in Vietnam (As of June 1968)* (Washington, D.C.: GPO, 1969), 95; Gen. W. C. Westmoreland, *A Soldier Reports* (Garden City, N.Y.: Doubleday, 1976), 105; Lt. Gen. P. B. Davidson, *Vietnam at War: The History, 1946–1975* (London: Sidgwick and Jackson, 1988), 324, 325.

29. Davidson, *Vietnam at War,* 324.

30. Race, *War Comes to Long An,* 108.

31. Brigadier O. D. Jackson, interview, 9 Mar. 1972, Sydney, 27, AWM 107, AHQ file 707/R2/39.

32. "Aid to South Vietnam," Joint Planning Committee Report no. 110/64, 11 Dec. 1964. The committee was required to consider, in conjunction with the Joint Intelligence Committee, both an anticipated American request for two hundred advisers and the question of stationing ground forces near the DMZ. See JPC Addendum no. 172/1964, 9 Dec. 1964, AWM 121, DMO &P file 161/A/2.

33. Revised paper by William Bundy and J. McNaughton, "Summary: Courses of Action in Southeast Asia," 26 Nov. 1964, *Pentagon Papers,* 656; Robert S. McNamara, "United States Policy in Vietnam," in Department of State Bulletin, 13 Apr. 1964, *Pentagon Papers,* 713.

34. McNamara, "United States Policy in Vietnam," 713.

35. Ibid.

36. Pham Van Dong, "Report to the Second Session of the Third National Assembly," 8 Apr. 1965, in *Selected Writings* (Hanoi: Foreign Languages Publishing House, 1977), 144; Le Duan, "Excerpt from the Report of the Meeting of Representatives of the Communist and Workers' Parties in November 1960 in Moscow to the Third Session of the Viet Nam Workers' Party Central Committee in December 1960," in *Selected Writings,* 17.

37. Paul M. Kattenburg repeated a widely accepted view when he wrote that the communist leadership during the Vietnam War "survived and won out largely because, from the start, it draped itself in the mantle and championed the cause of Vietnamese nationalism" ("The U.S. and Indochina: Then and Now," *Australian Outlook* 42, no. 2 [Aug., 1988]: 88).

38. Le Duan, "Excerpt from the Report," 14 (quotation), 25; Le Duan, *Letters to the South,* 25; Pham Van Dong, "Excerpts from the Report to the 6th Session of the National Assembly, 29 April 1963," in *Selected Writings,* 70; Pham Van Dong, "Report to the Second Session," 92, 147–50; Ho Chi Minh, *Patriotism and Proletarian Internationalism* (Hanoi: Foreign Languages Publishing House, 1979), 149, 154.

39. Pham Van Dong, "Report to the Second Session," 148.

40. Le Duan, "Excerpt from the speech delivered to the 9th session of the Vietnam Workers' Party Central Committee held in December 1963," in *Selected Writings,* 158–60. North Vietnam's solidarity with China and the Soviet Union, certainly at the time of writing in 1963, seemed not to be affected by the 1961 Sino-Soviet rift.

41. Ibid., 158.

42. The "lips and teeth" expression was used commonly at the time. Examples of the analogy are found in Pham Van Dong, "Report to the Second Session," 85; and Le Duan, "Excerpt from the speech," 159. Chinese utterances are found in Chen Yi, Foreign Minister of the People's Republic of China, reproduced in *The People of Vietnam Will Triumph! U.S. Aggressors Will Be Defeated* (Peking: Foreign Language Press, 1965); and "Resolution of the Third National People's Congress of the People's Republic of China adopted 20 Apr. 1965," ibid., copies with Official History (OHU) papers in the Australian War Memorial.

43. McNamara, "United States Policy in Vietnam," 713. Pham Van Dong, "Report to the Second Session," 150. See also Le Duan, *Letters to the South,* 20.

44. "Military Assistance to South Vietnam," Defence Committee Minute no. 37/1964, 21 May 1964, 4. AWM121, DMO&P file 161/A/2.

45. As a token and somewhat reluctant gesture, but to provide some positive response, an additional seventeen advisers were offered to bring the total strength of AATTV to one hundred.

46. Vo Nguyen Giap, *Big Victory, Great Task* (London: Pall Mall Press, 1968), 5–7. Local communist historians Pham Ngoc Danh, Tran Quang Toai, Dong Nai saw the battle similarly. See *30 Years War of Liberation, 1945–1975,* Executive Committee of the Dong Nai Province Branch of the Communist Party of Vietnam (Hanoi: Dong Nai Publishing House, 1986), 26. "Special war" was the terminology given by the Communists to the warfare waged by the RVN with US advisers before the introduction of US and allied combat forces.

47. Westmoreland, *Soldier Reports,* 110.

48. Cabinet Decision no. 659 (FAD), 17 Dec. 1964. Defence file 248/4/100 TS 1752, Department of Defence.

49. Prime Minister to President Johnson, 18 Dec. 1964, Defence file 248/4/100, TS 1752, Department of Defence.

50. Sharp and Westmoreland, *Report on the War in Vietnam,* 95.

51. J. Shulimson and C. M. Johnson, *U.S. Marines in Vietnam: The Landing and the Buildup, 1965* (Washington, D.C.: History and Museums Division, USMC, 1978), 4, 6.

52. Ibid., 7.

53. Republic of Vietnam armed forces were responsible for the defense of the air bases, but their effort was found to be inadequate and uncoordinated (Roger P. Fox, *Air Base Defense in the Republic of Vietnam, 1961–1973* [Washington D.C.: Office of Air Force History, 1979], 16). For a discussion of the measures that led the United States into assuming the responsibility for defense of the major air bases, see 11–23.

54. The initial role was "to occupy and defend critical terrain features in order to secure the airfield and, as directed, communications facilities, U.S. supporting installations, port facilities, landing beaches and other U.S. installations against attack. The U.S. Marine force will not, repeat will not, engage in day to day actions against the Viet Cong" ("Marine Combat Units Go To Da Nang," *Pentagon Papers,* 417).

55. The marine force was the 9th Marine Expeditionary Brigade (9th MEB). It initially consisted of two battalion landing teams (BLTs) built around the 1st Battalion, 9th Marines (BLT 1/9), and 3rd Battalion, 9th Marines (BLT 3/9). Battalion

landing teams were a combined-arms team composed of an infantry battalion with a battery of artillery, tanks, trucks, amphibian tractors, and engineers and other support—about 1,500 men. The 1st Battalion, 3rd Marines (1/3), based on Okinawa, replaced BLT 1/9 for the deployment to Da Nang. Thus the first two infantry battalions to move to Da Nang were 1/3 (by air) and 3/9 (by sea). The total strength of the initial Marine force at Da Nang was almost 5,000 troops. Brigadier General Frederick J. Karch commanded the brigade. By December, 1965, the Marine ground contingent in South Vietnam numbered more than 38,000 men, all assigned to Maj. Gen. Lewis W. Walt's III Marine Amphibious Force (Shulimson and Johnson, *U.S. Marines in Vietnam,* xi, 3, 6, 7, 9, 15).

56. "Marine Combat Units Go To Da Nang, March 1965," *Pentagon Papers,* 417.

57. Australian Embassy, Washington, to Defence Department, Canberra, message WA 63, 6 May 1965, Defence file 248/4/114, TS 1794, Department of Defence. Douglas Pike, a leading American historian of the Vietnam War, comes to similar conclusions. He claims that the most important point to make about the American formulation of strategy is that the nation first committed itself to the war and then began to think about it comprehensively ("Conduct of the Vietnam War: Strategic Factors, 1965–1968," in *Second Indochina War Symposium: Papers and Commentary,* ed. John Schlight [Washington, D.C.: Center of Military History, U.S. Army, 1986], 112). Pike also maintains that Hanoi's leaders did not have a clear understanding, either. For grand strategy it substituted a "blind, implacable faith in its cause to which it clung tenaciously" (ibid., 119 n 9).

58. External Affairs to Australian Embassy, Washington, cable no. 883, 9 Apr. 1965, 2, Defence file 248/4/111, TS 1784, Department of Defence.

59. Sir Robert Menzies, *Commonwealth Parliamentary Debates,* H of R, 29 Apr. 1985, 1060, 1061.

60. "Further Military Assistance to South Vietnam," Defence Committee Minute 15/1965 of meeting on 5 Apr. 1965, dated 6 Apr. 1965, AWM 121, DMO&P file 161/A/3.

61. J. Plimsoll, Minute, 28 Apr. 1965, Defence file 248/4/111, TS 1784, Department of Defence. This episode, its likely causes, and its ramifications were analyzed by the Australian official historian, Peter Edwards, in the *Sydney Morning Herald,* 6 June 1989, 19.

62. *Sydney Morning Herald,* 6 June 1989, 19.

63. "Strategic Basis of Australian Defence Policy," Defence Committee Minute no. 75/1964, 16 Oct. 1964, AWM 121, DMO&P 11/A/2.

64. As a matter of military prudence, SEATO contingency plans provided for the advent of military aggression by China.

65. "Strategic Basis of Australian Defence Policy," para. 37.

66. "Notes for the Minister for Defence," Defence file 248/4/116, TS 1796, Department of Defence.

67. Arthur Calwell, *Commonwealth Parliamentary Debates,* H of R, 4–26 May 1965, 1103, 1105

68. AAFV Quarterly Report to 30 Sept. 1965, 6, AHQ file 723/R5/18, Army Office. An additional five Australian journalists flew to Vietnam.

69. "A Troopship Leaving Sydney," *Sydney Morning Herald,* 28 May 1965, 2.

70. Le Duan, "To Comrade Xuan," May, 1965, in *Letters to the South,* 27. Xuan was secretary of the Central Office South Vietnam (COSVN).

71. Gen. Sir John Wilton, interview, 9, 13, and 14 Sept. 1976, Canberra, 16; Lt. Gen. Sir Thomas Daly, interview, 22 Nov. 1974 and 4 June 1975, Sydney, 12, AWM 107; Lt. Gen. Sir John Wilton, CGS, to Air Chief Marshal Sir Frederick Scherger, CCOSC, Minute CGS 126/1965, 20 July 1965, AWM 121, DMO&P file 161/A/4.

72. The only exception to this occurred with the formation of self-contained battle groups during the four years of the Pentropic organization.

73. Lt. Gen. Sir John Wilton, CGS, to Air Chief Marshal Sir Frederick Scherger, CCOSC, CGS 57/1965, 25 Mar. 1965, AWM 121, DMO&P file 161/A/3.

74. Wilton to Scherger, 20 July 1965; Wilton interview.

75. Wilton to Scherger, 20 July 1965.

76. Minute no. 6/1966 by the Defence Committee at a meeting on 10 Feb. 1966, "South Vietnam—Australian Military Assistance," 13, Defence file 248–4-145, AWM 121.

77. Such requirements included withdrawing from what Australian commanders might consider to be foolhardy or ill-considered operations ordered by the U.S. command, and not being involved in operations that closed on or crossed international boundaries.

78. Wilton interview.

79. A listing of the criteria for the selection of a province and the base area within the province is contained in Ian McNeill, "An Outline of the Australian Military Involvement in Vietnam July 1962–December 1972," *Defence Force Journal*, Sept.-Oct., 1980, 42–53.

80. In November, 1965, the port of Saigon had a three-week backlog of shipping. The U.S. secretary of defense, Robert S. McNamara, after a visit to Saigon that month, described the logistic problems being faced by American troops in Vietnam as "massive." During recent fighting in one area, the near exhaustion of fuel supplies was a major factor in forcing American troops to ease off their pressure on the enemy (Australian Embassy, Washington, to Foreign Affairs, cable 8653, 30 Nov. 1965, Defence file 248/4/138).

81. The following sources were used for evidence concerning the selection of Phuoc Tuy Province: Brigadier Mackay to CGS, "Report on Visit to South Vietnam by DMO&P," 27 Dec. 1965, AWM 121, DMO&P file 161/A/5; Presentation by Maj. Gen. K. Mackay at CGS Exercise, 1971, 11, 12, AWM 101 (10); Wilton interview, 24–26; Maj. Gen. K. Mackay, interviews, 8 Mar. 1972, 10–13, and 9 Oct. 1987, AWM 107; Jackson interview, 9 Mar. 1972, 44, 45. As commander of Australian forces in Vietnam in 1965, Jackson states that General Walt, commander of the III Marine Amphibious Force based at Da Nang in northern I Corps, asked that the Australian Task Force join the marines. Although Walt seemed enthusiastic, the suggestion did not appear to receive serious consideration.

82. The Long Dat provincial committee in former Phuoc Tuy Province in 1988 consisted mostly of former Vietcong. When interviewed by the author they said this assessment was about correct except that the divisional headquarters was not formed until May, 1967.

83. This last proposal, put forward by the defense minister, was not put into effect. The AATTV was fully integrated into the American advisory system and deployed principally in I Corps. In the years that followed, some argued that more of the team should be deployed in Phuoc Tuy Province under the command of the task force. No major move into Phuoc Tuy occurred until the closing stages of the task force's presence, although the team was spread over the whole of South Vietnam. Even when members moved into Phuoc Tuy, they were not placed under task force command or "embodied" into the task force (McNeill, *The Team*, app.: "Australian Army Training Team Vietnam—Moves to Concentrate Team in Phuoc Tuy"). The Caribou were under command of the U.S. 834th Air Division and were used throughout South Vietnam on transport and resupply missions. It would have been wasteful to place them under task force command, especially as resupply from the Australian logistics base at Vung Tau and the task force base in Phuoc Tuy was only twenty miles by road.

84. Cabinet Decision no. 60, 2 Mar. 1966, AWM 121, Defence file 248/4/145.

85. Ibid.
86. Jackson interview, 9 Mar. 1972, 45–51; presentation by Brigadier Jackson to CGS Exercise 1971, AWM.
87. Jackson to CGS Exercise 1971.
88. Wilton interview, 26, 27.
89. Lt. Gen. Sir John Wilton to Air Chief Marshal Sir Frederick Scherger, CGS Minute no. 39/1966, 21 Mar. 1966, AWM 121, DMO&P file 161/A/6.
90. Frank Frost, *Australia's War in Vietnam,* 181, 71, 182 (in order of quotations).
91. Ibid., 181, 182.
92. Ibid., 65.
93. Ibid.
94. Greg Lockhart, "Fear and Dependence: Australia's Vietnam Policy, 1965–1985," 21.
95. Greg Lockhart, "Into Battle: Counter Revolution," 38–59.
96. Maj. Gen. C. M. I. Pearson to OHU, 20 Apr. 1990, OHU papers.
97. Ibid.
98. Maj. Gen. C. M. I. Pearson, interview, 7 Apr. 1972, Canberra, 23, AWM 107.
99. Pearson to OHU, 20 Apr. 1990.
100. Ibid.
101. Ibid.
102. Brigadier R. L. Hughes, interview, 24 Mar. 1972, Canberra, AWM 107.
103. Presentation by Brigadier O. D. Jackson to CGS Exercise 1971, AWM101 (10).
104. Mackay, interview, 8 Mar. 1972, 23, 25.
105. Lt. Col. R. R. Hannigan (former GSO2 [Ops], to Brigadier Jackson), interview, 20 Sept. 1989, Sydney, 37, OHU papers.
106. Ibid., 38.
107. Jackson to CGS Exercise 1971, AWM101 (10).
108. Lockhart, "Into Battle," 57.
109. Robert J. O'Neill, *Vietnam Task: The 5th Battalion, Royal Australian Regiment, 1966–67.*
110. Ibid., 181, 182.
111. Capt. R. J. O'Neill, "An Analysis of the Operational Experience of 5 RAR in Vietnam May–Dec 1966," 4 Jan. 1967, copy in OHU papers.
112. D. M. Horner, *Australian Higher Command in the Vietnam War,* 76.
113. Ibid., 79.
114. Lt. Gen. T. J. Daly, CGS 44/1967, 6 Mar. 1927, AHQ file 569/R4/43, Department of Defence.
115. Pearson to OHU, 20 Apr. 1990.
116. There was also a battalion in Malaysia.
117. As occurred during a briefing of Westmoreland at the task force base at Nui Dat in early 1967. Westmoreland was obviously impatient and irritated by the methodical extension of the secure area and separation of the guerrillas from the population favored by Jackson rather than aggressively pursuing the main force in depth (Lt. Col. A.W. Piper [GSO2 (Int) to Brigadier O. D. Jackson], interview, 26 Feb. 1990, Canberra, 5, OHU papers).
118. One writer suggests Wilton was "timid," but this does not take into account the extent of Wilton's determination and the strength of his convictions (Horner, *Australian Higher Command in the Vietnam War,* 72).

119. Wilton interview, 30.
120. Maj. Gen. D. Vincent to Lt. Gen. T. J. Daly, 15 July 1967, AWM 101 (24), box 3. Vincent was COMAFV after Mackay.
121. Wilton interview, 34.
122. Frank Frost, "Conflict and Withdrawal, 1968–1972," 109.
123. Maj. Gen. D. B. Dunstan, interview, 4 Oct. 1973, Canberra, AWM 107.
124. Frost, "Conflict and Withdrawal."
125. Dunstan interview, 11.
126. Ibid.
127. Lt. Col. Nguyen Duc Thu, interview, 20 June 1988, Long Dat, Vietnam, OHU papers.
128. See Jane Ross, "Australia's Legacy: The Vietnam Veterans," 187–213.
129. Little has been written on the roles of either the RAAF or the RAN in Vietnam, although the balance lies with the air force. This addendum is drawn from what in the main there is: Jeffrey Grey, *Up Top: The Royal Australian Navy and Southeast Asian Conflicts, 1955–1972;* Chris Coulthard-Clark, *The RAAF in Vietnam: Australian Air Involvement in the Vietnam War, 1962–1975;* and Alan Stephens, *Going Solo: The Royal Australian Air Force 1946–1971.*

Chapter 3

The literature on anti–Vietnam War activism in Australia is in some areas fairly extensive, although varied in both quality and focus. The bibliography in this volume will guide the interested reader to relevant items. Here I have been content to provide specific references only for specific points or quotations within the text. By way of contrast, Peter Pierce argues in chapter 4 for a dearth of relevant material in the more literary genres.

1. See, for example, Bobbie Oliver, *Peacemongers: Conscientious Objectors to Military Service in Australia, 1911–1945* (Fremantle: Fremantle Arts Centre Press, 1997); and Hugh Smith, "Conscience, Law and the State: Australia's Approach to Conscientious Objection since 1901," *Australian Journal of Politics and History* 35, no. 1 (1989): 13–28.
2. The literature on conscription in the First World War is extensive. See F. B. Smith, *The Conscription Plebiscites in Australia, 1916–1917* (Melbourne: Melbourne University Press, 1966); and L. L. Robson, *The First AIF: A Study of Its Recruitment* (Melbourne: Melbourne University Press, 1970).
3. Stuart Macintyre, *The Reds: The Communist Party of Australia from Origins to Illegality* (Sydney: Allen and Unwin, 1998).
4. His arguments are developed at length in Edwards, *Crises and Commitments,* especially chaps. 15, 18, and 19.
5. See Terry H. Anderson, *The Movement and the Sixties: Protest in America from Greensboro to Wounded Knee* (New York: Oxford University Press, 1995).
6. For a discussion of the rise and decline of the Moratoriums, see Peter Edwards, *A Nation at War: Australian Politics, Society and Diplomacy during the Vietnam War, 1965–1975,* chaps. 12–14.
7. Ann Curthoys makes the point that the timing of demonstrations was increasingly coordinated with those in the United States after 1967 ("The Anti-War Movements," 93).
8. This is not to imply that the media by itself had a war-winning—or war-losing—impact on middle America, as some right-wing critics profess to believe. The issue of media impact is much more complex than much of this analysis allows, and most of its assertions have not been tested and probably cannot be proved in any case.

9. Kim Beazley, "Federal Labor and the Vietnam Commitment," 55.
10. Adam Garfinkle, *Telltale Hearts: The Origins and Impact of the Vietnam Antiwar Movement* (New York: Macmillan, 1995), 201.
11. Ann Curthoys, "'Shut Up, You Bourgeois Bitch': Sexual Identity and Political Action in the Anti–Vietnam War Movement."
12. Curthoys, "Anti-War Movements," 101–103.
13. Garfinkle, *Telltale Hearts,* 265–98.
14. This is one of the central themes in Robin Gerster and Jan Bassett, *Seizures of Youth: "The Sixties" and Australia.*
15. Peter Cochrane, "At War at Home: Australian Attitudes During the Vietnam Years," 185.
16. Curthoys, "'Shut Up, You Bourgeois Bitch,'" 332–33.
17. Charlotte Clutterbuck, "Protests and Peace Marches: From Vietnam to Palm Sunday."

Chapter 4

1. David Caute, *Sixty-Eight: The Year of the Barricades* (London: Hamish Hamilton, 1988).
2. Michael Hyde, ed., *It is Right to Rebel;* Michael E. Hamel-Green, "The Resisters: A History of the Anti-Conscription Movement, 1964–1972."
3. Bob Buick with Gary McKay, *All Guts No Glory: The Story of a Long Tan Warrior.* See also the selected bibliography in this volume.
4. Gerster and Bassett, *Seizures of Youth,* 1.
5. Frank Crowley, *Tough Times* (Melbourne: William Heinemann, 1986).
6. Geoffrey Dutton, ed., *Australia's Censorship Crisis* (Melbourne: Sun Books, 1970).
7. Roberto Rabel, "The Vietnam Antiwar Movement in New Zealand" (unpublished paper in the author's possession).
8. Patricia Dobrez, *Michael Dransfield's Lives: A Sixties Biography* (Melbourne: Miegunyah Press, 1999).
9. Brian Kiernan, "Perceptions 1915–1965," in *The Penguin New Literary History of Australia,* ed. Laurie Hergenhan (Ringwood: Penguin, 1988).
10. Donald Horne, "Introduction," in Michael Boddy and Robert Ellis, *The Legend of King O'Malley* (Sydney: Currency Press, 1974).
11. Jack Hibberd, *Three Popular Plays* (Melbourne: Outback Press, 1976), 5.
12. Peter Pierce, "Revaluing Australian Legends: Some Plays by Jack Hibberd," *Australian Literary Studies* 8, no. 3 (May, 1978).
13. Kiernan, "Perceptions 1915–1965."
14. This material is drawn from an unpublished article by David Nadel.
15. In 2000–2001, "Khe Sanh" is one of the chosen "battle" songs of the Australian cricket team apparently sung in dressing rooms after victories.
16. Thomas Pynchon, *Vineland* (London: Secker and Warburg, 1990).
17. Alan Gould, *The Enduring Disguises.*

Chapter 5

1. See, among numerous others, Gary McKay, *Vietnam Fragments: An Oral History of Australians at War;* Greg Langley, *A Decade of Dissent: Vietnam and the Conflict on the Australian Home Front;* Glen D. Edwards, *Vietnam: The War Within: Australian, American, New Zealand;* Barry Dickins, *Ordinary Heroes: Personal Recollections of Australians at War;* Stuart Rintoul, ed., *Ashes of Vietnam: Australian Voices;* Brian

Hennessy, *The Sharp End: The Trauma of a War in Vietnam;* Alistair Thomson, *Anzac Memories: Living with the Legend* (Melbourne: Oxford University Press, 1994).

2. For a more substantial discussion of the newer types of "history" with special regard to film, see Robert A. Rosenstone, *Revisioning History: Film and the Construction of a New Past* (Princeton, N.J.: Princeton University Press, 1995). For a wider scope, see Jeff Doyle, "The New (Film) Histories," in *Our Selection On: Writings on Cinemas' Histories,* ed. Jeff Doyle et al. (Canberra: National Film and Sound Archive/ADFA, 1998), 3–20.

3. For examples, see Jane Ross, "The Myth of the Digger in Australian Society"; and Jeff Doyle, "Bringing Whose War Home? Vietnam and American Myths in Australian Popular Culture."

4. See chap. 4 in this volume.

5. But see Seymour M. Hersh, *Against All Enemies: Gulf War Syndrome: The War Between America's Ailing Veterans and Their Government* (New York: Ballantine, 1998).

6. For more detail on the history of the VVAA, see Jane Ross, "Veterans in Australia: The Search for Integration," *Vietnam Generation* 3, no. 2 (1991): 50–73; Ambrose Crowe, *The Battle after the War: The Story of Australia's Vietnam Veterans;* Stephen Garton, *The Cost of War: Australians Return.*

7. See Ross, "Veterans in Australia," 50–73.

8. Ibid.

9. From December, 2000, to early 2001, major exhibitions at the Australian War Memorial and at the Australian National Gallery, both in Canberra, were devoted to Federation celebrations. The AWM focused on the way the imagery and history of the digger helped define the Australian identity and "forge" (one of the key terms) the reality of Federation. The more wide-ranging exhibition at the National Gallery provided many images of the bushmen and the digger as "icons" (a buzzword for representational markers) of national identity.

10. As recently as September, 1999, six veterans were "belatedly" awarded medals for gallantry after years of lobbying (*Canberra Times,* 2 Sept. 1999, 5).

11. Keith Beattie, *The Scar That Binds: American Culture and the Vietnam War* (New York: New York University Press, 1998).

12. For more detail on this section, see Ross, "Australia's Legacy," 199–204; John Dux and P. J. Young, *Agent Orange: The Bitter Harvest* Hodder and Stoughton, Sydney, 1980; and Crowe, *The Battle after the War.*

13. *Royal Commission on the Use and Effects of Chemical Agents on Australian Personnel in Vietnam,* vol. 8, 38.

14. Ibid., vol. 4, 399.

15. Ross, "Veterans in Australia."

16. *Australian,* 12–13 May 1990.

17. For a comprehensive study of the Repatriation system, see Clem Lloyd and Jacqui Rees, *The Last Shilling: A History of Repatriation in Australia.* Additional details specific to Vietnam veterans can be found in Ross, "Veterans in Australia," and "Australia's Legacy." A brief summary is given by one of the then commissioners, Maj. Gen. A. L. Morrison, "Repatriation," in *The Shock of Battle,* ed. Harry Heseltine, Occasional Papers 16 (Canberra: University College [ADFA], 1988), 117–22. In "Veterans in Australia," Ross notes that "the Repatriation System was established in Australia during the First World War. In fact, the commonly used term "Repat" is misleading, as the series of legislative acts are more concerned with social security than with the return of soldiers to their home country. "Repat" includes disability and service pensions, health services, home loans, workforce retraining, etc. The system has undergone changes over the years, and was most recently revamped in 1986 when the various acts were consolidated into the *Veterans Entitlement Act.* The Department of Veterans Af-

fairs (DVA) administers the system. At times, the DVA has been accused of being unsympathetic and obstructionist toward veterans, which is not surprising given that the DVA and veterans are frequently in an adversarial situation, with the veterans trying to show cause for the DVA to release funds, and the DVA guarding the public monies against what it sees as unfounded claims."

18. Administrative Appeals Tribunal, *Repatriation Commission v. Maree Smith* (1990), V 87/56.

19. *Case Control Study of Congenital Abnormalities and Vietnam Service.*

20. Australian Veterans Health Studies, *The Mortality Report,* pt. 1, *A Retrospective Cohort Study of Mortality Among Australian National Servicemen of the Vietnam Conflict Era, and an Executive Summary of the Mortality Report.*

21. The Royal Commission version of PTSD included the following symptoms: flashbacks to terrifying events, nightmares, irritability, rage reaction, dizzy spells, anxiety, insomnia, depression, guilt feelings, headaches, low back pain, ulcer, migraine, irritable bowel syndrome, irritable colon, hypertension, paranoia, suspicion, crowd phobia, and alcoholism (*Royal Commission,* vol. 8, 23–24). See also Jeffrey Streimer and Christopher Tennant, "Psychiatric Aspects of the Vietnam War," 230–61.

22. For more detail on this section, see Ross, "Australia's Legacy."

23. *Australian,* 10–11 Oct. 1987.

24. *Sydney Morning Herald,* 2 May 1987.

25. A thirty-minute documentary, *The Last March,* produced by Martyn Goddard et al., was broadcast by the Australian Broadcasting Corporation in 1988. For more comments on this documentary, see Doyle, "Bringing Whose War Home?" 97–141.

26. For another discussion of the dislocation of Australia in Vietnam that specifically uses the concept of the "funny place," see Peter Pierce, "'The Funny Place': Australian Literature and the War in Vietnam," in *Vietnam Generation* 3, no. 2 (1991): 98–108.

27. Peter Pierce charts similar patterns in his discussion of American literary influences in chapter 7 of this volume.

28. See Tom O'Regan, "The Enchantment with Cinema: Film in the 1980s," in *The Australian Screen,* ed. Albert Moran and Tom O'Regan (Ringwood: Penguin, 1989), 118–45.

29. It is worth noting the collateral evidence of Australian reaction to Vietnamese and other Asian refugees as detailed in James Coughlan, "International Factors Influencing Australian Governments' Responses to the Indochinese Refugee Problem," *Vietnam Generation* 3, no. 2 (1991): 84–97.

30. For a more complete history and analysis of the design and building of the Australian Vietnam Forces National Memorial, see chapter 8 in this volume.

31. The exhibition began as a Web site for the Australian Art of the Vietnam Experience virtual gallery, a project directed by Jeff Doyle designed to collect any and all images of the Australian involvement in Vietnam and its aftermath in virtual space, and where feasible as actual art, in order to halt the loss of this material. See: http://idun.itsc.adfa.edu.au/SOE/VIETNAM/vietnam.htm.

32. Following the publication of *Vietnam Days* in 1990, I was confronted personally at a seminar by, among others, Graham Walker, one of the chief archivists and writers of VVAA (internal) history. Fundamentally, I was challenged to "put up or shut up" about how "our" book had presented the veterans' case. (The author of the chapter that caused greatest offense in this regard, Jeffrey Grey, was also challenged by the VVAA in the letters pages of the *Bulletin.* He explained that he was engaged in history, not advocacy.) I accepted the challenge and spent some time at the VVAA Granville Branch with Tim McCombe, then serving as president of the New South Wales Branch. I have been given copies of almost

all the submissions, and have had access to much VVAA documentation and scientific papers on Agent Orange. My own position, I maintain, has always been one of sympathy, tempered by a "professional distance."

33. See Garton, *Cost of War.* See also, Pierce et al., eds., *Vietnam Days,* passim.

34. F. B. Smith, "Agent Orange: The Australian Aftermath," in Brendan O'Keefe and F. B. Smith, *Medicine at War: Medical Aspects of Australia's Involvement in Southeast Asian Conflicts, 1950–1972,* 283–363.

35. Crowe, *Battle after the War.*

Chapter 6

1. Douglas Pike, "Vietnam: Thinking About It Today," *Asia Record,* Feb., 1982, 2–7.

2. Bill Gammage, *The Broken Years: Australian Soldiers in the Great War* (Canberra: Australian National University Press, 1974 and subsequent editions); Patsy Adam-Smith, *The Anzacs* (Melbourne: Nelson, 1984 and subsequent editions).

3. See especially Gerald R. Stone, *War Without Honour;* and Ian Mackay, *Australians in Vietnam.*

4. (R. G. Neale), "Australia's Military Commitment to Vietnam" (paper tabled in the H of R, 13 May 1975). Professor Neale was director-general of the Australian Archives at the time.

5. Evan Whitton, "The Final Decision: A Battalion Instead of Instructors," *National Times,* 28 Apr., and 5 and 12 May 1975. See also "The Role Menzies Played in Vietnam," *National Times,* 22 May 1978. The latter was essentially a rehash of the earlier material, published after the death that year of Robert Menzies, the prime minister who led Australia into the war.

6. Michael Sexton, *War for the Asking: Australia's Vietnam Secrets.*

7. Peter King, ed., *Australia's Vietnam: Australia and the Second Indochina War.*

8. The best example is Lloyd Robson at Melbourne University, whose *The First AIF: A Study of its Recruitment 1914–1918* (Melbourne: Melbourne University Press, 1970) was a direct consequence of Robson's antiwar activism.

9. Barry York, *Student Revolt: La Trobe University 1967–73* (Canberra: Nicholas Press, 1989), and "Police, Students and Dissent: Melbourne, 1966–1972," *Journal of Australian Studies* 14 (May, 1984): 58–76; Hamel-Green, "The Resisters," 10–28; Kenneth Maddock, "Opposing the War in Vietnam—the Australian Experience," 137–49; Clutterbuck, "Protests and Peace Marches," 135–47; Ann Curthoys, "Mobilising Dissent: The Later Stages of Protest," 138–63. Summy, York, and Hamel-Green also wrote doctoral dissertations on Vietnam protest.

10. Malcolm Saunders, "The ALP's Response to the Anti–Vietnam War Movement: 1965–73," *Labour History* 44 (May, 1983): 75–91; "'Law and Order' and the Anti–Vietnam War Movement, 1965–72," *Australian Journal of Politics and History* 28, no. 3 (1982): 367–79; "The Trade Unions in Australia and Opposition to Vietnam and Conscription," *Labour History* 43 (1982): 64–82; "Australia's Withdrawal from Vietnam: The Influence of the Peace Movement," Social Alternatives 1, nos. 6–7 (1980): 56–62; and "Opposition to the Vietnam War in South Australia, 1965–73," *Journal of the Historical Society of South Australia* 10 (1982): 61–71. Saunders also wrote a masters thesis on antiwar activism.

11. Cochrane, "At War at Home," 165–85; Gerster and Bassett, *Seizures of Youth.*

12. Langley, *Decade of Dissent,* xi.

13. But see Sue Langford, "The National Service Scheme, 1964–1972," appendix in Edwards, *Nation at War,* 355–80.

14. Gregory Pemberton, *All the Way: Australia's Road to Vietnam;* Glen St. J. Barclay, *A Very Small Insurance Policy: The Politics of Australian Involvement in Vietnam 1954–1967.*

15. Lex McAulay, *The Battle of Long Tan: The Legend of Anzac Upheld; The Battle of Coral: Fire Support Bases Coral and Balmoral, May 1968; Contact: Australians in Vietnam;*

and *The Fighting First: Combat Operations in Vietnam, 1968–69: The First Battalion, The Royal Australian Regiment;* Bob Breen, *First to Fight: Australian Diggers, NZ Kiwis and US Paratroopers in Vietnam, 1965–66;* Terry Burstall, *The Soldiers' Story. The Battle of Xa Long Tan, Vietnam, 18 August 1966;* Gary Mackay, *In Good Company: One Man's War in Vietnam; Delta Four: Australian Riflemen in Vietnam;* and *Vietnam Fragments;* Barry Petersen with John Cribben, *Tiger Men: An Australian Soldier's Secret War in Vietnam;* John Shaddock Gibson, *Foxhound: Australian Infantry on Operations South Vietnam, 1967–68.*

16. O'Neill, *Vietnam Task;* Michael O'Brien, *Regulars and Conscripts: With the Seventh Battalion in Vietnam.*

17. Frost, *Australia's War in Vietnam;* Frost, "Conflict and Withdrawal"; Lockhart, "Into Battle."

18. Ian McNeill, "The Australian Army and the Vietnam War," 11–61.

19. David M. Horner, *Duty First: The Royal Australian Regiment in Peace and War,* chaps. 9–11; *SAS, Phantoms of the Jungle: A History of the Special Air Service,* chaps. 11–21; and *The Gunners: A History of Australian Artillery,* chap. 20. Of note as well is his *Australian Higher Command in the Vietnam War.*

20. McNeill, *The Team.*

21. Richard Bushby, *Educating an Army: Australian Army Doctrinal Development and the Operational Experience in South Vietnam, 1965–1972.*

22. C. E. W. Bean, *Official History of Australia in the War of 1914–1918,* 12 vols. (Sydney: Angus and Robertson, 1921–42); Gavin Long, *Australia in the War of 1939–1945,* 22 vols. (Canberra: Australian War Memorial, 1951–77); Robert J. O'Neill, *Australia in the Korean War, 1950–1953,* 2 vols. (Canberra: Australian War Memorial and Australian Government Publishing Service, 1981, 1985).

23. Peter Edwards, *Crises and Commitments,* and *Nation at War.*

24. Ian McNeill, *To Long Tan: Ground Combat Operations in Vietnam, 1962–66;* Coulthard-Clark, *RAAF in Vietnam;* Grey, *Up Top.* The medical history also treats Australian military medicine in three conflicts. See Brendan O'Keefe with F. B. Smith, *Medicine at War: Medical Aspects of Australia's Involvement in Southeast Asian Conflicts, 1950–1972.*

25. Peter Dennis and Jeffrey Grey, *Emergency and Confrontation: Australian Military Operations in Malaya and Borneo, 1950–1966.*

26. McNeill's second and the final series volume has been delayed by that author's sudden and premature death. It will be published by Allen and Unwin of Sydney as Ian McNeill, *A Province for a Battlefield: The Australian Army in the Vietnam War, 1967–72.*

27. John Murphy, *Harvest of Fear: A History of Australia's Vietnam War.*

28. Note that historically Australian usage has been to refer to such people as "returned servicemen" or servicewomen, or simply as "returned men." The Americanism "veteran" only came into popular usage after Vietnam.

29. The best example is Rintoul, ed., *Ashes of Vietnam.* See also Martin Cameron, *Australia's Longest War,* a book that is almost impossible to categorize.

30. Terry Burstall, *A Soldier Returns: A Long Tan Veteran Discovers the Other Side of Vietnam,* is a "therapeutic" book that evinces some serious flaws when it attempts to relate individual experience to wider issues. Kenneth Maddock, ed., *Memories of Vietnam,* is equally confused in relating cause and effect.

31. John J. Coe, ed., *Desperate Praise: The Australians in Vietnam.* Gary Mackay's participant-histories, with their robust assertion of what might be characterized as traditional soldierly values, have found a ready market in the 1990s.

32. Ross, "Australia's Legacy," 186–213, and "Veterans in Australia," 50–73; Jeffrey Grey, "Anzac, Vietnam, and the Veteran," 63–96. The latter attracted a hostile response from the national executive of the VVAA. See "Flak," *Bulletin,* 20 Aug.

1991, 9–10, and reply, ibid., 15 Oct. 1991, 15. On the other hand, a number of Vietnam veterans told me that they thought the VVAA's stance in general was "too self-pitying" and essentially counterproductive.

33. Rodney Tiffen, "News Coverage of Vietnam"; Lyn Gorman, "Television and War: Australia's Four Corners Program and Vietnam, 1963–1975," *War & Society* 15, no. 1 (May, 1997). Gorman points out that analysis of Australian television for content and balance in this period is made more difficult, where not impossible, by the widespread habit of reusing expensive commercial videotape on which programs were initially recorded for broadcast.

34. K. S. Inglis, *This is the ABC: The Australian Broadcasting Commission, 1932–1983.* Melbourne: Melbourne University Press, 1983.

35. An exception to this, one that involves a comparison with the Canadian public broadcaster, CBC, is Neville Petersen, "The Coverage of the Vietnam War in an Organisational Context: The ABC and CBC Experience," *Australian-Canadian Studies* 16, no. 2 (1998): 33–47.

36. Clyde Cameron, *The Cameron Diaries* (Sydney: Allen and Unwin, 1990), 801. The remark reflected a popular belief in the Australian Labor Party that postwar migrants from the Baltic states had voted against Labor because of the anticommunism engendered by Soviet occupation of their homelands. For reasons never adequately explained, Whitlam's government extended official recognition of the Soviet incorporation of these countries in July, 1974, which largely confirmed that antagonism. Cameron was the minister for industrial relations.

37. Nancy Viviani, *The Long Journey: Vietnamese Migration and Settlement in Australia; The Indochinese in Australia, 1975–1995: From Burnt Boats to Barbecues;* and "After the War was Over: Vietnamese in Australia," 215–31; Coughlan, "International Factors," 84–97.

38. Roberto Rabel, "'The Most Dovish of the Hawks': New Zealand Alliance Politics and the Vietnam War."

39. David McCraw, "Reluctant Ally: New Zealand's Entry into the Vietnam War," *New Zealand Journal of History* 15, no. 1 (1981): 49–60; and "The Demanding Alliance: New Zealand and the Escalation of the Vietnam War," *Australian Journal of Politics and History* 34, no. 3, 1989): 308–19; Ministry of Defence, *The New Zealand Army in Vietnam, 1964–1972* (Wellington: New Zealand Army, 1973); S. D. Newman, *Vietnam Gunners: 161 Battery RNZA, South Vietnam, 1965–71.*

40. Gary R. Brooker, *Two Lanyards in Vietnam;* Deborah Challinor, *Grey Ghosts: New Zealand Vietnam Vets Talk About Their War;* Michael Subritzky, *The Vietnam Scrapbook: The Second ANZAC Adventure;* Ian Macfarling, "New Zealand and the Vietnam Conflict," [Australian] Defence Force Journal 79 (Nov.-Dec., 1989): 8–19; Keith Sinclair, ed., *The Oxford Illustrated History of New Zealand* (Auckland: Oxford University Press, 1990).

Chapter 7

1. John Keegan, *The Face of Battle* (London: Jonathan Cape, 1976), 62.

2. Frank Moorhouse, *The Americans, Baby* (Sydney: Angus and Robertson, 1972), 58.

3. "David Alexander" [Lex McAulay], *When the Buffalo Fight.*

4. Robert Ludlum, *The Bourne Ultimatum* (London: Grafton, 1990), 121.

5. John Rowe, *Count Your Dead.*

6. Ibid., 99, 105, 108, 112, 113.

7. Paul Fussell, *The Great War and Modern Memory* (London: Oxford University Press, 1975), 312.

8. C. D. B. Bryan, "Barely Suppressed Scream," *Harper's,* June, 1984, 68.

9. David Morrell, *First Blood* (London: Barrie and Jenkins, 1972); Robert Stone, *Dog Soldiers* (London: Secker and Warburg, 1975); Newton Thornburg, *Cutter and*

Bone (London: Heinemann, 1976); James Webb, *Fields of Fire* (London: Granada, 1976); Peter Straub, *Koko* (London: Penguin, 1988); Michael Connelly, *The Black Echo* (London: Orion, 1993).

10. David Williamson, *Jugglers Three;* C. J. Cairncross, *The Unforgiven;* Gabrielle Lord, *The Sharp End.*
11. Michiko Kakutani, "Novelists and Vietnam: The War Goes On," *New York Times Review of Books,* 15 Apr. 1984, 8, 26, 39, 41.
12. Michael Peterson, *A Time of War* (London: Mandarin, 1990); John M. Del Vecchio, *The 13th Valley* (New York: Bantam, 1982).
13. Stephen Wright, *Meditations in Green* (New York: Charles Scribner's Sons, 1983).
14. Tim O'Brien, *Going After Cacciato* (London: Jonathan Cape, 1978).
15. Jack Fuller, *Fragments* (New York: William Morrow, 1984).
16. Michael Frazer, *Nasho,* 142.
17. Graham Greene, *The Quiet American* (London: Heinemann, 1955).
18. John Carroll, *Token Soldiers,* 142.
19. Michael Herr, *Dispatches* (New York: Knopf, 1977).
20. Del Vecchio, *13th Valley.*
21. Stephen Phillip Smith, *American Boys* (New York: Avon Books, 1975), 345.
22. Christopher Buonanno, *Beyond the Flag* (New York: Tower Publications, 1984).
23. Pollard, *Cream Machine,* 77.
24. Jeffrey Walsh, *American War Literature: 1914 to Vietnam* (London: Macmillan, 1982), 5.
25. Ernest Hemingway, *A Farewell to Arms* (New York: Scribners, 1929).
26. A. D. Horne, ed., *The Wounded Generation: America After Vietnam* (Upper Saddle River, N.J.: Prentice Hall, 1981), 163–64.
27. Greene, *Quiet American.*
28. James F. Mersmann, *Out of the Vietnam Vortex: A Study of Poets and Poetry Against the War* (Lawrence: University Press of Kansas, 1974), 207, 210.
29. Del Vecchio, *13th Valley,* 258, 510.
30. Gustav Hasford, *The Short-Timers* (New York: Harper and Row, 1979).
31. Frazer, *Nasho,* 258.
32. Hasford, *Short-Timers,* 123, 154.
33. Buonanno, *Beyond the Flag,* 152.
34. Wright, *Meditations in Green,* 251.
35. Ibid., 176–77.
36. Herr, *Dispatches,* 28, 58.
37. James Tulip, "Poetry Since 1965," in *The Penguin New Literary History of Australia,* ed. Laurie Hergenhan (Melbourne: Penguin, 1988).
38. Norman Bartlett, *Island Victory* (Sydney: Angus and Robertson, 1955), "David Forrest" [David Denholm], *The Last Blue Sea* (London: Heinemann, 1959).
39. Cook, *Wine of God's Anger,* 147.
40. Thomas Keneally, *Passenger.*
41. Shirley Cass, Michael Wilding et al., eds, *We Took Their Orders and Are Dead.*
42. *Mersmann, Out of the Vietnam Vortex,* 225.
43. Frazer, *Nasho,* 186.
44. Peter Bourne, *Men, Stress, and Vietnam,* 170.
45. *San Francisco Examiner,* 9 Apr. 1968.

46. John Hellmann, *American Myth and the Legacy of Vietnam* (New York: Columbia University Press, 1986).
47. Tim O'Brien, "How to Tell a True War Story," in *The Things They Carried* (London: Collins, 1990).
48. Joseph Heller, *Catch-22* (New York: Simon and Schuster, 1961).
49. James Webb, *A Country Such as This* (London: Grafton, 1983).
50. Mark Baker, *'Nam* (New York: William Morrow, 1981).
51. Hugh Lunn, *Vietnam: A Reporter's War,* 35, 53.
52. Hugh Atkinson, *The Most Savage Animal,* 84.
53. Robert Riggan, *Free Fire Zone* (New York: W. W. Norton, 1984).
54. Buonanno, *Beyond the Flag,* 5, 11.
55. Wright, *Meditations in Green,* 193.
56. Robert Gray, *Collected Poems* (Sydney: Angus and Robertson, 1990).
57. Bruce Dawe, *Condolences of the Season.*
58. Robert Olen Butler, *A Good Scent From a Strange Mountain* (New York: Henry Holt, 1992).
59. See, for example, Don Pendleton, *Dirty War* (Toronto and New York: Worldwide, 1985); Eric Helm, *Tet* (Toronto and New York: Worldwide, 1988); Dennis K. Philburn, *Freedom Bird* (New York: Tom Doherty, 1987); Peter Corris, *The Vietnam Volunteer* (Lismone: Southern Cross University Press, 2000).

Chapter 8

I was granted access to the documents, sketches, and architectural design briefs by a number of interested parties whose willingness and aid I gratefully acknowledge: Ken Unsworth, AM; Peter Tonkin and other members of the firm Tonkin Zulaikha Harford; Brigadier Colin Kahn, DSO, and Andrew Baird of the NCPA; and Peter Poulton of the AVFNMC.

1. For thoroughly researched documentation of the earlier welcome home marches see Ross, "Australia's Legacy," 187–213, and "Veterans in Australia," 50–73. Stuart Rintoul's collection of interviews, *Ashes of Vietnam,* offers almost totally negative responses to the Vietnam War and includes several accounts of the after-midnight drop. More recently, Kenneth Maddock's collection, *Memories of Vietnam,* 134–35, offers an account by Neil Matthews of an early welcome home march in Adelaide for the 9th Battalion, RAR, which toured in 1968–69, and which, while it acknowledges a "new" memory of some of the events, still maintains the difficulty of readjustment as the primary focus of the homecoming experience.
2. This information is derived from *The Wall: Images and Offerings from the Vietnam Veterans' Memorial* (New York: Collins, 1987), and Lydia Fish, *The Last Firebase: A Guide to the Vietnam Veterans' Memorial* (Shippensburg, Pa.: White Mane, 1987).
3. See Jan C. Scruggs and Joel C. Swerdlow, *To Heal a Nation* (New York: Harper and Row, 1985), and Rick Atkinson, *The Long Gray Line: West Point's Class of 1966* (London: Collins, 1990), chap. 17, "Walls," 449–80.
4. "America Remembers," *National Geographic,* May, 1985, 577. Most of the studies of the Wall quoting Lin use as their primary source the "Winning Designer's Statement," reproduced by the Vietnam Veterans' Memorial Fund, Incorporated. See, for example, R. Campbell, "An Emotive Place Apart," *American Institute of Architects Journal* 72 (May, 1983): 151.
5. Fredrick Hart, "Statement Read to U.S. Commission of Fine Arts," 20 Oct. 1982, as quoted in Fish, *Last Firebase,* 13.
6. See, for example, the photographs by Sal Lopes and others in *The Wall.*

7. *National Memorial to the Australian Vietnam Forces: Conditions for a Two-Stage Design Competition* (Canberra: National Capital Planning Authority, 1989), 16.
8. Ibid.
9. Ibid., 16–17.
10. Ibid., 17.
11. Ibid., 19.
12. Ibid., 21.
13. Ibid., 22.
14. "Fuzzy wuzzy" refers to the natives of Papua New Guinea, whose coarse wiry hair explains, if forgivably for its time, the not-so-submerged racism, while their merciful actions in helping wounded Australians back to medical camps is legendary and earned them the appellation "angel." The most famous image of the Kokoda Trail campaign is of a blinded digger being supported by such a man.
15. These comments were made to the author in a series of interviews conducted in July and August, 1991, at Unsworth's studios in Sydney.
16. For a brief skirmish with some of the more colorful and, one might observe, more quotable language of the war as it appears in the literary and cinematic products of Australia, see Pierce, Grey, and Doyle, eds., *Vietnam Days,* especially chapters 3, 5, and 6.
17. Although the implications and use I make of it are my own, much of this section is a summary of the reading of the Washington Vietnam Memorial in its context provided by C. L. Griswold in "The Vietnam Veterans Memorial and the Washington Mall: Philosophical Thoughts on Political Iconography," *Critical Inquiry* 12, no. 4 (summer, 1986): 688–719.
18. Ibid., 713.

SELECT BIBLIOGRAPHY

A Note on Archives and Archival Practices in Australia

All records generated by the Australian federal government are subject to the *Archives Act (1983)*, which provides for material to be made accessible to the public thirty years after its creation—the so-called thirty-year rule. Australia also possesses a *Freedom of Information Act (1982)*, but unlike in the United States, the provisions of this legislation do not cover records generated before its enactment.

As a result, records relating to Australia's war effort remain partially closed to public researchers. The official historian of Australia's involvement in Southeast Asian conflicts, Peter Edwards and his staff, had full and unhindered access to all such material for the writing of the history, but nonofficial historians are generally constricted in their access by the relevant legislation. Exceptions are made by individual departments concerning their own records, but this is on a case-by-case basis and cannot be assumed.

The one significant exception to this state of affairs involves material used in evidence before the Evatt Royal Commission on the use of herbicides, pesticides, and other chemicals by the Australian Army. These records, all of which are operational in nature, were released for public access in 1982, and are located at the Australian War Memorial in Canberra in a temporary record series, AWM 181. This series comprises some one hundred shelf feet of documents and contains important operational records generated by Headquarters, 1st Australian Task Force; MACV combined campaign plans for 1966–72; intelligence summaries and some unit records; as well as some administrative files. The unifying principle lies in the observation that all this material contains references to the use of chemical agents in Phuoc Tuy Province. The main series of operational records, some sixteen hundred shelf feet of material, is contained in AWM 95 and is subject to the thirty-year rule. This is the case for all other Australian government records relating to Australia's Vietnam War, such as those generated by the Departments of External Affairs or Labour and National Service. Helen Creagh has compiled a lengthy, unpublished guide to the series titled "Search and Research: Operation Mitchell: Information collected in the search to compile the Report on the Use of Herbicides and Insecticides and other chemicals by the Australian Army in South Vietnam," which can be found in *Archives and Manuscripts* 11 (May, 1983): 7–13. The materials in AWM 181 are gradually being folded back into the AWM 95 series as the passage of the thirty-year rule renders the exempt material open to public access.

Private records and those created by nongovernment agencies are subject to no such restrictions, although private embargoes or normal copyright rules may apply. There are important collections relating to the various antiwar and anticonscription movements held in state and university libraries throughout Australia. For example, the records of the Campaign for Peace in Vietnam, a pressure group formed in 1967 and based in the state of South Australia, are held in the State Library of South Australia in Adelaide, the state capital, as Record Group 124. They occupy nearly thirty shelf feet. Most states spawned a branch of the Vietnam Moratorium Campaign, formed in 1970, and these records are held in the State Library in South Australia's case, and in the University of Melbourne Library in the case of the state of Victoria.

The National Library of Australia in Canberra holds a number of important collections of anti–Vietnam War material. Prominent among these are the records of the Save Our Sons group (MS 3821), the Vietnam Moratorium Committee (MS 4969), and the Women's International League for Peace and Freedom (MS 7755). The papers of significant individuals in the protest movements are often valuable sources of material. At the National Library, to give but two examples, the papers of Ian Turner (MS 6206), a radical Melbourne academic, contain three boxes of anti–Vietnam War records, while the collection donated by Andrew Reeves (MS 8076) concentrates particularly on student radicalism and antiwar agitation. A further source of antiwar material is to be found in trade union records, many of which are held by the Noel Butlin Archive of Business and Labour based at the Australian National University in Canberra.

Private groups that supported government policy in Vietnam are much less well documented. Perhaps the principal organization with relevant papers in the public domain is the Returned and Services League (RSL), which is the equivalent of the American Legion and the Veterans of Foreign Wars. The records of its federal body likewise are held by the National Library (MS 6609).

There are considerable, though as yet relatively untapped, U.S. sources for the Australian participation in the Vietnam War. Among them are the Records of the United States Military Assistance Command Vietnam, Free World Military Assistance Forces, Command Reporting Files (Record Group 319 at the National Archives in Washington D.C.), and the Command History United States Military Assistance Command Vietnam (Record Group 472 in the National Archives in Washington, D.C.). There are undoubtedly more references scattered through other U.S. repositories, but it is difficult to identify many of these without working through large quantities of records on a file-by-file basis.

Government Publications and Other Official Documents

As well as the following short list, one of the most essential resources for Australian Parliamentary matters are the daily Hansard transcripts of all matters before the two houses (Representatives and Senate) of the Australian Parliament, usually cited, for example, as *Commonwealth Parliamentary Debates,* H[ouse]of R[epresentatives] vol. 43, 1964. A specific speech or report will be listed under the date it was given.

After the March: Strengthening Support for the Veterans. Report of the House of Representatives Standing Committee on Community Affairs. Canberra, 1988.

Australian Veterans Health Studies. *The Mortality Report,* pt. 1, *A Retrospective Cohort Study of Mortality Among Australian National Servicemen of the Vietnam Conflict Era, and an Executive Summary of the Mortality Report.* Canberra: Australian Government Publishing Service, 1984.

Australian Veterans Health Studies. *The Mortality Report,* pt. 3, *The Relationship Between Aspects of Vietnam Service and Subsequent Mortality Among Australian National Servicemen of the Vietnam Conflict Era.* Canberra: Australian Government Publishing Service, 1984.

"Brief History: Australian Force in Vietnam 1962–1970." Legislative Research Service, Parliamentary Library, Defence, Science, and Technology Group, Canberra, 1970.

Case Control Study of Congenital Anomalies and Vietnam Service. Canberra: Australian Government Publishing Service, 1983.

Fairfax, Denis, *Navy in Vietnam. A Record of The Royal Australian Navy in the Vietnam War.* Canberra: Australian Government Publishing Service, 1980.
Fitzgerald, Stephen et al. *The Committee to Advise on Australia's Immigration Policies.* Canberra: Australian Government Publishing Service, 1988.
[Grey, R. A.] *Patrolling and Tracking.* Canberra: Army Headquarters, 1966.
Harries, Owen. *Australia and the Third World.* Canberra: Australian Government Publishing Service, 1979.
[Menzies, Sir Robert, Right Rev. J. S. Moyes, et al.] *Vietnam: Exchange of Letters between the Prime Minister, the Rt. Hon. Sir Robert Menzies, K.T., C.H., M.P., and the Rt. Rev. J.S. Moyes, C.M.G., and certain Archbishops and Bishops.* Canberra: Prime Minister's Department, 20 April 1965.
[Neale, R. G.] "Australia's Military Commitment to Vietnam." Paper tabled in accordance with the Prime Minister's Statement to the House of Representatives, 13 May 1975. (Parliamentary Papers are normally published, but on this occasion publication did not eventuate.)
Odgers, George. *Mission Vietnam: Royal Australian Air Force Operations, 1964–1972.* Canberra: Australian Government Publishing Service, 1974.
———. *Australian Experience in Joint Armed Service Activities.* Historical Monograph 10, Canberra: Directorate of Instructions, Orders and Manuals, Administrative Services Branch, Department of Defence, 1979.
"Report on the Uses of Herbicides and Insecticides and Other Chemicals by the Australian Army in South Vietnam." Canberra: Department of Defence, November, 1982.
Royal Commission on the Use and Effects of Chemical Agents on Australian Personnel in Vietnam [Evatt Royal Commission]. 8 vols. Canberra: Australian Government Publishing Service, 1985.
Tracey, Michael P. *Australians in Vietnam: An Account of the War in Vietnam and the 30th Anniversary Commemorations of the Battle of Long Tan.* Canberra: Department of Defence, 1996.
Viet Nam Since the 1954 Geneva Agreements. Department of External Affairs. Vol. 1. Canberra: Australian Government Publishing Service, 1964.
Viet Nam First Half of 1965. Department of External Affairs. Vol. 2. Canberra: Australian Government Publishing Service, 1965.
Viet Nam: Questions and Answers. Minister of External Affairs. Canberra: Australian Government Publishing Service, May, 1966.
Viet Nam: Documents on Communist Aggression. Department of External Affairs. Canberra: Australian Government Publishing Service, n.d.

Fiction, Poetry, and Drama

"Alexander, David" [Lex McAulay]. *When the Buffalo Fight.* Melbourne: Hutchinson, 1980.
Allen, Robert. *Saigon: South of Beyond.* Sydney: Angus and Robertson, 1990.
Astley, Thea. *Beachmasters.* Ringwood: Penguin, 1985.
Atkinson, Hugh. *The Most Savage Animal.* London: Hart-Davis, 1972.
Auchterlonie, Dorothy. *The Dolphin.* Canberra: Australian National University Press, 1967.
Beilby, Richard. *The Bitter Lotus.* Sydney: Angus and Robertson, 1978.
Bich, Nguyen Ngoc, ed. "From an Anthology of Vietnamese Poetry." *Quadrant* 14, no. 3 (May-June, 1970).
Bojtschuck, R. H. *Operation Sea Dragon.* Nerang, Queensland: Ryebuck Publications, 1986.
Brass, Alister. *Bleeding Earth.* Sydney: Alpha Books, 1967.

Cairncross, C. J. *The Unforgiven.* Melbourne: Sun Books, 1977.
Campbell, David. *The Branch of Dodona.* Sydney: Angus and Robertson, 1970.
Carroll, John. *Token Soldiers.* Melbourne: Wildgrass Books, 1983.
Cass, Shirley, Michael Wilding et al., eds. *We Took Their Orders and Are Dead.* Sydney: Ure Smith, 1971.
Clanchy, John. *Homecoming.* St. Lucia: University of Queensland Press, 1989.
Coe, John N., ed. *Desperate Praise: The Australians in Vietnam.* Perth: Artlook, 1982.
Cook, Kenneth. *The Wine of God's Anger.* Melbourne: Cheshire Lansdowne, 1968.
Connell, R. *Firewinds.* Sydney: Wentworth Press, 1968.
Corris, Peter. *The Vietnam Volunteer.* Lismore: Southern Cross University Press, 2000.
D'Alpuget, Blanche, *Monkeys in the Dark,* Sydney and London: Aurora Press, 1980.
———. *Turtle Beach.* Ringwood: Penguin, 1981.
Dawe, Bruce. *Condolences of the Season.* Melbourne: Cheshire, 1971.
Dowse, Sara. *Schemetime.* Ringwood: Penguin, 1990.
Drewe, Robert. *A Cry in the Jungle Bar.* Sydney: Collins, 1979.
Duke, Jas H. *Poems of Peace and War.* Melbourne: Collective Effort Press, n.d.
———. *Vietnam Neighbours.* Sydney: Jas H. Duke, 1966.
Frazer, Michael. *Nasho.* Melbourne: Aries, 1984.
George, Rob. *Sandy Lee Live at Nui Dat.* Sydney: Currency Press, 1983.
Giles, Mike. *Rest and Recreation.* In *Seven One-Act Plays.* Sydney: Currency Press, 1983.
Gould, Alan. *The Enduring Disguises.* Sydney: Angus and Robertson, 1988.
Gow, Michael. *Away.* Sydney: Currency Press, 1986.
Grant, Bruce. *Cherry Bloom.* Sydney and London: Aurora Press, 1980.
Harrison-Ford, Carl, ed. *Fighting Words: Australian War Writing.* Melbourne: Lothian Press, 1986.
Hope, A. D. *"Antechinus": Poems 1975–1980.* Sydney: Angus and Robertson, 1981.
John, Rosemary. *Luck of the Draw.* Sydney: Currency Press, 1986.
Kap, Pothan. *A Time to Die.* Sydney: Jacaranda Press, 1967.
Keneally, Thomas. *Passenger.* London and Sydney: Collins, 1979.
Kevans, Dennis. *The Great Prawn War and Other Poems.* Sydney: Dennis Kevans, 1982.
Kim, D'Ono. *My Name is Tian.* Sydney: Angus and Robertson, 1968.
Koch, Christopher J. *Across the Sea Wall.* London: Heinemann, 1965.
———. *The Year of Living Dangerously.* Melbourne: Nelson, 1978.
———. *Highways to a War.* Melbourne: William Heinemann, 1995.
Krauth, Nigel. *Freedom Highway.* Sydney: Allen and Unwin, 1999.
Laird, John, ed. *The Australian Experience of War: Illustrated Stories and Verse.* Sydney: Mead and Beckett, 1988.
Lockhart, Greg. "A Poetry Reading." *Vietnam Today* [Newsletter of the Australian Vietnam Society], August, 1987, 10–12.
———. "The Trunk: An Australian Memoir of the Vietnam War." *Overland,* December, 1988, 62–67.
Loewald, Uyen. *Child of Vietnam.* Melbourne: Hyland House, 1987.
———. "Child of Vietnam: Uyen Loewald Writes About Growing Up in Vietnam, Prior to the Vietnam War." *Meanjin* 46, no. 1 (March, 1987): 67–81.
Lord, Gabrielle. *The Sharp End.* Sydney: Sceptre, 1998.
Malouf, David. *Fly Away Peter.* London: Chatto and Windus, 1979.
———. *The Great World.* London: Cape, 1990.

Moffitt, Ian. *The Retreat of Radiance.* Sydney: Collins and London, 1982.
Moorhead, Finola. *Still Murder.* Ringwood: Penguin, 1990.
Moorhouse, Frank. *The Americans, Baby.* Sydney: Angus and Robertson, 1972.
Morphett, Tony. "Objector." *Overland,* May, 1966, 17–18.
Morrison, R. H., ed. "Vietnam Voices: A Retrospect." *Overland,* autumn, 1973, passim. (Contains works by: Dorothy Auchterlonie, Bruce Beaver, Mona Brand, David Campbell, C.B. Christesen, Laurence Collinson, Michael Dransfield, Len Fox, Michael Hamel-Green, Charles Kaiser, John Levett, Brian Medlin, Rod Moran, R.H. Morrison, G. Pitts, Christopher Pollnitz, Craig Powell, Roland Robinson, Leon Slade, Norman Talbot, Andrew Taylor, and Chris Wallace-Crabbe.)
Mukherjee, Bharati. "Loose Ends." In *The Middleman and Other Stories.* Melbourne: McPhee Gribble, 1989.
Murray, Les. *The Ilex Tree.* Sydney: Angus and Robertson, 1965.
Nagle, William. *The Odd Angry Shot.* Sydney: Angus and Robertson, 1975.
Nowra, Louis. *Palu.* Sydney: Picador, 1987.
Page, Geoff. *Smalltown Memorials.* St. Lucia: University of Queensland Press, 1975.
Collecting the Weather. Sydney: Makar Press, 1978.
Benton's Conviction. Sydney: Angus and Robertson, 1985.
Pollard, Rhys. *The Cream Machine.* Sydney: Angus and Robertson, 1972.
Rowe, John. *Count Your Dead.* Sydney: Angus and Robertson, 1968.
Savage, Georgia. *Ceremony at Long Nho.* Ringwood: Penguin, 1995.
Stowe, Randolph. *Visitants.* London: Secker and Warburg, 1979.
Sweeney, Gerald. *Invasion.* Sydney: Angus and Robertson, 1982.
Townsend, Christine. *Travels with Myself.* Sydney: Wild and Woolley, 1976.
Wallace-Crabbe, Chris, and Peter Pierce, eds. *Clubbing of the Gunfire.* Melbourne: Melbourne University Press, 1984.
Williamson, David. *Jugglers Three.* In *Five One Act Plays.* Sydney: Currency Press, 1974. (Rewritten substantially and performed in 1997–98 as *Third World Blues.*)

Unit Histories

These were usually published by the unit and distributed within its ranks rather than for commercial sale. In recent years, a number of unit histories have appeared through trade publishing houses, while the original "tour books," as they were known colloquially, are now highly prized on the Australian secondhand and antiquarian book market.

Battle, Capt. M. R. *The Year of the Tigers: The Second Tour of 5th Battalion, the Royal Australian Regiment in South Vietnam, 1969–1970.* Sydney: 5th Battalion, RAR, 1970.
Church, J. M. *Second To None: 2 RAR as the ANZAC Battalion, 1970–71.* Sydney: Army Doctrine Centre, 1995.
Clarke, C. J., ed. *Yours Faithfully: Second Tour of 3rd Battalion, the Royal Australian Regiment in South Vietnam, 1969–71.* Sydney: 3rd Battalion, RAR, 1972.
Clunies-Ross, Maj. A. *The Grey Eight in Vietnam: The History of the Eighth Battalion, the Royal Australian Regiment, November 1969–November 1970.* Brisbane: 8th Battalion, RAR, 1971.
Grey, R. A., ed. *Seven in Seventy: Second Tour of 7th Battalion, the Royal Australian Regiment: Notes on Operations, Vietnam, 1970–1971.* [Sydney:] 7th Battalion RAR, [1971].

Johnson, Maj. L. D., ed. *The History of 6 RAR/NZ (ANZAC) Battalion.* Vol. 2, *1967–1970.* Townsville: 6th Battalion, RAR, 1972.

[Morrison, A. L.] *9th Battalion Royal Australian Regiment: Vietnam Tour of Duty 1968–1969: On Active Service.* Brisbane: 9th Battalion, RAR, Association, 1992.

Newman, Maj. K. E. *The ANZAC Battalion: A Record of the Tour of 2nd Battalion, The Royal Australian Regiment, 1st Battalion, The RNZIR. In South Vietnam 1967–68.* Sydney: 2nd Battalion, RAR, and 1st Battalion, RNZIR, 1968.

O'Brien, Michael. *Conscripts and Regulars: With the Seventh Battalion in Vietnam.* Sydney: Allen and Unwin, 1995.

O'Neill, Robert J. *Vietnam Task: The 5th Battalion, Royal Australian Regiment, 1966–67.* Melbourne: Cassell, 1968.

Rickards, G. F. B. *Twelve in Focus: 12th Field Regiment in South Vietnam 1971: A Memento for All Ranks of the Tour in South Vietnam.* Sydney: 12th Field Regiment Royal Australian Artillery, 1971.

Roberts, A. R. *The Anzac Battalion, 1970–71: Second Tour of the 2nd Battalion, the Royal Australian Regiment in South Vietnam.* Sydney: 2nd Battalion, RAR, Anzac Battalion, 1972.

Sayce, R. L., and M.D. O'Neill, eds. *The Fighting Fourth: 4RAR/NZ 1970–72: A Pictorial Record of the Second Tour in South Vietnam.* Sydney: 4th Battalion, RAR, 1972.

Stuart, R. F., ed. *3 RAR in South Vietnam, 1967–1968: A Record of the Operational Service of the Third Battalion, the Royal Australian Regiment in South Vietnam, 12th December 1967–20th November 1968.* Sydney: 3rd Battalion, RAR, [1968].

Vendetta: Vietnam, 1969–70. Sydney: Wentworth Press, 1970. (Tour book produced by the ship's company of HMAS *Vendetta,* the only *Daring* Class destroyer from the RAN to serve on the gun line in Vietnam.)

Webb, J. R. *Mission in Vietnam: First Tour of 4th Battalion, the Royal Australian Regiment in South Vietnam.* Townsville: 4th Battalion, RAR, 1969.

Williams, Ian McLean. *Vietnam: A Pictorial History of the Sixth Battalion, the Royal Australian Regiment, 1966–1967.* Sydney: 6th Battalion, RAR, 1967.

Cinematic and Radio/Television Productions

For Australia, Vietnam was by no means the media war it is commonly held to have been (and seemingly remains) for the United States, but there was a moderate and, as the war progressed, increasing, electronic media response. Little of this had been touched on in any detail, nor listed in any comprehensive manner, until the work of Ann-Mari Jordens in a paper delivered at the 1987 Macquarie University Conference. It would, however, be impossible to list every reference to Vietnam made by the television or radio media during the war and subsequently, as it came to feature weekly, if not nightly, in the various network news and current affairs programs. In the case of the numerous short films made by the commonwealth and state bodies, a number of these may exist in variant prints. Occasionally, differing dating and production details appear within the catalogues. In addition, scenes from some of the earlier films reappear as if contemporary in later films, and have often been edited for use within other commercial current affairs material—again without noting their "file footage" status. The list given below is therefore even more selective and imperfect than the term "select bibliography" might imply.

Action in Vietnam. Short film. Commonwealth Film Commission, for The Directorate of Defence Information, 1968. (Restricted access.)

Anzacs. Television miniseries. Produced by Geoff Burrowes. Burrowes-Dixon Co., P.L., 1985.

Army Advisers in Vietnam. Directorate of Public Relations, Department of the Army, 1970.

Army Nurses in Vietnam. Short film. Directorate of Public Relations, Department of the Army, 1972. Short film.

Army Officers. Short film. Department of the Army, Commonwealth Film Unit, 1966.

Arts Vietnam: A Protest to Stop the War. Short film. Sasha Ivanovich, 1968.

Australian Task Force, Vietnam. Short film. Commonwealth Film Commission, for The Directorate of Defence Information, 1967. (Restricted access.)

Australians at War. Television documentary series, episode 9 of 11. TEN Network, 1976.

Australians Remember. Short film. Film Australia Production Co., sponsored by the Australian War Memorial, 1977.

Beginnings. Short film. Acme Films, for the Aquarius Foundation, 1970.

"British Broadcasting Commission TV Vietnam Documentary." Michael Charlton. *Impact* ABC TV, 1966.

Call for Youth. Short film. Christopher Productions and Youth Campaign Against Conscription, 1966.

Cambodia Year 10. Television documentary. John Pilger, 1990.

Changing the Needle. Film. Directed by Martha Ansara for Jequerity P.L. with assistance from Creative Development Branch, Australian Film Commission, 1981.

Connections, 26 April 1990, Australian Broadcasting Corporation Radio National, "Phone-in" on the effects of Vietnam, producers Roger Penny & Christian Peterson.

Deathcheaters. Film. Directed by Brian Trenchard Smith. 1976.

Democratic Process. Short film. Jada Films, 1979.

Demonstrator. Feature film. Warwick Freeman. 1971.

Diggers in Vietnam. Short film. Commonwealth Film Commission, for The Directorate of Defence Information, 1968. (Restricted access.)

Diggers Relaxing. Short film. Department of the Army, 1969.

Dustoff Vietnam. Short film. Directorate of Public Relations, Department of the Army, 1970.

Every Day, Every Night. Short film (originally video). Directed by Kathy Mueller. Swinburne Film and Television School, 1983.

Front Line. Film. David Bradbury, sponsored by the Australian Film Commission, Tasmanian Film Corporation, and Australian War Memorial, 1978.

Frontline. Neil Davis, 1989. Television documentary and videocassette.

Gallipoli. Feature film. Produced by R & R Film. Directed by Peter Weir. 1981.

Hearts and Minds. Short, partly animated, film. Petty Film Productions, 1967.

Hit the U.S. Aggressors. Television documentary (banned from Australian TV May-June, 1966).

It's a New World for Sure. Australian Broadcasting Corporation TV Documentary Series, including two programs on the Sixties radical movements, 1987.

Land of Fire. Film. Martha Ansara, 1981.

The Last March. Television documentary. Produced by Martyn Goddard et al. Australian Broadcasting Corporation TV, 1988.

Living in the Field. Short film. Department of the Army, 1968.
Malaya Posting. Short film. Department of Army, 1962.
Minh: A Vietnamese. Short film. Film Australia, 1979.
Mobile Advisory Teams in Vietnam. Short film. Directorate of Public Relations, Department of the Army, 1971.
"My Lai." Television documentary. Australian Broadcasting Corporation TV, *Four Corners* Documentary, 1990.
National Service Corps Training—Armoured Corps. Short film. Directorate of Public Relations, Department of the Army, 1966.
National Service Corps Training—Cooks Corps. Short film. Directorate of Public Relations, Department of the Army, 1966.
National Service Corps Training—Electrical and Mechanical Engineers. Short film. Directorate of Public Relations, Department of the Army, 1966.
National Service Corps Training—Medical Assistants. Short film. Directorate of Public Relations, Department of the Army, 1966.
National Service Corps Training—Provosts. Short film. Directorate of Public Relations, Department of the Army, 1966.
National Service Corps Training—Survey Regiment (Bendigo). Short film. Directorate of Public Relations, Department of the Army, 1966.
National Service Officer. Short film. Directorate of Public Relations, Department of the Army, 1967.
No Trouble. Televised stage play. Australian Broadcasting Corporation TV, Melbourne Theatre Company, Media World, and the Commonwealth Employment Service, 1987.
The Odd Angry Shot. Feature film. Directed by Tom Jeffrey, script by William Nagle from his novel, *The Odd Angry Shot* (1975). Samson Productions, 1979.
On the Gunline. Short film. Department of the Navy, 1969.
Once Upon a War. Short film. Patricia Penn, 1970.
One Crowded Hour: Neil Davis Combat Cameraman, 1934–1985. Presented by Tim Bowden. Australian Broadcasting Corporation Radio broadcast, 1987. Audiocassette (companion to Bowden's book of the same title).
One Shot, One Kill. British Broadcasting Commission, 1967, shown on the *Inside Australia* series.
Or Forever Hold Your Peace. Film. Richard Brennan and others, 1970.
Ordinance Support for Australian Force Vietnam. Short film. Army Design Establishment, 1970.
The Quiet Mutiny. Short film. John Pilger, 1970.
The Quiet War. Short film. Australian Broadcasting Commission, 1967.
"Power to the People." 5 May 1990, documentary, Geraldine Doogue et al, for the *Hindsight* series, Australian Broadcasting Corporation TV [Australian Broadcasting Corporation Radio National held a phone-in forum the day following the broadcast].
The President Visits Brisbane. Premier's Department Queensland, Queensland Government Film Unit, 1967.
Public Enemy Number One. Produced by David Bradbury and Steward Young. Creative Development Branch, Australian Film Commission, 1980.
Ranger Advisors—Vietnam. Short film. Directorate of Public Relations, Department of the Army, 1972.
Red Cross Civilian Relief in Vietnam. Short film. Cine Service, for the Australian Red Cross Society, 1967.

Rescue Vietnam. Short film. Mathais, Kenyan, and Merton Pictures, for Australian Red Cross Society, 1968.

"Right as Rain." Radio drama. David Knox, Australian Broadcasting Corporation Radio, 17 December 1989.

Rintoul, Stuart. *Ashes of Vietnam.* ABC radio broadcast and audiocassette (after the 1987 book of the same title by Rintoul), 1988.

Sad Song of Yellow Skin. Film. Directed by Michael Rubbo (Australian) for the Canadian National Film Board, 1976.

The Siege of Fire Base Gloria. Feature film. Directed by Brian Trenchard-Smith. Script byWilliam Nagle. 1989. (Ostensibly a U.S. film, shot in the Philippines, the director, and scriptwriter are Australians or Australian-trained. and much of the technical processing was done in Sydney.)

The Soldier. Short film. Australian Broadcasting Commission TV, 1967.

Special Air Service in Vietnam. Short film. Directorate of Public Relations, Department of the Army, 1971.

A Street to Die. Film. Produced and directed by Bill Bennett. 1985.

Sword of Honour. Television miniseries. Produced by Simpson-LeMesurier. ATN 7 Network, 1987. Videocassette.

Task Force Vietnam. Short film. Directorate of Public Relations, Department of the Army, 1969.

This Day Tonight. Australian Broadcasting Commission TV news and current affairs program, active in the Vietnam period.

Three Bridges to Cross. Film. Australian Broadcasting Commission TV and Japan Broadcasting Corporation, 1966.

The Trespassers. Feature film. Directed by John Duigan. 1976.

The Unlucky Country. Short film. Australian Commonwealth Film Unit, 1967.

Vietnam. Television miniseries. Produced by Kennedy-Miller. Directed by Chris Noonan and John Duigan. Script by Terry Hayes, Chris Noonan, John Duigan, and others. Ten Network TV, 1987. Videocassette.

"Vietnam Documentary." Produced by Reg Boulter and Douglas Mann. Special Broadcasting System TV, August, 1989.

"Vietnam Retrospect." Australian Broadcasting Corporation, 1988. Audiocassette.

Vietnam Interpreters. Short film. Department of the Army, 1967.

Vietnam Scene. Short film. Department of the Army, 1967.

Vietnam Today. 6 programs on 2SER Macquarie University Radio Station, 6 June–25 July 1987. Selections from the Vietnam Conference at Macquarie University, 27 April–1 May 1987. (See Maddock and Wright, eds., *War: Australia and Vietnam,* below.)

"Vietnamese Gangs in Melbourne." News report, *A Current Affair,* September, 1990.

The Vung Tau Ferry. Short film. Department of the Navy, 1971.

Warriors, Friends or Foes? Television documentary series, episode 3. 1988.

"White Paper No. 1—Conscription." Television debate. ATN 7 Network, Sydney University, and Ampol Petroleum Australia, 23 April 1966.

Winter of Our Dreams. Feature film. Directed by John Duigan, 1981.

You Can't See Round Corners. Feature film. Directed by David Cahill. 1968. (Based on a 1967–68 television soap opera, which was an updated version of Jon Cleary's 1947 novel *You Can't See Round Corners.* The novel deals with draft resistance and absenteeism in the Second World War; the television and film versions present the hero as a Vietnam draft resister.)

In addition, single episodes of various serial (or soap opera) dramas and situation comedies have been devoted to Vietnam and/or Vietnam veterans. These include: *A Country Practice,* 1989; *Col'n Carpenter,* 1990; *The Flying Doctor,* 1990; and *Winners,* 1985. Occasional "sketches" in television comedy programs have depicted Vietnam film stereotypes (especially Ramboesque crazed killers). These include: *The Comedy Company,* 1990; *Let the Blood Run Free,* 1990; and *The Big Gig: Tuesday Night Live,* 1989–90. *See also* Ann-Mari Jordens. "Cultural Influences: The Vietnam War and Australia," *Journal of the Australian War Memorial* 15 [October, 1989]: 3–14, and several entries for Jeff Doyle below.

Books and Articles

Aarons, Laurie. "Anti-War Perspectives—A Communist View." *Australian Left Review* 29 (March, 1971): 20–30.

———. "The Life and Times of Wilfred Burchett: Reply to Robert Manne" ["The Fortunes of Wilfred Burchett." *Quadrant* 29, no. 8 (August, 1985): 7–15], *Australian Left Review* 94 (June, 1985): 41.

Adena, Michael J., et al. "Mortality Among Vietnam Veterans Compared with Non-Veterans and the Australian Population." *Medical Journal of Australia* 143, nos. 12 and 13 (9–23 December 1985): 541–44.

Henry S. Albinski. *Politics and Foreign Policy in Australia: The Impact of Vietnam and Conscription.* Durham, N.C.: Duke University Press, 1970.

———. "The Armed Forces and the Community in Post-Vietnam Australia." *Politics* 14, no. 2 (November, 1979): 198–209.

Alomes, Stephen. "Cultural Radicalism in the Sixties." *Arena* 62 (1983): 28–54.

Altman, Dennis. "Australia and Vietnam: Some Preliminary Speculations." *Australian Quarterly* 42, no. 2 (June, 1970): 61–69.

Anderson, Tim. "1968 in Australia: Anti Vietnam War Demonstrations and Their Impact on Politics." *Socialist (Melbourne),* August, 1988, 8–9.

Armstrong, Bruce, and Fiona J. Stanley. "Birth Defects and Vietnam Service." *Medical Journal of Australia* 140, no. 7 (31 March 1984): 388–89.

Arndt, H. W. "The Vietnam Debate Revisited—A Perspective for the 1990s." *Quadrant* 33, no. 10 (October, 1989): passim. (Includes comments by Coral Bell, Jim Cairns, Gregory Clark, Kenneth Gee, Frank Knopfelmacher, F. P. Serong, and John Wheeldon.)

Bailey, Mark. *Aspects of the Australian Army Intelligence System During Confrontation and Vietnam.* Canberra: Australian Defence Studies Centre, 1994.

Ball, Desmond. "The Official History of Vietnam and its Critics." *Quadrant* 37, no. 11 (November, 1993): 40–44.

Barclay, Glen St. J. *Friends in High Places.* Oxford: Oxford University Press, 1985.

———. *A Very Small Insurance Policy: The Politics of Australian Involvement in Vietnam, 1954–1967.* St. Lucia: University of Queensland Press, 1988.

———. "Problems in Australian Foreign Policy, July-December 1968: Problems of War, Problems of Peace." *Australian Journal of Politics and History* 15, no. 1 (April, 1969): 1–9.

———. "Future Australian-American Relations." *Australian Outlook* 30, no. 3 (1976): 459–73.

———. "In the Sticky Flypaper: The United States, Australia and Indonesia, 1959–1964." *U.S. Naval War College Review* 34, no. 4 (July-August, 1981): 67–80.

———. "A Very Small Insurance Premium: The Politics of Australian Involvement in Vietnam, 1961–67." *World Review* 25, no. 4 (December, 1986): 4–24.

Basham, Richard. "Betrayed By Secrecy: The Nixon-Thieu Letters and the Fall of Vietnam." *Quadrant* 32, no. 6 (June, 1988): 42–45.

Bassett, Jan. "Who Cares for the Caregiver?" *Vietnam Generation* 3, no. 2 (1991): 74–83.

Beale, Howard. *This Inch of Time.* Melbourne: Melbourne University Press, 1977.

Beazley, Kim E. "Labor and Foreign Policy. *Australian Outlook* 20, no. 2 (1966):125–34.

Beazley, Kim C. "Federal Labor and the American Installations: Prelude to Government." *Australian Outlook* 33, no. 2 (1987): 166–81.

———. "Federal Labor and the Vietnam Commitment." In *Australia's Vietnam: Australia in the Second Indochina War,* ed. Peter King. Sydney: Allen and Unwin, 1983.

Beddie, Brian. "The Australian Armed Forces in Transition." *Armed Forces and Society* 5, no. 3 (spring, 1979): 414–30.

Beed, Terence W., Murray Goot, Stephen Hodgson, and Peggy Ridley. *Australian Opinion Polls, 1941–1977.* Sydney: Hale and Iremonger, 1978.

Bell, Coral. *Dependent Ally: A Study in Australian Foreign Policy.* Melbourne: Oxford University Press, 1988.

Bell, Philip. "Remembering Vietnam: The Vietnam War in Cinema and Television." *Current Affairs Bulletin* 65, no. 2 (July, 1988): 16–22.

Berry, J. W. "Who Are the Marchers?" *Politics* 3, no. 2 (November, 1968): 163–75.

———. 'The Vietnam Marchers." In *Australian Politics: A Second Reader,* ed. H. Mayer. Melbourne: Cheshire, 1969.

Bertrand, Ina. "From Silence to Reconciliation: The Representation of the Vietnam War in Australian Film and Television." *Historical Journal of Film, Radio, and Television* 8, no. 1 (1988): 75–89.

Beveridge, D. W. "The Ground War in Vietnam." [Australian] *Defence Force Journal* 76 (May-June, 1989): 36–46.

Blaxland, J. C. *Organising an Army: The Australian Experience, 1957–1965.* Canberra: Strategic and Defence Studies Centre, 1989.

Blue, R. S. *United and Undaunted: The History of the Clearance Diving Branch of the RAN.* Sydney: Naval Historical Society of Australia, 1976.

Booker, Malcolm. *The Last Domino: Aspects of Australia's Foreign Relations.* Sydney: Collins, 1976.

Boman, Bruce. "The Vietnam Veteran Ten Years On." *Australian and New Zealand Journal of Psychiatry* 16 (September, 1982): 107–27.

Bourne, Peter G. *Men, Stress, and Vietnam.* Boston: Little, Brown, 1970. (There is a separate chapter of observations on the Australians).

Bowden, Tim. *One Crowded Hour: Neil Davis Combat Cameraman, 1934–1985.* Sydney: Collins, 1987.

Bowers, C. F. "The Catholic Church in Sydney & the Vietnam Conflict." *Australian Left Review* 71 (October, 1979): 30–37.

Breen, R. J. *First to Fight: Australian Diggers, NZ Kiwis, and U.S. Paratroopers in Vietnam, 1965–66.* Sydney: Allen and Unwin, 1988.

———. "Problems of an Expeditionary Force: First Battalion, The Royal Australian Regiment in 1965." [Australian] *Defence Force Journal* 60 (September-October, 1986): 29–38.

Brodie, Scott. *Tilting at Dominoes.* Sydney: Child and Associates, 1987. Republished as *Australia in the Vietnam War.* Sydney: PR Press, 1990.

Brooker, Gary R. *Two Lanyards in Vietnam.* Canterbury, N.Z.: Gary R. Brooker, 1994.

Browne, Margaret. *Australia at War: Vietnam.* Sydney: Hodder and Stoughton, 1984. (Text aimed at the upper primary/lower secondary school market.)

Browne, Peter, and Sarah Henry. "The Issue That Won't Go Away: Agent Orange." *Australian Society* 7, no. 6 (June, 1988): 44–47.

Buick, Bob, with Gary McKay. *All Guts, No Glory: The Story of a Long Tan Warrior.* Sydney: Allen and Unwin, 2000.

Burchett, Wilfred. *At the Barricades: Forty Years on the Cutting Edge of History.* New York: Times Books, n.d. [1981].

———. "Interview with Wilfred Burchett." *Australian Left Review* 40 (May, 1973): 3–7.

Burgess, Pat. *Warco: Australian Reporters at War.* Melbourne: Heinemann, 1986.

———. "A Correspondent's Report." In *War: Australia and Vietnam,* ed. Kenneth Maddock and Barry Wright. Sydney: Harper and Row, 1987.

Burnside, Ian. "DDGs in Vietnam: HMAS *Perth,* 26 September 1970 to 30 March 1971." In *Reflections on the RAN,* ed. T. R. Frame, J. P. V. Goldrick, and P. D. Jones. Sydney: Kangaroo Press, 1991.

Burstall, Terry. *The Soldiers' Story. The Battle of Xa Long Tan, Vietnam, 18 August 1966.* St. Lucia: University of Queensland Press, 1986.

———. *A Soldier Returns: A Long Tan Veteran Discovers the Other Side of Vietnam.* St. Lucia: University of Queensland Press, 1990.

———. *Vietnam: The Australian Dilemma.* St. Lucia: University of Queensland Press, 1993.

Bushby, Richard. *Educating an Army: Australian Army Doctrinal Development and the Operational Experience in South Vietnam, 1965–1972.* Canberra: Strategic and Defence Studies Centre, 1998.

Cable, R. W. *An Independent Command: Command and Control of the 1st Australian Task Force in Vietnam.* Canberra: Strategic and Defence Studies Centre, 2000.

Cairns, J. F. *Vietnam: Is It the Truth We Want?* Melbourne: Victorian Branch, Australian Labor Party, 1965.

———. *Living with Asia.* Melbourne: Lansdowne Press, 1966.

———. *The Eagle and the Lotus.* Melbourne: Lansdowne Press, 1969.

———. *Silence Kills: Events Leading up to the Vietnam Moratorium on 8 May.* Melbourne: Vietnam Moratorium Committee, 1970.

———. *Vietnam: Scorched Earth Reborn.* Melbourne: Widescope, 1976.

———, and Bill Hartley. "An Interview with Bernie Tufts." *Australian Left Review* 30 (May, 1971): 8–20.

Cameron, Martin. *Australia's Longest War.* N.p.: n.p., 1987.

———. *A Look on the Bright Side.* N.p.: n.p., 1988.

Carey, Alex. *Of Professors and Pacification.* N.p.: Alex Carey, 1968.

———. *Australian Atrocities in Vietnam.* Sydney: Vietnam Action Committee, 1968.

———. "Rewriting the Vietnam War: Portrayal of Events as a Noble Experience." *New Journalist* 32 (May, 1979): 21–22.

———. "Rewriting the Vietnam War, 1: The Semantics of Aggression." *New Journalist* 32 (May, 1979): 23–26, 30–31.

———, and Marion Hosking. "Rewriting the Vietnam War, 2: Lest We Forget." *New Journalist* 32 (May, 1979): 27–29.

Carver, George A. Jr. "The Real Revolution in South Vietnam." *Quadrant* 9, no. 5 (September-October, 1965): 43–53.

Cass, Shirley. "How I Turned My Nuclear Dread Into Rational Fear: A Private View." *Australian Society* 1 (February, 1983): 30–31.

Catley, Bob. "Vietnam: Aggression from the West." *Australian Left Review* (October, 1972): 13–15.

Chalk, G., and S. Cullum. "Morbidity Among National Service Registrants." *Medical Journal of Australia* 6 (April, 1968): 604–607.

Challinor, Deborah. *Grey Ghosts: New Zealand Vietnam Vets Talk About Their War.* Auckland: Hodder Moa Beckett, 1998.

Chamberlain, Max. "Australian War Statistics: Problems of Quantifying a Legend." *Australian Historical Statistics* 6 (January, 1983): 47–57.

Champion, Rafe. "Second Thoughts on Vietnam." *Quadrant* 32, no. 6 (June, 1988): 54–55.

Charlesworth, Max, and Val Noone. "Christians, the Vietnam War, and the Theory of the Just War: The Response of the 'Pax' Group." In *War: Australia and Vietnam,* ed. Kenneth Maddock and Barry Wright. Sydney: Harper and Row, 1987.

Clark, Gregory. *In Fear of China.* Melbourne: Lansdowne Press, 1967.

———. "The Australian Department of Foreign Affairs: What's Wrong with Our Diplomats." *Australian Quarterly* 47, no. 2 (June, 1975): 21–35.

———. "Vietnam, China, and the Foreign Affairs Debate in Australia: A Personal Account." In *Australia's Vietnam: Australia in the Second Indochina War,* ed. Peter King. Sydney: Allen and Unwin, 1983.

Clutterbuck, Charlotte. "Protests and Peace Marches: From Vietnam to Palm Sunday." In *War: Australia and Vietnam,* ed. Kenneth Maddock and Barry Wright. Sydney: Harper and Row, 1987.

Cochrane, Peter. "At War At Home: Australian Attitudes During the Vietnam Years." In *Vietnam Remembered,* ed. Gregory Pemberton. Sydney: Weldon, 1990.

Colbatch, Hal G. P. "A Literature of Nothingness: Creative Literature Generated by the Vietnam War." In *War: Australia and Vietnam,* ed. Kenneth Maddock and Barry Wright.Sydney: Harper and Row, 1987.

Coleman, Peter. "Editorial: The Bourbons of Protest: Lack of Australian Comment by Anti–Vietnam War Movement." *Quadrant* 29, no. 6 (June, 1985): 7–8.

———, and James McAuley, eds. "Vietnam: After the Moratorium." *Quadrant* 14, no. 3 (May-June, 1970).

Connolly, Keith. "Vietnam on Film." *Cinema Papers* 21 (May-June, 1979): 334–38.

Cooksey, R. J. "Australian Public Opinion and Vietnam Policy." *Dissent,* autumn, 1968, 5–6.

Coughlan, James E. "International Factors Influencing Australian Governments' Responses to the Indochinese Refugee Problem." *Vietnam Generation* 3, no. 2 (1991): 84–97.

Coulthard-Clark, Chris. *The RAAF in Vietnam: Australian Air Involvement in the Vietnam War, 1962–1975.* Sydney: Allen and Unwin, 1995.

———. *Hit my Smoke: Targeting the Enemy in Vietnam.* Sydney: Allen and Unwin, 1997.

Creagh, Helen. "Search and Re-search: Operation Mitchell: Information collected in the search to compile the Report on the Use of Herbicides and Insecticides and other chemicals by the Australian Army in South Vietnam." *Archives and Manuscripts* 11 (May, 1983): 7–13.

Crowe, Ambrose. *The Battle after the War: The Story of Australia's Vietnam Veterans.* Sydney: Allen and Unwin, 1999.

Cuddy, Dennis L. "The American Role in Australian Involvement in the Vietnam War." *Australian Journal of Politics and History* 28, no. 3 (1982).

Cugley, J. A. M., and R. D. Savage. "Cognitive Impairment and Personality Adjustment in Vietnam Veterans." *Australian Psychologist* 19, no. 2 (July, 1984): 205–16.

Curthoys, Ann. "Mobilising Dissent: The Later Stages of Protest." In *Vietnam Remembered,* ed. Gregory Pemberton. Sydney: Weldon, 1990.

———. "The Anti-War Movements." In *Vietnam: War, Myth, and Memory,* ed. Jeffrey Grey and Jeff Doyle. Sydney: Allen and Unwin, 1992.

———. '"Shut Up, You Bourgeois Bitch": Sexual Identity and Political Action in the Anti–Vietnam War Movement." In *Gender and War: Australians at War in the Twentieth Century,* ed. Joy Damousi and Marilyn Lake. Melbourne: Cambridge University Press, 1995.

Dennis, D. J. *One Day at a Time: A Vietnam Diary.* St. Lucia: University of Queensland Press, 1992.

Dennis, Peter, and Jeffrey Grey. *Emergency and Confrontation: Australian Military Operations in Malaya and Borneo, 1950–1966.* Sydney: Sydney: Allen and Unwin, 1996.

Dickins, Barry. *Ordinary Heroes: Personal Recollections of Australians at War.* Melbourne: Hardie Grant, 1999.

Docker, John. "'Those Halcyon Days': The Moment of the New Left." In *Intellectual Movements and Australian Society,* ed. Brian Head and James Walter. Melbourne: Oxford University Press, 1988.

Donnelly, Roger. The Scheyville Experience, 1965–1973: The Officer Training Unit Scheyville. St. Lucia: University of Queensland Press, 2001.

Donovan, John W., Robert MacLennan, and Michael Adena. "Vietnam Service and the Risk of Congenital Anomalies: A Case-Control Study." *Medical Journal of Australia* 140, no. 7 (31 March 1984): 394–97.

Doyle, Jeff. "Bringing Whose War Home? Vietnam and American Myths in Australian Popular Culture." In *Vietnam Days: Australia and the Impact of Vietnam,* ed. Peter Pierce et al. Ringwood: Penguin, 1991.

———. "Dismembering the Anzac Legend: Australian Popular Culture and the Vietnam War." *Vietnam Generation* 3, no. 2 (1991): 109–25.

———. "Short-Timers' Endless Monuments: Comparative Readings of the Australian Vietnam Veterans' National Memorial and the American Vietnam Veterans' Memorial." In *Vietnam: War, Myth, and Memory,* ed. Jeffrey Grey and Jeff Doyle. Sydney: Allen and Unwin, 1992.

Drewe, Robert. "A Cry in the Jungle Bar: Australians in Asia." *Meridian* 5, no. 2 (1986): 133–39.

Dux, John, and J. P. Young. *Agent Orange: The Bitter Harvest.* Sydney: Hodder and Stoughton, 1980.

Eather, Steve. *Get the Bloody Job Done: The Royal Australian Navy Helicopter Flight—Vietnam and the 135th Assault Helicopter Company, 1967–1971.* Sydney: Allen and Unwin, 1998.

East, C. H. A. "The Australian Infantryman: Better Than His Father?" *Australian Infantry* 18, no. 1 (January, 1972): 28–31.

Eccles Smith, Peter. *Letters from a Vietnam Hospital.* Sydney: A. H. and A. W. Reed, 1969.

Edwards, Glen D. *Vietnam: The War Within: Australian, American, New Zealand.* Adelaide: Glen D. Edwards, 1992.

Edwards, Peter. *Crises and Commitments: The Politics and Diplomacy of Australia's Involvement in Southeast Asian Conflicts, 1948–1965.* Sydney: Allen and Unwin, 1992.

———. *A Nation at War: Australian Politics, Society and Diplomacy during the Vietnam War, 1965–1975.* Sydney: Allen and Unwin, 1997.

———. "Malaya and Vietnam: Some Preliminary Thoughts by the Official Historian." *Journal of the Australian War Memorial* 3 (October, 1983): 10–12.

———. "Official History: Does It Merit Suspicion?" *Canberra Historical Journal,* n.s., 17 (March, 1986): 17–21.

———. "Foreign Policies." In *Australians from 1939: Australians, A Historical Library.* Sydney: Fairfax, Syme, and Weldon, 1987.

———. "Australia and Its Official War Histories." In *Australians on Peace and War: Proceedings of a Conference on "Perspectives on War and Peace in Australian Society."* Canberra: Australian Defence Studies Centre, 1987.

———. "The Post-1945 Conflicts: Korea, Malaya, Borneo, Vietnam." In *Australia: Two Centuries of War and Peace,* ed. Michael McKernan and Margaret Browne. Canberra: Australian War Memorial, 1988.

———. "Some Reflections on the Australian Government's Commitment to the Vietnam War." In *Vietnam: War, Myth and Memory,* ed. Jeffrey Grey and Jeff Doyle. Sydney: Allen and Unwin, 1992.

Ekins, Ashley. "'Not One Scintilla of Evidence?' The Media, the Military and the Government in the Vietnam Water Torture Case." *Australian Journal of Politics and History* 42, no. 3 (1996): 345–64.

English, Michael. *The Battle of Long Khanh: 3 RAR Vietnam, 1971.* Sydney: Army Doctrine Centre, 1995.

Evans, Michael, and Alan Ryan, eds. *The Human Face of Warfare: Killing, Fear, and Chaos in Battle.* Sydney: Allen and Unwin, 2000.

Fairbairn, Geoffrey. "The Cairns Line on Vietnam: A Campaign of Evasive Obfuscation." *Bulletin,* 31 July 1965, 35–36.

———. "The Nature of Revolutionary Guerrilla Warfare." In *Vietnam: Seen from East and West,* ed. S. Ray. Sydney: Nelson, 1966.

———. "Thoughts on Vietnam." *Quadrant* 12, no. 2 (March-April, 1968): 28–33.

———. "Vietnam Notebook." *Quadrant* 14, no. 3 (May-June, 1970): 44–53.

Field, B., and C. Kerr. "Reproductive Behaviour and Consistent Patterns of Abnormality in Offspring of Vietnam Veterans." *Journal of Medical Genetics* 25 (1988): 819–26.

Filer, David. *The New Zealand Armed Services: Their Development in Relation to Defence Policy, 1946–1972.* Canterbury [New Zealand]: David Filer, 1972.

Finn, Peter. *Vietnam Dispatches.* Perth: Access Press, 1998.

Fogarty, Michael. "Showing the Flag: Naval Diplomacy to Saigon, 1956–63." *Journal of the Australian Naval Institute* 20, no. 1 (February-April, 1994): 23–39.

Forward, Roy. "Conscription, 1954–68." In *Conscription in Australia,* ed. Roy Forward and Bob Reece. St. Lucia: University of Queensland Press, 1967.

Freudenberg, Graham. "The Australian Labor Party and Vietnam." *Australian Outlook* 33 (August, 1979): 157–65.

Frost, Frank. *Australia's War in Vietnam.* Sydney: Allen and Unwin, 1987.

———. "Australia and Vietnam, 1950–1980, Part 1: Australia and Vietnam, 1950–1972." *Dyason House Papers* 6, no. 3 (March, 1980): 1–5.

———. "Australia's War in Vietnam, 1962–1972." In *Australia's Vietnam: Australia in the Second Indochina War,* ed. Peter King. Sydney: Allen and Unwin, 1983.

———. "Conflict and Withdrawal, 1968–1972." In *Vietnam Remembered,* ed. Gregory Pemberton. Sydney: Weldon, 1990.

Gale, Betty. "South Vietnam: The Hopeless War." *Outlook* (Sydney), 9 June 1964, 3–5.

Garton, Stephen. *The Cost of War: Australians Return.* Melbourne: Oxford University Press, 1996.

Gee, Kenneth. "Betrayal in Vietnam: Journal of a Vietcong, by Truong Nhu Tang." *Quadrant* 31, no. 5 (May, 1987): 69–71, 73–74.

———. "The Vietnam War: The Macquarie Conference Retrospective." *Quadrant* 31, no. 7 (July, 1987): 14–16.

———. "It Was Right to Be There: Australians in Vietnam." *Quadrant* 31, no. 10 (October, 1987): 8–12.

Gelder, Malcolm van, and Michael J. Eley. "ANZACs, Chockos, and Diggers: A Portrait of the Australian Enlisted Man." In *Life in the Rank and File,* ed. David R. Segal and H. Wallace Sinaiko. Washington, D.C.: Pergamon-Brassey's, 1986.

Gerster, Robin. *Big-Noting: The Heroic Theme in Australian War Writing.* Melbourne: Melbourne University Press, 1987.

———. "Occidental Tourists: The Ugly Australian in Vietnam War Narrative." In *Vietnam Days: Australia and the Impact of Vietnam,* ed. Peter Pierce et al. Ringwood: Penguin, 1991.

———. "A Bit of the Other: Touring Vietnam." In *War and Gender: Australians at War in the Twentieth Century,* ed. Joy Damousi and Marilyn Lake. Melbourne: Cambridge University Press, 1995.

———, and Jan Bassett. *Seizures of Youth: "The Sixties" and Australia.* Melbourne: Hyland House, 1991.

Giblett, Noel, ed. *Homecomings: Stories from Australian Vietnam Veterans and Their Wives.* Sydney: Vietnam Veterans' Counselling Service, 1987.

Gibson, John Shaddock. *Foxhound: Australian Infantry on Operations South Vietnam, 1967–68.* Sydney: Hippo Books, 1997.

Gilbert, Alan D. "Religion and Politics: The Churches and the Vietnam War." In *Australians from 1939: Australians, A Historical Library.* Sydney: Fairfax, Syme, and Weldon, 1987.

———, and Ann-Mari Jordens. "Traditions of Dissent." In *Australia: Two Centuries of War and Peace,* ed. Michael McKernan and Margaret Browne. Canberra: Australian War Memorial, 1988.

Gittings, John, and A. Singh. *Viet Nam Briefing.* Sydney: Morgan Publishing, 1965.

Glover, Rupert G. *New Zealand in Vietnam: A Study of the Use of Force in International Law.* Palmerston North, N.Z.: Dunmore Press, 1986.

Goot, Murray, and Rodney Tiffen. "Public Opinion and the Politics of the Polls." In *Australia's Vietnam: Australia in the Second Indochina War,* ed. Peter King. Sydney: Allen and Unwin, 1983.

Gorman, Lyn. "Television and War: Australia's Four Corners Program and Vietnam, 1963–1975." *War & Society* 15, no. 1 (May, 1997): 119–50.

Graham, Brigadier S.C. "Observations on Operations in Vietnam." *Australian Army Journal* 235 (December, 1968).

Grant, Bruce. *The Boat People: An "Age" Investigation.* Ringwood: Penguin, 1979.

Gration, Peter. "Reflections on 1 ATF [1st Australian Task Force] in Vietnam." *Journal of the Australian War Memorial* 12 (April, 1988): 45–46.

Gray, Anne. "Artists' Visions of Vietnam." In *Vietnam Days: Australia and the Impact of Vietnam,* ed. Peter Pierce et al. Ringwood: Penguin, 1991.

Green, Jan. "A Soldier's Wife's Story." In *War: Australia and Vietnam,* ed. Kenneth Maddock and Barry Wright. Sydney: Harper and Row, 1987.

Grenville, K., ed. *The Saving of South Vietnam.* Sydney: Alpha Books, 1972.

Grey, Jeffrey. *Up Top: The Royal Australian Navy and Southeast Asian Conflicts, 1955–1972.* Sydney: Allen and Unwin, 1998.

———. *A Military History of Australia.* 2nd rev. ed. Melbourne: Cambridge University Press, 1999.

———. "Australia and the Vietnam War: What the Books Have Told Us." *Overland,* December, 1988, 57–61.

———. "Anzac, Vietnam, and the Veteran." In *Vietnam Days: Australia and the Impact of Vietnam,* ed. Peter Pierce et al. Ringwood: Penguin, 1991.

———, and Jeff Doyle, eds. *Vietnam: War, Myth, and Memory.* Sydney: Allen and Unwin, 1992.

Griffiths, Guy. "DDGs in Vietnam: HMAS *Hobart,* 7 March to 27 September 1967." In *Reflections on the RAN,* ed. T. R. Frame, J. P. V. Goldrick, and P. D. Jones. Sydney: Kangaroo Press, 1991.

Groenewegen, P. D. "The Public Finance of Australia's Participation in the Vietnam War." *Australian Quarterly* 42, no. 4 (December, 1970): 63–73.

Guyatt, Chris. "The Anti-Conscription Movement, 1964–66." In *Conscription in Australia,* ed. Roy Forward and Bob Reece. St. Lucia: University of Queensland Press, 1968.

Hall, Robert A. *Combat Battalion: The Eighth Battalion in Vietnam.* Sydney: Allen and Unwin, 2000.

Ham-Tieu, Anne Nguyen-Thi. "Remembering and Forgetting." In *War: Australia and Vietnam,* ed. Kenneth Maddock and Barry Wright. Sydney: Harper and Row, 1987.

Hamel-Green, Michael E. "Conscription and Legitimacy, 1964–72." *Melbourne Journal of Politics* 7 (1974–75): 11–12.

———. "The Resisters: A History of the Anti-Conscription Movement, 1964–1972." In *Australia's Vietnam: Australia in the Second Indochina War,* ed. Peter King. Sydney: Allen and Unwin, 1983.

Harries, Owen. "The Australian Debate on Vietnam." *Quadrant* 10, no. 3 (May-June, 1966): 39–46.

———. "After the Moratorium." *Quadrant* 14, no. 3 (May-June, 1970): 40–43.

———. "Decency, Peace, and Historical Inevitability: The Vietnam Debate Revisited." *Quadrant* 19, no. 3 (June, 1975): 8–11.

Hawkes, Raymond. "Readjustment Issues of Returned Vietnam Veterans." *Australian Social Work* 40, no. 3 (September, 1987): 12–16.

Heeson, T. I. *Historical Notes on 1 ALSG WKSP Det RAEME Bien Hoa, South Vietnam, 3 May 1965–13 May 1966: A Personal View.* N.p.: T. I. Heeson, 1982.

Henderson, Gerard. "Vietnam and the Victorian Universities." *Twentieth Century* 24, no. 1 (spring, 1969): 5–16.

———. "In Hanoi's Fields: Ten Years after the Fall of Phnom Penh and Saigon." *Quadrant* 29, no. 5 (May, 1985): 53–58.

Hennessy, Brian. *The Sharp End: The Trauma of a War in Vietnam.* Sydney: Allen and Unwin, 1997.

Hopkins, Maj. Gen. R. N. L. *Australian Armour: A History of the Royal Australian Armoured Corps, 1927–1972.* Canberra: Australian War Memorial and Australian Government Publishing Service, 1978.

Horner, David M. *Australian Higher Command in the Vietnam War.* Canberra Papers on Strategy and Defence 40. Canberra: Strategic and Defence Studies Centre, Australian National University, 1986.

———. *SAS, Phantoms of the Jungle: A History of the Special Air Service.* Sydney: Allen and Unwin, 1990.

———. *Duty First: The Royal Australian Regiment in Peace and War.* Sydney: Allen and Unwin, 1990.

———. *The Gunners: A History of Australian Artillery.* Sydney: Allen and Unwin, 1995.

———. "A Complex Command: The Role of the Commander, Australian Force Vietnam." *Journal of the Australian War Memorial* 13 (October, 1988): 19–30.

[Howson, Peter]. *The Howson Diaries: The Life of Politics.* Ed. Don Aitken. Melbourne: Viking, 1984.

Hudson, W. J. "Strategy for Survival." In *Australia: Two Centuries of War and Peace,* ed. Michael McKernan and Margaret Browne. Canberra: Australian War Memorial, 1988.

Hutchinson, Garrie. *Not Going to Vietnam: Journeys Through Two Wars.* Sydney: Sceptre, 1999.

Hutton, Drew. "Anarchism and the Anti-Militarist Movement in Australia." *Social Alternatives* 2 (February, 1982): 17–22.

Hyde, Michael, ed. *It Is Right to Rebel.* Sydney: Free Association Press, 1972.

Inglis, Ken. *This is the ABC: The Australian Broadcasting Commission, 1932–1983.* Melbourne: Melbourne University Press, 1983.

———. "The Digger's Grave: Conflicting Proposals on the Vietnam Dead." *Nation,* 19 February 1966, 13–15.

———. "Anzac and the Australian Military Tradition." In Peter Dennis et al., *Revue Internationale d'Histoire Militaire, Edition Australienne* 72 (Canberra: Australian Commission of Military History, 1990): 1–24.

Isaksson, O. H. *Encounters in Asia: A Soldier's Story.* Australians in Asia Paper no. 19. Brisbane: Griffith University, 1997.

Jones, Peter. "Buying the DDGs." In *Reflections on the RAN,* ed. T. R. Frame, J. P. V. Goldrick, and P. D. Jones. Sydney: Kangaroo Press, 1991.

Jordens, Ann-Mari. "Conscription." In *Australians: A Historical Dictionary,* ed. Graeme Aplin, S.G. Foster, and Michael McKernan. Sydney: Fairfax, Syme, and Weldon, 1987.

———. "A Dream Turns Sour: Official War Artists in Vietnam." *Journal of the Australian War Memorial* 11 (October, 1987): 17–24.

———. "An Administrative Nightmare: Aboriginal Conscription, 1965–72." *Aboriginal History* 13 (1988).

———. "Cultural Influences: The Vietnam War and Australia." *Journal of the Australian War Memorial* 15 (October, 1989): 3–14.

———. "Conscription and Dissent: The Genesis of Anti-War Protest." In *Vietnam Remembered,* ed. Gregory Pemberton. Sydney: Weldon, 1990.

———. "Not *Apocalypse Now:* Government-Sponsored Entertainers in Vietnam, 1965–71." *Labour History* 58 (1990): 65–75.

Kay, John, with David and Anthony Syme. *Vietnam: An End to War?* Sydney: John Kay and CAPS, 1966.

Kent, David. "From the Sudan to Saigon: A Critical Review of Historical Works." *Australian Literary Studies* 12, no. 2 (October, 1985).

King, Peter, ed. *Australia's Vietnam: Australia in the Second Indochina War.* Sydney: Allen and Unwin, 1983.

Knopfelmacher, Frank. "Traitor Burchett: As I Please." *Quadrant* 27, no. 11 (November, 1983): 7–8.

———. "Peace with Freedom: Australian Efforts to Counteract the Revolt Against the Vietnam War." *Quadrant* 29, no. 7 (July, 1985): 55–56.

Kristianson, G. L. *The Politics of Patriotism. The Pressure Group Activities of the Returned Servicemen's League.* Canberra: Australian National University Press, 1966.

Krupinski, Jerzy, and Graham Burrows, eds. *The Price of Freedom: Young Indochina Refugees in Australia.* Sydney: Pergamnon Press, 1986.

Lambert, Anthony. "It's a Good Time for the Great Taste of Vietnam: Use of the Vietnam War in the Television Business." *B&T,* 16 October 1987, 26–27.

Langley, Greg. *A Decade of Dissent: Vietnam and the Conflict on the Australian Home Front.* Sydney: Allen and Unwin, 1992.

Larsen, Lt. Gen. Stanley Robert, and Brig. Gen. James Lawton Collins Jr. *Allied Participation In Vietnam.* Vietnam Studies. Washington D.C.: Department of the Army, 1975.

Leach, David. "DDGs in Vietnam: HMAS *Perth,* 19 September 1968 to 19 April 1969." In *Reflections on the RAN,* ed. T. R. Frame, J. P. V. Goldrick, and P.D. Jones.Sydney: Kangaroo Press, 1991.

Lockhart, Greg. "Fear and Dependence: Australia's Vietnam Policy, 1965–1985." In *War: Australia and Vietnam,* ed. Kenneth Maddock and Barry Wright. Sydney: Harper and Row, 1987.

———. "Into Battle: Counter Revolution." In *Vietnam Remembered,* ed. Gregory Pemberton. Sydney: Weldon, 1990.

Losik, Robert. "The American Alliance—The Debit Side." *Australian Journal of Defence Studies* 3 (May, 1979): 36–46.

Lloyd, Clem, and Jacqui Rees. *The Last Shilling: A History of Repatriation in Australia.* Melbourne: Melbourne University Press, 1994.

Lunn, Hugh. *Vietnam: A Reporter's War.* St. Lucia: University of Queensland Press, 1985.

Macfarling, Ian. "New Zealand and the Vietnam Conflict." [Australian] *Defence Force Journal* 79 (November-December, 1989): 8–19.

Mackay, Gary and Graeme Nicholas. *Jungle Tracks: Australian Armour in Vietnam.* Sydney: Allen and Unwin, 2001.

Maddock, Kenneth, ed. *Memories of Vietnam.* Melbourne: Random Century, 1991.

———. "Opposing the War in Vietnam—the Australian Experience." In *Vietnam and the Antiwar Movement: An International Perspective,* London: Avebury, 1989.

———, and Barry Wright, eds. *War: Australia and Vietnam.* Sydney: Harper and Row, 1987.

Mann, L. "Attitudes Towards My Lai and Obedience to Orders: An Australian Survey." *Australian Journal of Psychology* 25, no. 1 (April, 1973): 17–21.

Manne, Robert. "The Fortunes of Wilfred Burchett: A New Assessment." *Quadrant* 29, no. 8 (August, 1985): 27–45.

Marlowe, Shauna. *A Nurse in Vietnam.* Sydney: Shauna Marlowe, 1967.

McAulay, Lex. *The Battle of Long Tan: The Legend of Anzac Upheld.* Melbourne: Hutchinson, 1986.

———. *The Battle of Coral: Fire Support Bases Coral and Balmoral, May 1968.* Melbourne: Hutchinson, 1988.

———. *Contact: Australians in Vietnam.* Melbourne: Hutchinson, 1989.

———. *The Fighting First: Combat Operations in Vietnam, 1968–69: The First Battalion, The Royal Australian Regiment.* Sydney: Allen and Unwin, 1991.

———. "Anzac and the Vietnam Digger." *Journal of the Australian War Memorial* 16 (April, 1990): 52–53.

McCraw, David. "Reluctant Ally: New Zealand's Entry into the Vietnam War." *New Zealand Journal of History* 15, no. 1 (1981): 49–60.

———. "The Demanding Alliance: New Zealand and the Escalation of the Vietnam War." *Australian Journal of Politics and History* 34, no. 3 (1989): 308–19.

McCulloch, Jock. *The Politics of Agent Orange: The Australian Experience.* Melbourne: Heinemann, 1984.

———. "The Unlucky Veterans." *Australian Society,* 1 February 1984, 16–17.

———. "The Politics of Writing about Agent Orange." *Social Alternatives* 5, no. 2 (April, 1986): 33–35.

———. "Whistling in the Dark: The Royal Commission into Agent Orange." In *War: Australia and Vietnam,* ed. Kenneth Maddock and Barry Wright. Sydney: Harper and Row, 1987.

McDougall, Derek. "The Australian Press Coverage of the Vietnam War in 1965." *Australian Outlook* 20 (December, 1966): 303–10.

McGregor, Peter. "Australia and Vietnam: Retribution and Reconciliation." *National Outlook* 10, no. 8 (September, 1988): 24–26.

MacGregor, Sandy. *No Need for Heroes.* Sydney: CALM Pty, 1993.

McHugh, Siobhan. *Minefields and Miniskirts: Australian Women and the Vietnam War.* Sydney: Doubleday, 1993.

Mackay, Gary. *In Good Company: One Man's War in Vietnam.* Sydney: Allen and Unwin, 1987.

———. *Vietnam Fragments: An Oral History of Australians at War.* Sydney: Allen and Unwin, 1992.

———. *Delta Four: Australian Riflemen in Vietnam.* Sydney: Allen and Unwin, 1996.

———. *Bullets, Beans, and Bandages: Australians at War in Vietnam.* Sydney: Allen and Unwin, 1999.

Mackay, Ian. *Australians in Vietnam.* Adelaide: Rigby, 1968.

McKernan, Michael. "Writing About War." In *Australia: Two Centuries of War and Peace,* ed. Michael McKernan and Margaret Browne. Canberra: Australian War Memorial, 1988.

McNamara, E. G. "Australian Military Operations in Vietnam." *Journal of the Royal United Services Institute* (London) 113 (December, 1968): 310–16.

McNarn, Maurie. "From Imperial Appendage to American Satellite: *Australian* Foreign Policy and Australian Involvement in Vietnam." Australian *National University Historical Journal* 14 (1979–1980): 73–86.

McNeill, Ian. *The Team: Australian Army Advisers in Vietnam, 1962–1972.* Canberra: Australian War Memorial, 1984.

———. *To Long Tan: Ground Combat Operations in Vietnam, 1962–66.* Sydney: Allen and Unwin, 1993.

———. "Petersen and the Montagnards: An Episode in the Vietnam War." *Journal of the Australian War Memorial* 1 (October, 1982): 33–46.

———. "General Sir John Wilton: A Commander for His Time." In *The Commanders: Australian Military Leadership in the Twentieth Century,* ed. David M. Horner. Sydney: Allen and Unwin, 1984.

———. "Australian Army Advisers: Perceptions of Enemies and Allies." In *War: Australia and Vietnam,* ed. Kenneth Maddock and Barry Wright. Sydney: Harper and Row, 1987.

———. "The Australian Army and the Vietnam War." In *Vietnam Days: Australia and the Impact of Vietnam,* ed. Peter Pierce et al. Ringwood: Penguin, 1991.

Mediansky, F. A. "Defence Reorganisation, 1957–1975." In *Australia in World Affairs, 1971–1975,* ed. W. J. Hudson. Sydney: Allen and Unwin, 1980.

Menzies, Robert G. *Afternoon Light: Some Memories of Men and Events.* Melbourne: n.p., 1967.

———. *The Measure of the Years.* London: n.p., 1970.

Millar, T. B. *Australia in Peace and War: External Relations, 1788–1977.* Canberra: Australian National University Press, 1978.

———. "Australian Defence, 1945–1965." In *Australia in World Affairs, 1961–1965,* ed. Gordon Greenwood and Norman Harper. Melbourne: Cheshire, 1968.

———. "Indo-China: The Implications for Australian Security." *Quadrant* 19, no. 4 (July, 1975): 4–9.

Miller, J. D. B. *Australia in Vietnam: Necessary Insurance or Burnt Fingers?* London: Round Table, 1970.

Morgan, Patrick, and Warren Osmond. "The State of Student Power." *Current Affairs Bulletin* 46, no. 8 (September 1970): 114–28.

Mount, Frank. "Corruption and the Vietnam War." *Social Survey* 24 (September, 1975): 232–43.

Munster, G. J, and J. R. Walsh, eds. *Documents on Australian Defence and Foreign Policy, 1968–75.* Sydney: G. J. Munster and J. R. Walsh, 1975. (This book was ordered to be withdrawn from sale after the government successfully challenged the publication of classified materials contained within it.)

Murphy, John. *Harvest of Fear: A History of Australia's Vietnam War.* Sydney: Allen and Unwin, 1993.

———. "'Like Outlaws': Australian Narratives from the Vietnam War." *Meanjin* 2 (1987): 157–62.

———. "The Fragmented Visions of Various Single Issue Movements in Politics. In *Staining the Wattle.* Ringwood: Penguin, 1988.

Newman, S. D. *Vietnam Gunners: 161 Battery RNZA, South Vietnam, 1965–71.* Wellington: Moana Press, 1988.

Nicol, J. D. "The Morale of the Australian Infantry in South Vietnam, 1965–1972." *British Army Review* 127, (summer 2001): 37–46.

Noone, Val. "Narrabri: The War and a Country Town." *Retrieval* 26 (August-September, 1975): 9–13.

———. "Melbourne Catholics and the 1965 Increase in Australian Military Intervention in Vietnam." *Journal of Religious History* 16, no. 4 (December, 1991): 456–81.

O'Farrell, Terry. *Behind Enemy Lines: An Australian SAS Soldier in Vietnam.* Sydney: Allen and Unwin, 2001.

O'Hara, J. "Press Coverage of the First Vietnam Moratorium Demonstration in Melbourne." *Melbourne Journal of Politics* 6 (1973): 18–38.

O'Keefe, Brendan, and F. B. Smith. *Medicine at War: Medical Aspects of Australia's*

Involvement in Southeast Asian Conflicts, 1950–1972. Sydney: Allen and Unwin, 1994.

O'Neill, Robert. *The Strategy of General Giap Since 1964.* Canberra: Australian National University Press, 1969.

———. *General Giap: Politician and Strategist.* Melbourne: Cassell, 1969.

———. "Australian Military Problems in Vietnam." *Australian Outlook* 23, no. 1 (1969): 45–57.

———. "Soldiers and Historians: Trends in Military Historiography in the Nineteenth and Twentieth Centuries." *Journal of the Royal Historical Society* 56, no. 1 (March, 1970): 36–47.

———. "Australia and Vietnam." In *Selected Readings in Australian Foreign Policy,* ed. D. Pettit. Melbourne: Sorrett, 1973.

———. "Defence Policy." In *Australia in World Affairs, 1971–1975,* ed. W. J. Hudson. Sydney: Allen and Unwin, 1980.

O'Toole, Brian, Michael Adena, and Michael P. Jones. "Risk Factors for Mortality in Australian-Vietnam Era National Servicemen: A Case Control Study." *Community Health Studies* 12, no. 4 (1988): 408–17.

Palmos, Frank. *Ridding the Devils.* Sydney: Bantam Books, 1990.

Patterson, Lee. "Drink and Drugs in Australia's Armed Forces." *Australian Playboy,* December, 1979, 71–76.

Pemberton, Gregory. *All the Way: Australia's Road to Vietnam.* Sydney: Allen and Unwin, 1987.

———, ed. *Vietnam Remembered.* Sydney: Weldon, 1990.

———. "Australia's Road to Vietnam, 1945–1965." In *Vietnam Remembered,* ed. Gregory Pemberton. Sydney: Weldon, 1990.

———. "The Vietnam War and Its Supporters." *Quadrant* 38, no. 4 (April, 1994): 51–52.

Pennington, Vic. *The Team in Vietnam . . . The Lighter Side.* Adelaide: Wakefield Press, 1992.

Petersen, Barry, with John Cribben. *Tiger Men: An Australian Soldier's Secret War in Vietnam.* Melbourne: Macmillan, 1988.

Petersen, Neville. "The Coverage of the Vietnam War in an Organisational Context: The ABC and CBC Experience." *Australian-Canadian Studies* 16, no. 2 (1998): 33–47.

Phillips, Dennis. *Ambivalent Allies: Myth and Reality in the Australian-American Relationship.* Ringwood: Penguin, 1988.

———. "Ambivalent Allies: Myth and Reality in the Australian-American Relationship." *Australian Journal of American Studies* 6, no. 2 (1987): 1–7.

Pierce, Peter. "The Australian Literature of the Viet Nam War." *Meanjin* 39, no. 3 (1980): 290–303.

———. "Perceptions of the Enemy in Australian War Literature." *Australian Literary Studies* 12, no. 2 (May, 1985): 166–81.

———. "Australian and American Literature of the Vietnam War." In *Vietnam Days: Australia and the Impact of Vietnam,* ed. Peter Pierce et al. Ringwood: Penguin, 1991.

———. "'The Funny Place': Australian Literature and the War in Vietnam." *Vietnam Generation* 3, no. 2 (1991): 98–108.

Pierce, Peter, Jeffrey Grey, and Jeff Doyle, eds. *Vietnam Days: Australia and the Impact of Vietnam,* Ringwood: Penguin, 1991.

Pogson, Gary, and Michael Sassella. "Repatriation Benefits for Agent Orange Victims?" *Legal Service Bulletin* 7 (December, 1982): 263–65.

Rabel, Roberto. "Australia's War in Vietnam." *New Zealand International Review* 13, no. 6 (November-December, 1988): 27.

———. "'The Most Dovish of the Hawks': New Zealand Alliance Politics and the Vietnam War." In *Vietnam: War, Myth, and Memory,* ed. Jeffrey Grey and Jeff Doyle. Sydney: Allen and Unwin, 1992, 14–30.

Read, Susan. "How Electors Confound the Pundits: The Vietnam War, 1969." *Politics* 10, no. 2 (November, 1975): 200–206.

Renouf, Alan. *The Frightened Country.* Melbourne: Macmillan, 1979.

Richardson, J. L. "Australian Strategic and Defence Policies." In *Australia in World Affairs, 1966–1970,* ed. Gordon Greenwood and Norman Harper. Melbourne: Cheshire, 1974.

Rintoul, Stuart, ed. *Ashes of Vietnam: Australian Voices.* Melbourne: William Heinemann, 1987.

Rivett, Kenneth. "Towards a Policy on Refugees." *Australian Outlook* 33, no. 2 (August, 1979).

Robertson, Alec. "CPA in the Anti-War Movement." *Australian Left Review* 27 (October-November, 1970): 39–49.

Rodan, Paul. "Harold Holt's Foreign Policy, 1966–1967." *Australian Journal of Politics and History* 25, no. 3 (1979): 310–18.

Ross, Jane. *The Myth of the Digger.* Sydney: Hale and Iremonger, 1985.

———. "The Australian Army: Some Views from the Bottom." *Australian Quarterly* 46, no. 3 (1974): 35–47.

———. "The Conscript Experience in Vietnam." *Australian Outlook* 29, no. 3 (1975): 315–22.

———. "Australian Soldiers in Vietnam: Product and Performance." In *Australia's Vietnam: Australia in the Second Indochina War,* ed. Peter King. Sydney: Allen and Unwin, 1983.

———. "The Myth of the Digger in Australian Society." In *Australians on Peace and War,* ed. Hugh Smith. Canberra: Australian Defence Force Academy, 1987.

———. "Australia's Legacy: The Vietnam Veterans." In *Vietnam Remembered,* ed. Gregory Pemberton. Sydney: Weldon, 1990.

———. "Veterans in Australia: The Search for Integration." *Vietnam Generation* 3, no. 2 (1991): 50–73.

Rowe, John. *Vietnam: The Australian Experience.* Sydney: Time-Life Books in association with John Ferguson, 1987.

Santamaria, B.A. *Australia at the Crossroads: Reflections of an Outsider.* Melbourne: Melbourne University Press, 1987.

———. "Australian Security & Vietnam." In *Vietnam: Seen from East and West,* ed. S. Ray. Sydney: Nelson, 1966.

———. "Burchett: Dissent or Treason?" *Quadrant* 30, no. 1 (January-February 1986): 52.

Saunders, Kay, and Helen Taylor. "The Impact of Total War Upon Policing: The Queensland Experience." In ed. Mark Finnane. *Policing in Australia: Historical Perspectives.* Sydney: New South Wales University Press, 1987.

Saunders, Malcolm. *A Bibliography of Books, Articles, and Theses on the History of the Australian Peace Movement.* Peace Research Centre Monograph 1. Canberra: Australian National University, 1987.

———. "Australia's Withdrawal from Vietnam: The Influence of the Peace Movement." *Social Alternatives* 1, nos. 6 and 7 (1980): 56–62.

———. "'Law and Order' and the Anti–Vietnam War Movement: 1965–72." *Australian Journal of Politics and History* 28, no. 3 (1982): 367–79.

———. "A Note on the files of the Campaign for Peace in Vietnam." *South Australiana* 21 (September, 1982): 105–10.

———. "Opposition to the Vietnam War in South Australia, 1965–73." *Journal of the Historical Society of South Australia* 10 (1982): 61–71.

———. "The Sydney Peace Movement, 1966–73." *Flinders Journal of History and Politics* 8 (1982): 91–104.

———. "The Trade Unions in Australia and Opposition to Vietnam and Conscription: 1965–1973." *Labour History* 43 (1982): 64–82.

———. "The Anti-War Movement in Australia: 1962–1973." *Chatta* 9, no. 1 (March, 1983): 5–18.

———. "The ALP's Response to the Anti–Vietnam War Movement: 1965–73." *Labour History* 44 (May, 1983): 75–91.

———. "Looking back on Australia's Vietnam: Review Article." *Flinders [University] Journal of History and Politics* 10 (1984): 133–46.

———, and Ralph Summy. *The Australian Peace Movement: A Short History.* Canberra: Peace Research Centre, Australian National University, 1986.

———. "Salient Themes of the Australian Peace Movement: An Historical Perspective." *Social Alternatives* 3 (October, 1982): 23–32.

———. "One Hundred Years of an Australian Peace Movement: 1885–1984. Part I: From the Sudan Campaigns to the Outbreak of the Second World War." *Peace and Change* 10, no. 3 (fall, 1984): 39–56.

———. "One Hundred Years of an Australian Peace Movement: 1885–1984. Part II: From the Second World War to Vietnam and Beyond." *Peace and Change* 10, no. 4 (winter, 1984): 57–75.

Sekuless, Peter, and Jacqueline Rees. *Lest We Forget: The History of the Returned Services League, 1916–86.* Sydney: Rigby, 1986.

Savage, David. *Through the Wire: Action with the SAS in Borneo and the Special Forces in Vietnam.* Sydney: Allen and Unwin, 1999.

Sexton, Michael. *War for the Asking: Australia's Vietnam Secrets.* Ringwood: Penguin, 1981.

Shulze, Terry. "Vietnam Post Traumatic Stress Disorder and Criminal Behaviour." *Law Society Journal* 25, no. 7 (August, 1987): 38–40.

Smith, F. B. "Agent Orange: The Australian Aftermath." In Brendan O'Keefe with F. B. Smith, *Medicine at War: Medical Aspects of Australia's Involvement in Southeast Asian Conflicts, 1950–1972.* St. Leonards, New South Wales: Allen and Unwin, 1994.

Smith, Hugh. "Defence Policy." In *Independence and Alliance: Australia in World Affairs, 1976–80,* ed. P. J. Boyce and J. R. Angel. Sydney: Allen and Unwin, 1983.

———. "Conscience, Law and the State: Australia's Approach to Conscientious Objection since 1901." *Australian Journal of Politics and History* 35, no. 1 (1989): 13–28.

———. "Conscientious Objection to Particular Wars: Australia's Experience during the Vietnam War, 1965–1972." *War & Society* 8, no. 1 (May, 1990): 118–34.

Stephens, Alan. *Going Solo: The Royal Australian Air Force, 1946–1971.* Canberra: Australian Government Publishing Service, 1995.

Stone, Gerald L. *War Without Honour.* Melbourne: Jacaranda Press, 1966.

Streimer, Jeffrey, and Christopher Tennant. "Psychiatric Aspects of the Vietnam War: The Effect on Combatants." In *War: Australia and Vietnam,* ed. Kenneth Maddock and Barry Wright. Sydney: Harper and Row, 1987.

Stretton, Alan. *Soldier in a Storm: An Autobiography.* Sydney: Collins, 1978.

Subritzky, Michael. *The Vietnam Scrapbook: The Second ANZAC Adventure.* Papakura, N.Z.: Three Feathers Publishing, 1995.

Summy, Ralph. "Militancy and the Australian Peace Movement: 1960–1967." *Politics* 5, no. 2 (November, 1970): 148–62.

Thayer, Carlyle A. *War By Other Means: National Liberation and Revolution in Viet Nam, 1954–1960.* Sydney: Allen and Unwin, 1989.

Thieme, John. "Re-mapping the Australian Psyche: The Asian Novels of C. J. Koch." *Southerly* 47, no. 4 (1987): 451–61.

Thurgar, Jack, and Charles Wright, comps. *Welcome Home.* Canberra: Jack Thurgar and Charles Wright, 1988.

Tiffen, Helen. "Asia and the Contemporary Australian Novel." *Australian Literary Studies* 11, no. 4 (1984): 468–79.

Tiffen, Rodney. "News Coverage of Vietnam." In *Australia's Vietnam: Australia in the Second Indochina War,* ed. Peter King. Sydney: Allen and Unwin, 1983.

———. "The War the Media Lost: Australian News Coverage of Vietnam." In *Vietnam Remembered,* ed. Gregory Pemberton. Sydney: Weldon, 1990.

Towers, Mike. *A Jungle Circus: Memories of Vietnam.* Sydney: Allen and Unwin, 1999.

Tran Quoc Trung. "A Page of History One Should Not Take Pride In." In *War: Australia and Vietnam,* ed. Kenneth Maddock and Barry Wright.Sydney: Harper and Row, 1987.

Tran Quong Viet. "A Perspective on Vietnam Since the Fall of Saigon." In *War: Australia and Vietnam,* ed. Kenneth Maddock and Barry Wright. Sydney: Harper and Row, 1987.

Turner, Ian. "The Vietnam Moratorium." *Meanjin Quarterly* 2 (1970): 244.

Turner, L. C. F. "Australian Historians and the Study of War, 1964–74." In *Historical Disciplines and Culture in Australasia: An Assessment,* ed. John Moses. St. Lucia: University of Queensland Press, 1979.

Viviani, Nancy. *The Long Journey: Vietnamese Migration and Settlement in Australia.* Melbourne: Melbourne University Press, 1984.

———. "After the War Was Over: Vietnamese in Australia." In *Vietnam Remembered,* ed. Gregory Pemberton. Sydney: Weldon, 1990.

———. *The Indochinese in Australia, 1975–1995: From Burnt Boats to Barbecues.* Melbourne: Oxford University Press, 1996.

Walker, Graham. "The Vietnam Veterans Association of Australia." In *War: Australia and Vietnam,* ed. Kenneth Maddock and Barry Wright. Sydney: Harper and Row, 1987.

Walters, Ian. *Dasher Wheatley and Australia in Vietnam.* Darwin: Northern Territory University Press, 1998. [This is the only published study of one of Australia's four Victoria Cross recipients in Vietnam.]

Warner, Denis. *The Last Confucian: Vietnam, South-East Asia, and the West. New York:* Macmillan, 1963. Reprint, Sydney: Angus and Robertson, 1964.

———. *Reporting South East Asia.* Sydney: Angus and Robertson, 1966.

———. *Not With Guns Alone.* Melbourne: Hutchinson, 1977.

———. *Wake Me If There's Trouble: An Australian Correspondent at the Front Line: Asia at War and Peace, 1944–1964. Ringwood:* Penguin, 1995.

———. *Not Always on Horseback: An Australian Correspondent at War and Peace in Asia, 1961–1993.* Sydney: Allen and Unwin, 1997.

———. "How Vietnam Correspondents Turned Victory into Defeat." *Quadrant* 22, no. 2 (March, 1978): 72–74.

Watt, Alan. *Vietnam: An Australian Analysis. Melbourne:* Cheshire, 1968.

———. "Australia at War in Vietnam: Public Unease and Uncertainty." *Round Table* 244 (October, 1966): 354–62.

Welburn, M. C. J. *The Development of Australian Army Doctrine, 1945–64.* Canberra: Strategic and Defence Studies Centre, 1994.

Whitlam, E. G. *Beyond Vietnam.* Melbourne: Victoran Fabian Society, 1968.

Williams, Jean R. *Cry in the Wilderness: Guinea Pigs of Vietnam.* Nambour, Queensland: Jean R. Williams, 1995.

York, Barry. *Student Revolt: La Trobe University, 1967–1973.* Canberra: Nicholas Press, 1989.

———. "Police, Students and Dissent: Melbourne, 1966–1972." *Journal of Australian Studies* 14 (May, 1984): 58–77.

———. "Sources of Student Dissent: La Trobe University, 1967–72." *Vestes* 7, no. 1 (1984): 21–31.

———. "The Australian Anti-Vietnam Movement, 1965–1973." *Melbourne Journal of Politics* 15 (1983–84): 24–41.

———. "Baiting the Tiger: Police and Protest During the Vietnam War." In *Policing in Australia: Historical Perspectives,* ed. Mark Finnane. Sydney: University of New South Wales Press, 1987.

———. "Power to the Young: The Vietnam Protest Movement. In *Staining the Wattle.* Ringwood, Penguin, 1988.

INDEX

Bold face type indicates maps.